THE SOCIAL HISTORY OF EDUCATION

GENERAL EDITOR: VICTOR E. NEUBURG

Second Series — No. 4

ESSAYS UPON

EDUCATIONAL SUBJECTS

THE SOCIAL HISTORY OF EDUCATION

General Editor: Victor E. Neuberg

Second Series

No. 1.   Sir Thomas Bernard
Of the Education of the Poor (1809)

No. 2.   Eighteenth Century Education: Selected Sources
Edited by Victor E. Neuburg
The five pamphlets included in this volume exemplify eighteenth century approaches to popular education. They include a facsimile of one of the more important reading primers used in charity schools, an early manual of their organization and a highly significant sermon preached by Joseph Butler, Bishop of Bristol. An Appendix contains some useful material on reading methods.

No. 3.   G. Griffith
Going to Markets and Grammar Schools, 2 vols (1870)

No. 4.   A. Hill (Editor)
Essays Upon Educational Subjects (1857)

No. 5.   Literacy and Society
Comprising:
Introduction by Victor E. Neuburg
  (i) W. H. Reid: *The Rise and Dissolution of Infidel Societies in this Metropolis . . . etc. (1800)*
  (ii) W. J. Linton: *James Watson. A Memoir of the days of the fight for a free press, 2nd edition (1880)*
Appendix
Catalogue of James Watson's publications

No. 6.   Nineteenth Century Education: Selected Sources
Edited by Victor E. Neuburg
The subjects included in this selection cover Penny Readings, Ragged Schools, the training of working women and working class recreations; as well as a contemporary biography of J. G. Brooks who undertook much voluntary educational work.

No. 7.   J. A. St. John
The Education of the People (1858)

No. 8.   J. C. Symons
School Economy (1852)

ESSAYS UPON
EDUCATIONAL SUBJECTS

READ AT THE

EDUCATIONAL CONFERENCE
OF JUNE 1857

EDITED BY

ALFRED HILL

THE WOBURN PRESS
1971

Published by

WOBURN BOOKS LIMITED

10 WOBURN WALK, LONDON WC1 0JL

First edition   1857
New impression   1971

ISBN 7130 0013 9

Printed in Great Britain by Clarke, Doble & Brendon Ltd.
Plymouth and London

ESSAYS

UPON

EDUCATIONAL SUBJECTS

READ AT THE

EDUCATIONAL CONFERENCE

OF JUNE 1857.

WITH A SHORT

ACCOUNT OF THE OBJECTS

AND

PROCEEDINGS OF THE MEETING.

(Published by Authority of the Committee.)

EDITED BY

ALFRED HILL,

BARRISTER-AT-LAW;

ONE OF THE HONORARY SECRETARIES.

LONDON:

LONGMAN, BROWN, GREEN, LONGMANS, & ROBERTS.

1857.

PREFACE.

THAT the main defect in the present state of popular education in this country is not so much the lack of schools, as the insufficient attendance of the children of the working classes (many never coming at all, and most others being withdrawn before they have had time to derive much benefit), is a truth which has for some years past been impressing itself more and more upon those who are best informed on the subject.

Early in the present year, therefore, at the suggestion of the Rev. Canon Moseley, of Bristol, the Educational Conference was projected—*firstly*, to ascertain the extent of the evil; and, *secondly*, to consider the question of remedy.

To admit of full latitude of suggestion and discussion, it was determined to adopt a course of proceeding which had proved eminently successful at the Bristol Meeting of the National Reformatory Union,—viz. to inaugurate the proceedings by a public meeting; then to employ a day in the reading and discussion of papers in sections (on the plan of the British Association); and to wind up with another public meeting, at which the results of the proceedings of the sections should be discussed, and re-solutions founded thereon, submitted, and decided upon.

His Royal Highness the Prince Consort, with the deep interest which he always shows in matters of social improvement, graciously consented to be nominated Pre-sident of the Conference, and opened the inaugural meet-ing with a most appropriate and able speech.

The precise scheme of the Conference, and the names of the gentlemen who countenanced its promotion, will be learned from the following copy of the prospectus :—

"EDUCATIONAL CONFERENCE.

" A CONFERENCE of the Friends of the Education of the Working Classes, on the 'EARLY AGE AT WHICH CHILDREN ARE TAKEN FROM SCHOOL,' will be held in London on the 22nd, 23rd, and 24th of June, 1857.

" President.

H.R.H. The Prince Consort.

" Committee.

The Marquis of Lansdowne.	Rev. Canon Moseley.
Lord Bishop of Oxford.	E. Baines, Esq.
Lord Lyttelton.	Harry Chester, Esq.
Lord Stanley, M.P.	J. C. Colquhoun, Esq.
The Right. Hon. William Cowper, M.P.	Henry Dunn, Esq.
	Joseph Kay, Esq.
Sir James Kay Shuttleworth, Bart.	S. Morley, Esq.
Sir Thomas Phillips.	John Reynolds, Esq.
Very Rev. The Dean of West-minster.	Rev. F. C. Cook.
	Rev. William Rogers.
Very Rev. The Dean of Salisbury.	Rev. F. Temple.
Venerable Archdeacon Sinclair.	Rev. John Scott.
Edward Akroyd, Esq. M.P.	

" Treasurer.

The Ven. Archdeacon Sinclair.

"Chairman of Sub-Committee of Management.

Rev. Canon Moseley.

"Honorary Secretaries.

Alfred Hill, Esq.   The Rev. John G. Lonsdale.

"THE FIRST MEETING

of the Conference will be held at WILLIS's ROOMS, on Monday, June 22nd, when the Chair will be taken by H.R.H. the President, at Three o'clock.

"THE SECOND DAY.

The Conference will be divided into Four Sections, each to meet at 12 o'clock, at the Thatched House Tavern.

" SECTION A.

Chairman : The LORD BISHOP OF OXFORD.
Secretary : The REV. B. WATKINS.

To inquire into the fact of the alleged early removal of Children from School in the Agricultural, Manufacturing, and Mining Districts of England, Scotland, and Wales ; and to inquire into the causes of such early removal and its results.

" SECTION B.

Chairman : RT. HON. WM. COWPER, M.P.
Secretary : REV. J. D. GLENNIE, Junr.

To institute similar inquiries in respect to the Education of Foreign Countries.

" SECTION C.

Chairman : SIR JAMES KAY SHUTTLEWORTH, Bart.
Secretary : REV. NASH STEPHENSON.

To consider the expedients which have been proposed for keeping the Children of the " Working Classes " longer at school ; under the heads of —

"First, CERTIFICATE SCHEMES.

" In respect to which are to be considered,—

1st. *The circumstances under which the Certificates are to be granted.*	(*a*) The authority which is to grant them. (*b*) The qualifications of those who are to receive them.
2ndly. *The means of giving effect to the Certificates when granted.*	(*a*) By pledges from the employers of labour that they will give a preference to those candidates for their employment who hold the certificates. (*b*) By seeking out suitable situations for the holders of certificates, and watching over their interests when so employed ; and with that view establishing corresponding committees in town and rural districts.

"Secondly, PRIZE SCHEMES.

" In respect to which are to be considered, —

1st. *How the Prize Fund is to be raised.*	Whether by subscriptions to a common fund, or by local subscriptions applied for the benefit of the locality where, or the religious community by which, they are raised ?
2ndly. *The conditions under which the Prizes are to be awarded.*	(*a*) By what authority ? (*b*) With what qualifications, as to age, character, and attainments? (*c*) By what means the qualifications are to be determined ?
3rdly. *The nature of the Prizes.*	(*a*) Whether money prizes ; (*b*) Apprentice premiums ; or (*c*) Books, clothes, tools, &c. &c. ?

" SECTION D.

Chairman: The Very REV. the DEAN OF SALISBURY.
Secretary: JOHN THACKRAY BUNCE, ESQ.

To inquire into the merits of such other expedients as shall be proposed for the consideration of the Conference, and particularly those known as

"HALF-TIME SCHEMES.

" Being schemes for the occupation of children half their time at school, and half at labour; the same arrangement being proposed to be made by parents and employers *voluntarily*, as under the provisions of the Factory Bill is made (in respect to certain children) compulsorily.

" In respect to which are to be considered, —

" 1. What are the times to be prescribed for the attendance of the Children at School,—certain hours of each day, or certain days of each week ?

" 2. Whether the time at School ought to be equal to the time at Work, or less or more than it ?

" 3. Whether a portion of the school-time may be taken in the Evening ?

"4. Whether the appeal in favour of the half-time scheme should be addressed to the Parents or the Employers of the Children ?

" THE FINAL MEETING

of the Conference will be held at Eleven o'clock on Thursday, the 24th June, at Willis's Rooms.

" A summary of the proceedings of the Sections will be laid before this Meeting, and Resolutions will be proposed to it founded thereon.

" The discussion of every subject will be preceded by the reading of a Paper on that subject before one of the Sections.

" *The following Noblemen and Gentlemen have promised their support to the proposed Conference, or have expressed in general terms their approval of it.*

His Grace the Archbishop of Canterbury.
The Most Noble the Marquis of Lansdowne, K.G.
The Earl Ducie.
The Earl Granville.
The Earl Nelson.
The Right Honourable Lord John Russell, M.P.
The Lord Stanley, M.P.
The Bishop of London.
The Bishop of Winchester.
The Bishop of Lichfield.
The Bishop of Oxford.
The Bishop of Bath and Wells.

The Bishop of Lincoln.
The Bishop of Salisbury.
The Bishop of St. Asaph.
The Bishop of Gloucester and Bristol.
The Bishop of Manchester.
The Lord Kinnaird.
The Lord Lyttelton.
The Right Hon. Sidney Herbert, M.P.
The Right Hon. Wm. Cowper, M.P.
The Right Hon. Sir John Pakington, Bart., M.P.
The Hon. and Rev. S. Best.
The Hon. and Rev. G. M. Yorke.

Sir Stafford Northcote, Bart.
Sir J. P. Kay Shuttleworth, Bart.
The Dean of Westminster.
The Dean of Bristol.
The Dean of Hereford.
The Dean of Salisbury.
The Venerable Archdeacon Sinclair.
The Venerable Archdeacon Allen.
The Rev. Chancellor Harrington.
Mr. Commissioner Hill, Q.C.
Sir Erskine Perry.
Sir Thomas Phillips.
The Rev. Canon Anderson.
The Rev. Canon Fry.
The Rev. Canon Girdlestone.
The Rev. Canon Lonsdale.
The Rev. Canon Moseley.
The Rev. Canon Richson.
The Rev. Prebendary Guthrie.
The Rev. E. Chapman, M.A.
The Rev. Geo. Craik, D.D.
The Rev. Dr. Craik, Glasgow.
The Rev. J. H. Hinton, M.A.
The Rev. Norman M'Leod, Glasgow.
The Rev. John Scott, M.A.
The Rev. Nash Stephenson.
The Rev. W. T. Morrison, M.A.
The Rev. W. Whitehead.
The Rev. Henry Wilkinson.
Joseph Allen, Esq.
Edward Baines, Esq., Leeds.

J. T. Bunce, Esq.
Richard Cobden, Esq.
Harry Chester, Esq.
J. C. Colquhoun, Esq.
S. P. Davis, Esq.
Henry Dunn, Esq.
William Ellis, Esq.
Robert Foster, Esq.
Rowland Hill, Esq.
Frederick Hill, Esq.
Alfred Hill, Esq.
Julian Hill, Esq.
Joseph Kay, Esq.
Horace Mann, Esq.
J. H. Markland, Esq., D.C.L.
John Martin, Esq.
William Miall, Esq.
William Miles, Esq.
Samuel Morley, Esq.
Professor Pillans.
Windham Postal, Esq.
Charles Ratcliffe, Esq.
Alexander Redgrave, Esq.
John Reynolds, Esq.
Hugh Seymour Tremenheere, Esq.
Mr. Sheriff Watson, Aberdeen.
E. D. Wilks, Esq.
J. F. Winfield, Esq.
William Wells, Esq.
James Wilson, Esq.
George Wilson, Esq."

Owing to the number of valuable papers which were sent in, it was found necessary, at the last moment, to constitute a fifth section, at which the Hon. and Rev. Grantham H. Yorke kindly consented to preside, and Mr. Charles Ratcliffe to act as Secretary.

From the whole number of papers read, the following have been selected by the Committee on account of their valuable and practical character, and are accompanied by a very brief account of the proceedings at the public meetings.

It should be mentioned, that a general report by the Committee of the Conference, of the facts and suggestions which have been elicited, will be made and published at an early period.

CONTENTS.

PART I.

PART II.

PAPERS ON THE ATTENDANCE, ETC., AT SCHOOLS ON THE CONTINENT.

PART III.

PAPERS CHIEFLY ON PRIZE AND CERTIFICATE SCHEMES.

PART IV.

PAPERS ON HALF-TIME SCHEMES, AND EVENING AND FACTORY SCHOOLS.

PART V.

PAPERS NOT FALLING UNDER THE ABOVE HEADS.

PART VI.

ESSAYS

UPON

EDUCATIONAL SUBJECTS,

ETC.

PART I.

PAPERS CHIEFLY ON THE FACT OF THE NON-
ATTENDANCE AND EARLY REMOVAL OF CHILDREN
FROM SCHOOL IN THIS COUNTRY.

—◆—

*On the Evidence afforded by the Reports of Her Majesty's
Inspectors as to the early Age at which Children are
taken from School.* By the Rev. M. MITCHELL, H. M.
Inspector of Schools.

IN the composition of this paper it will be my purpose,
first, to establish the fact that the children of the working
classes do leave school at too early an age.

I propose, secondly, to show the actual education they
do or may receive even under this condition.

And, thirdly, I shall suggest such remedies as appear
to me to be possible, or again, such expedients as may
ameliorate the defects consequent on the early age at
which school instruction in this class ceases.

The result obtained from the summaries of Her Majesty's Inspectors of Schools is as nearly as possible a true fact, viz., that in every hundred children of the poorer classes at present attending school there are about 33, or one-third, who are 10 years of age; while only one-fiftieth remain at school to 14 years. Thus, if we take 12 years to be the period of school life from the age of 2 to 14, the apprentice age, we shall find there are 66 children who remain, in every hundred, beyond their 10th year, and about 6 who stop the whole period up to 14.

And this remarkably agrees with the Report of the Census of 1851, as quoted by Mr. Moseley, viz. that boys of all classes attending school between 10 and 15 equal 36 per cent., *i. e.* more than two-thirds; and I think also it developes another fact, viz. that contrary to general idea — the school age is not on the decline, as most of the elder children are sons of small shopkeepers, gentlemen's servants, clerks, and mechanics of better class, such as engineers, carpenters.

I consider ten years to be the present normal age at which the English labourer's school period ceases.

The next question is, to what extent do we educate a boy of ten years? And this I propose to solve by exhibiting to you papers collected from all parts of the Eastern district. You will find that if a child be well taught at ten years of age, he may be able to write fairly from dictation out of an ordinary reading book; he will be decently acquainted with the four simple and compound rules; will have a sort of idea of grammar; and a certain knowledge of general geography and map drawing. He will also read fairly and intelligently, and have a certain knowledge of the Bible and History of England as contained in elementary works. Advancing to the question, to what extent the education of such child can be carried? I hold, that enough attention has not been and is not even now paid to the acquisition of quick, easy, and complete methods of instruction. The art of education is as yet only in its infancy, and I believe that by the present improved, and to be improved, systems — by the complete education of teachers—the proper furnishing and fitting of schools—the due supply of books and apparatus—and the saving of time and labour now very frequently most fruitlessly expended,—it will ultimately result that the boy finishing school life at 10 years will really be better educated than the boy of 13 is now, even as the education of the boy of 10 now is very, very far, superior to that which the boy of 14 received only 20 years back. Something also may be hoped from the improved condition and education of the parents of this class in the next generation.

I enter now on my third topic: viz. the remedies I would propose for defects.

All people interested in this subject know, that an idea very extensively prevails that the parents of the working classes are indifferent to the education of their children, and that it often happens that the most indifferent are those who have received such education as the old National Schools afforded. These complaints are constant: and when I look at the actual instruction too frequently offered in the schools for the working-classes, I can only rejoice that parents are so sensible, for more complete waste of time than one too frequently grieves over in these schools it is hardly possible to imagine. The same complaint, however, is sometimes with justice made by managers, even where the schools are excellent: a case, however not often occurring, since a really good, unfettered, simple-hearted, earnest, disinterested, unproselytising education rarely fails to succeed in commanding the attention of those for whom it is intended — and ordinarily where it is otherwise, if you carefully observe, you may discover some snake in the grass—some unpopularity whose origin is local, not educational. Unpopular managers and unaccommodating regulations make unpopular schools. The working-class may be led but won't be driven ; and it may be even doubted if John Bull would associate with John Barleycorn, if he was once induced to distrust him—or to imagine that he wanted to get the upper hand. Still it is not to be denied that there are certain impediments to education, and the retaining of children at school, not thus derived —and of these some might be legally removed, while others must be left to the operation of public opinion. In regard to Parliamentary or legal measures, I feel inclined to discountenance every regulation which includes direct compulsion. I do not conceive that direct compulsion would at present be tolerated, and I do not believe that education would be favoured by any such means. In a free country, instruction should rather be looked upon as a blessing and a privilege. I think, however, that indirect compulsion, or, perhaps, inducements, might be successfully applied.

By indirect compulsion, to be obtained from Parliament, I mean the according certain advantages to educated persons, and the withholding certain positions from the uneducated—to which may be added the decided removal of every obstacle to educational progress. Thus, in some districts the Guardians of the Poor refuse relief to an applicant if he has a child of eight or ten years of age at school. As we have seen that ten years is the age to which two-thirds of the children of that class are retained at school, I would propose that the law should sanction, under every circumstances, the continuance of all labourers' children at school to that period, and that under no circumstance should a child be compelled to work before he comes to that age, unless by parental authority, and by the wish and consent of his natural and legal guardians. There appear also to be certain manufactures which require the help of children — some of them even those of the tenderest years — such as artificial flowermaking. I conceive there would be small difficulty in compelling the employers to act by these, as the cotton and woollen manufacturers are compelled in similar cases, and that the children under ten years of age be retained three hours in each day at school.

You will remember that three hours is the time now mostly allotted to intellectual instruction in all girls' schools —the rest being spent in needlework, and consequently children thus circumstanced would be in the same position as all females in their situation of life. It will not be difficult, I conceive, to induce the Legislature to interfere thus far ; what I am about to proceed to will require greater consideration.

It may also be desirable to open certain electoral privileges to all persons who had received a certain amount of education, denying them to those not possessed of this qualification. It is a question of detail to what extent the education should be carried that would entitle to such a privilege; but whatever the standard, and however many might be admitted or excluded, it could hardly be believed that any persons possessing those privileges, and really qualified to form an opinion and judgment in matters of policy, would be excluded.

The exceptions of ill-educated men being able to entertain just political views are so very rare that little heed need be given to their case, which will not extend beyond a single generation.

If a vote were the privilege accorded to education, I think many parents would be induced to maintain their children at school in the desire that they should not be deprived of possible future advantages. It would be a stimulus also to the exertion of the children themselves. Another proposition I would make is, " that no person should be permitted to be employed in any occupation in which the lives of Her Majesty's subjects might be endangered, unless possessed of a certain amount of education."

A proposition of this kind would include all policemen —all railroad employés—all drivers of carts and omnibuses in towns—all engineers of steam-engines—all those engaged in gas works—as petty officers on board ships —all overlookers of factories or mines. Everyone indeed who should be elevated to any position of authority. The law might be made not absolute; but in case employers should prefer to engage persons for any of these duties not so educated, that then, whatever penalty might be incurred from loss or damage, should be levied both on the employer and the employed.

I would also consider parents responsible, as well as the child, for all crimes committed before—say fifteen years of age, if it should be proved that they had not sufficiently attended to his education.

I believe that these propositions are perfectly practicable; and that in making such provisions Parliament would really be doing as much as in a free State could be endured. Thus there would be no compulsion, but only an indirect influence exerted; and it is only fair that if damage ensues from anyone's carelessness and indifference, he should be made responsible for his neglect, just as a man who keeps an untamed bull or a savage dog; and the Legislature would be thus simply exercising its just power of protection to its subjects.

A step has been taken in this direction as respects the soldier. The following letter appeared in the "Times" on the 19th June:—

"It is scarcely less essential to the soldier to be able to read and write, and keep his own accounts, than to be acquainted with his drill.

"H. R. H. is pleased to direct, that in future every soldier shall attend school until he is reported on as sufficiently advanced in reading, writing, and arithmetic.

"No man is to be considered eligible for promotion to corporal who has not been dismissed the school, and for promotion to the rank of sergeant higher qualifications may be expected.

"Those men who avail themselves most intelligently of the means of improvement within their reach, will be generally preferred for promotion, and neglect to do so will be regarded as a disqualification.

"G. A. WETHERALL.

"Horse Guards, June 19th."

Thus far as to what the Legislature may be called upon to do.

Let us now proceed to such means as may be used without any application to the Legislature — depending on private influence or public opinion. The chief proposition of the present day to induce children to remain at school is some sort or other of " prize scheme." Some of my colleagues have taken up this idea under various forms very warmly. Notwithstanding the apparent or real success of their plans as far as they go (remember they have only been in work for three or four years), and under very limited circumstances, I confess to an entire and absolute disapproval of the use of any such means. I do not consider that they are legitimate. Believing the system to be false, I do not conceive it can be permanent. In the first place, people will soon become tired of subscribing for such a purpose, and therefore the scheme cannot be supported continually; and, secondly, if it could I consider the system injurious. One of the chief advantages derived to the progress of education in the present day has been the doing away with all these factitious sorts of aids; and the making a boy value his education for itself, and not for the paltry rewards of childhood, such as either places in the top of his class, medals or books, the value of which in after years he learns completely to despise; and the best schools we have are those in which no such meretricious honours are conferred.

A school education should be so regarded habitually as a thing which eventually is to make the boy a man — a man of power; and if your education is a true one, and the teacher know his work, and be earnest and true-hearted in it, it is in this light his scholars will regard it; and if they do so regard it, it will be with something of contempt that they will receive your paltry five shilling present, and those soft encomiums which usually accompany the same. It is because we have no faith in the power of education in its value and advantages, in its loveliness and attractability, that we propose such wretched subsidiary means.

Nothing has so tended to lower the true opinion of education as the eleemosynary conditions under which it has been offered; and the prevalence of this idea—that education is a charity and not a right — is the great impediment to its progress.

Let us then have faith in education; let us not do despite unto its spirit; let us not bring in to aid it any false or lowering principles or practices; let us make it really valuable, and it will be valued. Our appeals to the working-class to induce them to educate their children have been directed mostly to the advantages of education. I would in addition appeal to the pleasures, and make education conduce also to more agreeable results. It has often struck me that one cause of the indifference manifested on this subject by the working-class, especially the agricultural, is the very little opportunity ever afforded them

of calling it out into practical life. They learn to read,
and there is the end. An appetite is created, and nothing
is ever offered to satisfy it.

I maintain that you would do more to promote education by the establishment of good, *i. e.* liberally selected,
libraries in country parishes, than by all your "prize
schemes." Establish a good library of reference, of
standard works, of fiction, of fact, of history for the past,
of the newspaper for the present. Let your room be
well warmed and ventilated, and fairly furnished, and
freely opened, with no more restrictions than is offered
in a London club. And let there be now and then the
sympathising mind to point out rather than insist on
the road to knowledge; and I'll be bound — if your
schoolmaster is a good one, and your school in good
order—it won't be long before you need any other prize
than a temporary admission to these privileges to secure,
as far as is possible, the education of your village or
neighbourhood.

From my condemnation of prizes I exclude the certificates of Her Majesty's Inspectors, now granted to certain
scholars. These are not to be included in the same
category. They involve not competition; are open to
every scholar; and may be most useful in after life as a
certificate of character to the holders. It is also a great
deal to be said for them that they have the authority of
the Government, and belong to the whole kingdom, and
are not merely the charitable gift of the gentlemen belonging to one district or holding one set of opinions.

More it seems to me might be made of these certificates
than has yet been attempted; and they might be distributed to the youths, with more of form and solemnity,
in large public places, attended by the chief magistrates
and dignitaries of Church and State of the neighbourhood, at once honoured and conferring honour.

Such are the means I should propose for the promotion of education, and consequent retaining of the children at school.

But you will observe that previous to the adoption of such plans, our first care must be bestowed upon the present schools themselves. I believe a bad school to be a great curse.

Care should be taken then that a good building be provided within reasonable distance of every child, and that it be furnished with all necessary means and appliances for the complete instruction of its pupils, and that the teacher thereof be fully competent to his work.

Two thirds at least of all our school-going children, we have seen, remain till ten years of age before they leave school. I conceive that for their education up to this age, in agricultural places, a well-trained woman is all in all sufficient; that, in fact, she is the best teacher; and if the child's education commenced at 3 years under such training and circumstances, and ended at 10 or even 9, the child ought to have, and, as we have seen, actually has, acquired a very considerable amount of such elementary knowledge as would enable him, by the helps I am now going to describe, to carry his education forward.

I shall speak of the National School. I confine myself to the boy who leaves school at 10 years. He will then have learned to write a little, to read fairly, and to cipher the four first rules moderately. He will also have been orally instructed in elementary geography, and have acquired some facts in history; while, again, he will be able in church schools to say the Catechism, and possess a certain acquaintance with the Scriptures. He leaves school; he goes to work, and, in the course of a year, he knows nothing at all.

I think that to a certain extent this might be remedied, and that, if we could invent means of giving him from two to three hours a day of real instruction after 10 years, he would not only retain his previous acquirements, but even carry them onwards; indeed I am sure if he remained at school for three hours a day five days in the week for secular knowledge, and one hour and a half on the Sunday for religious knowledge — the time being methodically and properly applied — he would, at fourteen years of age, be quite as well educated as might be required for him as a citizen, in order to know and perform all the duties of the station to which God has called him.

The main question is, how can this latter part of his education be arranged? His parents cannot afford to allow him to forego working altogether—but they might see the advantage if they could arrange to allow him to attend school for three hours out of the twelve, leaving him nine hours for work.

Attempts have been made to adopt this idea, but, as far as I know, not successfully — at any rate not generally successfully. I shall detail to you such plans as I have heard of, and add an untried one of my own.

There is the ordinary halftime system — a boy drops in in the middle of the day at either of the school ordinary working hours, without method or order.

Education on such plan must be desultory and imperfect — in fact, I fear, hardly of any value.

There is a plan of forming schools of children, by certain employers of labour with large estates — these work in the day certain hours, and in the evening receive instruction.

There is the alternate plough-boy system of the Bishop of Winchester, which proposes alternate days of work and instruction.

And there is the plan I now propose, — that a master be employed from 6 to 9 A.M. in the instruction of boys from 10 to 14, and of youths from 14 to 18 in the evening from 6 to 9 P.M.; the mistress holding her school in the same rooms from $9\frac{1}{2}$ to $12\frac{1}{2}$ A.M., and from 2 to 5 P.M.

By adopting this plan, boys of tender years would receive their instruction in the morning, and go to work afterwards; while youths would work first and be instructed last, and there would be no break in the day. The boy having had his three hours of school, would be at the service of the plough, the sheep, or the birds all the rest of his time. This is a compromise of the question ; but both parties may be expected to yield something for so good a cause, and half a loaf is better than no bread. Of course I am only speaking of agricultural boys, though such a division of time might also in many cases be adopted for town boys.

In conclusion, allow me to observe that there is everything to encourage the promoters of education. It was reported to me by a clergyman in Essex, that at a late confirmation there was but one in twenty candidates that could not read, while twenty years ago there was only one in twenty that could. We are sometimes asked what has been done to improve the people by education. My reply is, that he must be either very ignorant of the past, or very unobservant of the present, who is unable to discover the immense progress that has been made in character, morality, and politeness, by the working classes of late years. None can go amongst their great gatherings without feeling this to be a fact. Perhaps it is not all as good as we should wish. But you now see little drunkenness — you hear little blasphemy or swearing — they mostly turn aside with disgust from any improprieties of language or behaviour, and they do no damage to the parks and places into which they are admitted. Out of seventeen cases of ill conduct, mostly very slight ones, at Hampton Court last year, eight were committed by the upper orders. Two gentlemen alone were charged with drunkenness.

There is then some hope for us—only let us believe— let us act, and the work must advance.

The Evidence afforded by Schools not under Government Inspection as to the Early Age at which Children are taken from School. By JOHN FLINT, late Assistant Diocesan Inspector of Schools in Derbyshire, and Organising Master of the National Society.

THE first question to be determined to-day in this section appears to be this: "Is it or is it not the fact that the children of the labouring classes leave school at an earlier age than they did formerly?"

I apprehend that no one, however limited may have been his acquaintance with our elementary schools, will venture to give any other than an affirmative reply to this question. It scarcely admits of even the semblance of a doubt; and unless I interpret incorrectly the views of the supporters of the Conference, there will be little hesitation to-day in asserting, once for all, that, at the present time, and during the last eight or ten years (the latter number is perhaps nearer the truth), the age to which the children of the working-classes remain under instruction is, and has been, gradually but steadily diminishing.

Appealing to my own experience in the matter, I am of opinion that the average age of the scholars in the first classes of our schools has decreased during the last twelve years from 12, 13, and 14, to 9, 10, and 11 years; that is to say, the child, who would formerly have remained under instruction until he had attained the age of 12 or 13, or 14, now quits school at the age of 9 or 10, or 11, as the case may be. I conclude that not quite one-fourth of the aggregate number in schools continue their attendance to the age of 12, and that even these are children not of the poor but of the small farmer, shopkeeper, foreman, and respectable artisan, who are intended for apprenticeship and clerkships. I believe that something less than two-fourths of the entire number of children under instruction have completed their school-life at an age somewhere between 10 and 11, but nearer the former than the latter, and that the remaining number, 35 per cent. perhaps, have finished their school-training at the age of 9. To any one only moderately enthusiastic in the cause of education the complaints everywhere made by school-managers and teachers with reference to the immense falling off in the age to which children remain at school are most depressing. Those who have devoted time, money, and energy to the work of educating the children of the labouring-classes seem, after a time to be thrown, as it were, completely back upon themselves; and after employing every stratagem in its behalf, to be driven to the conclusion that the age of 10 must be accepted as the normal condition of the withdrawal of children from school.

To economise time I shall state a few facts connected with schools in various parts of England. I have recently completed the inspection of about 200 schools in Derbyshire, situated in mining, manufacturing, agricultural, and a few in pottery districts. Of scholars above the age of 10 there were in the Deanery of Alfreton, 34·99 per cent.; in that of Ashbourne, 31·3; in Eyam, 33·7; Wirksworth, 21·2; Ockbrooke, 19·36, and Derby, 13·3. These numbers tend to establish a very important fact, viz., that the age to which the children of the working-classes leave school depends very much upon the labour-market, for in the deanery in which the percentage above 10 is the highest, employment cannot easily be obtained for very young children; while, on the contrary, in the Deanery of

Derby, in which there is the lowest percentage of scholars above 10 years of age, I have ascertained that they are able to procure employment and earn wages in a variety of ways.

Let us now turn our attention to another part of England — the county of Cornwall. In this county there are three distinct classes of the labouring population: the first being engaged in agricultural pursuits, the second in mining operations, and the third in the fisheries along the coasts. In East Cornwall, which is mainly an agricultural district, few of the children remain at school beyond the age of 10. The girls very seldom attend school after attaining the age of 11, and the majority leave before this time. I had no personal knowledge of the Cornish schools at that period, but I am informed on good authority that eight years ago the greater number of the scholars remained under instruction until they were 11½ or 12 years of age. In West Cornwall, which is principally the mining portion of the county, the majority of the boys quit school soon after they attain the age of 9. Very few indeed attend until they are 11.

In the Wolds and at the foot of the Wolds in Yorkshire, thirty-one schools were inspected, in 1855, by Diocesan agency. The percentage of scholars, between the ages of 10 and 12, was in that year 23·5, and only 5 per cent. had reached the age of 13. With one or two exceptions, the same circle of schools has undergone a tour of inspection during the current year. The result may be thus stated: there are now only 21·5 per cent. between the ages of 10 and 12, as compared with 23·5 in 1855, and only 3·7 per cent. of the age of 13 to be contrasted with the former percentage of 5.

In many parishes in the central parts of Huntingdonshire, boys begin to be unsettled as early as 7 years of age, frequently absenting themselves from school for long periods in order to engage in daily labour. Few of the children remain after the age of 10.

In Shropshire, children rarely attend beyond the age of $10\frac{1}{2}$, and the majority leave before they are 10. This remark must be confined, however, to schools in the agricultural portions of the county. I regret to say that when I was engaged in the neighbourhood of Lilleshall, Broseby, Coalbrook Dale, Iron Bridge, and other similar centres of mining and manufacturing industry, I did not pay sufficient attention to school statistics to be enabled to discuss their peculiarities with any degree of certainty.

In many of the schools in and near Winchester, Portsmouth, and Southampton, many of the scholars of the more respectable class attend school to the advanced ages of 15 and 16; but taking the number of such into our estimate, and including the ordinary schools of the county, we may say that the greater number of the children quit school before the age of 10.8.

In the county of Somerset the majority of the children leave before they are 10 years old.

In schools in the neighbourhood of Horsham, Petworth, Midhurst, and in all that part of Sussex, 11 is the limit of the children's school-life; more, however, leave before than at this age. In the schools near Lewes and in neighbouring districts of the county, I am informed (for I cannot speak from personal knowledge of the southern portion of Sussex) that the boys seldom remain until they are quite 10 years of age.

In eleven schools in Devonshire examined this year, the average age of the boys was $9\frac{8}{11}$, and of the girls $10\frac{4}{11}$, and these are about the ages at which they quit school.

In the mining districts of South Wales the boys leave rather under than over 10. In the agricultural portions of the same part of the principality there is a slight improvement on this state of things.

In schools in the neighbourhood of the granite quarries of Guernsey, the first classes consist of boys, many of whom are 12, 13, and even 14 years of age. The men in this part of the island earn high wages by quarrying and stone-breaking (in fact preparing stones for the London and other paviors), while in the agricultural districts of that island the children in the higher classes of the schools are very young indeed, probably 9, and a few 10 years old. In arranging these estimates, I have kept in view schools *not* under government inspection. In cases in which I have entertained doubts respecting the accuracy of my own views, I have sought and obtained reliable information from the Secretaries of Local Boards of Education, and Diocesan Inspectors of Schools. In one or two instances I am entirely dependent on others for my statistics. I am unwilling to occupy your time by extending my observations to schools in other parts of the country, but I may perhaps be excused for repeating my former statement, viz., I believe that scarcely one-fourth of the aggregate number of children in our schools continue their attendance to the age of 12, that even these are not the children of the poor, and that considerably less than two-fourths complete their school-life at an age somewhere between 10 and 11, while a large proportion leave at the excessively tender age of 9.

It is part of the business of this section to inquire into the causes of the early removal of children from school. At first sight it would seem to be a very simple operation to make such a generalisation of the facts of the case, as should serve to throw light on this branch of the subject, and admit of a ready solution of [the problem which the section has proposed to itself. The facts themselves, however, appear at times to be very conflicting, and to follow no fixed law. If you confine your observations to a particular district, and collate all the information bearing on the school-life of the children which it affords, it is probable you will be tempted to arrive too quickly at the conclusion that you have detected a principle of general application, running through the entire strata of evidence thus accumulated. At times it seems to you to crop out at the surface in bold, well-defined outline. On turning, however, to some other quarter for additional proofs of the truth of the principle which has presented itself for adoption, you are surprised to find a new class of facts starting up and staring you in the face, apparently irreconcilable with what seemed to you at first to be a very perfect and conclusive theory. For example, compare the schools near the granite quarries in Guernsey with those in the agricultural parts of the island. In the former the boys are of an advanced age, and their parents receive high wages, while in the latter the children in the higher classes are very young, and their parents' incomes are small. Reasoning on this fact a person might very easily be induced to suppose, that when their wages are high parents are more likely to keep their children longer at school than when their earnings are small. Belief in the soundness of this theory would be increased if the same law could be proved to hold good in one or two other localities. Suddenly, however, it is discovered that high wages (as among the iron-stone pits of North Derbyshire) are by no means accompanied by an extension of the school-life of the scholars, on the contrary that they tend to curtail it; while again, in the agricultural districts of South Wales, where the parents' earnings are small, the children remain rather longer at school than in the mining districts, where the wages are higher. It would seem, therefore, that the facts connected with the early removal of children from school are discordant, and calculated to lead one astray. But in all such cases, the one fact to be determined is the extent of the existing demand in each

locality for the labour of children. The entire question
of school-age resolves itself in a great measure into one of
demand in the labour-market, and a due consideration of
this will, under all circumstances, account for and harmonise facts which at first sight appear to be conflicting. It
must be universally admitted that during the last ten,
twelve, or even fifteen years, every department of industry has received a marvellous impetus, and that the
capabilities of the English people have sought and found
an adequate expression in a widely-spread spirit of competition. Indeed this word seems to be stamped upon
everything which is purely the offspring of human skill
and exertion. We appear like a nation which had suddenly received a special revelation as to the best mode of
developing unlimited natural resources within a very
limited period. One of the chief objects in life of the
present day is to effect the greatest possible results by the
least possible expenditure of time. Improvement after
improvement has been devised to economise labour in
general and that of adults in particular, and one striking
effect of this policy has been to throw open numerous avenues for the admission of juvenile labourers into the arena
of industrial activity. In many departments of industry
the assistance rendered by children has become essential
to the interest of the employer. " Education may be a
very good thing in its way," says the manufacturer and
agriculturist, " but we *must* have the children." This de-
claration (as teachers have told me) has frequently derived
the irresistible force with which it has appealed to the
parent's mind from the accompanying intimation, that
unless the services of the child are given up those of the
parent will no longer be required. In the mining, manufacturing, agricultural, and pottery districts, the labour
of children is in frequent or constant demand,—a demand,
too, which owes much of its influence with parents to the

charm of a ready-money payment with which it is attended. I have spoken thus briefly of the *first*, and, as I think, *chief* cause of the early withdrawal of children from school. To mention another, I would observe, that this demand for juvenile labour derives its power from the fact of its having been preferred by the employer at a most critical period of our national history; in other words, before we had called into existence a force to meet and counteract it. It intervened at a time when the great work of educating our population had advanced but a very small way indeed. It experienced no check; on the contrary, there was everything to favour its influence. It engaged the sympathies of an uneducated race of parents, who cared little or nothing for school-training, because a taste for education had not been created among them generally. The work of forming this taste was commenced too late in England, or rather the demand for children's labour was made too soon; at all events a sufficient time did not elapse between the beginning of the educational movement, and the increased pressure brought to bear upon us by employers. I say "increased," because a certain amount of juvenile labour has always been in request. It was natural that parents, in the absence of a feeling in favour of education, should at once incline to the immediate pecuniary advantage to accrue to them from the industry of their children; in short, to prefer the substance to what appeared to them to be a mere shadow. The nation was behind time. It had hardly arrived at the dawn of its intellectual day, when the meridian of industrial activity and improvement overtook it, attended by a host of claims antagonistic to the cause of school-training. A crisis has ensued in consequence. On the one side there is the demand for the labour of children preferred by the employer, on the other, the ready acquiescence of uneducated parents in that demand. Had it occurred later, and been exerted on an *educated* population, the effect would have been different from what it was. What it really would have been it is perhaps impossible to say, but I incline to believe that the sympathy of the labouring classes on the side of education would have been so overpowering that the parent would almost naturally have come to prefer the prospective well-being of his child to immediate gain. Education would have been considered a necessary qualification, and English parents would perhaps have felt as much reverence for it, and have been as inclined to make present sacrifices to secure it for their families, as the Irish or the Scotch. Our case stands thus at this moment : imperfect reading, imperfect writing, imperfect arithmetic, and very imperfect spelling, are considered by the working classes the limits of the knowledge required by their children; and as these may be gained much sooner than formerly, so much sooner than formerly are the children withdrawn from school. And it must not be forgotten that this knowledge, being necessarily very imperfect, is soon lost, as anyone who knows the working of our night schools can testify. Children have been paid for coming to school before this, but the plan has failed when the sum which could be realised by work has been found greater than that obtained by attendance at school. Were the Prize scheme to be applied in such cases, I confess I should tremble very much for its success. To state a case in point I will read, with your permission, an extract from a letter received a few days ago from a clergyman who has the care of a parish in a mining district. He is a kind and energetic man, and his schools are very fairly conducted, so that the evil to which he refers cannot be attributed to any personal disqualifications on his part for ensuring success, or to the defective education afforded his parishioners :—

" The pensioners in this school, belonging to my parish, receive 9*d*. each per week, which sum is given to them in clothing. They are admitted at the age of *seven*, and if they remain their full time (6 years) they are entitled to 10*l*. from another charity to apprentice them out to some trade. If they serve their apprenticeship faithfully, there is again another charity, open, I believe, to the whole county, which gives them 10*l*. more towards setting them up in business. Thus you will see that there is every possible inducement for parents to keep their children at school. Nevertheless, it is very seldom that any of them are allowed to remain their *first* time [that is to say, the 6 years]. Formerly (that is before the iron-stone mines were opened), the average age at which they left, as nearly as I can ascertain, was 13, but now it is not 11. Children cannot by law be put to work at the collieries under 10, but this does not apply to the iron-stone mines, at which they are taken as soon as they are capable of doing anything. I cannot say that I consider the poverty of the parents to be the general cause of their early removal. The real cause is that parents, for the sake of present gain, are content to sacrifice the future, and too often, I fear, the eternal, welfare of their children. At this present time there are no less than eight vacant apprenticeships for which there are no applicants. The parish contains a population of 623 souls. You, sir, must be well aware how disheartening it is to those engaged in their education to see the most promising lads continually removed just at a time when their previous instruction is beginning to tell upon them, with a certainty that in a few months what little knowledge they may have acquired, will all have vanished away. For my own part I am quite convinced that without some legislative enactment, such as I believe is now in operation with respect to factories, education in these parts must retrograde. All educational measures will be utterly useless, unless some check be placed upon the employment of juvenile labour."

It must not be forgotten that employers have urged with much force, what at first appears to be a very cogent reason for engaging the services of children at an early age. They assert that unless they commence manual labour early in life they will be totally useless as labourers when they grow up, in fact that labour requires a long apprenticeship. It is easy to perceive the truth of this doctrine, but it has its limits. Doubtless it would be impolitic to allow the period of moral and intellectual training to encroach on that required for a due training in industrial pursuits ; and the zealous advocates of national education must be careful that their zeal in favour of the former, does not tempt them to overlook the imperative claims of the latter. It appears to me, however, that the argument advanced by employers involves the assumption of a point which has not yet been proved. If they mean to defend the common practice of engaging the services of children, at the tender age of 9 or 10 years, on the ground that it is essential to their future qualifications as labourers, they virtually beg the entire question at issue. They are, at least, bound to establish the fact that a child who commences labour at the age of 12 or 13 will not become as good a labourer as one who begins work at the age of 9 or 10. And, assuming that there is no foundation for the fact, they would simply have to prove this by citing the actual results of experiments on both sides of the case. But they have not yet done this, at least I am not aware that they have ever adduced any detailed evidence calculated to determine the absolute conditions of industrial competency in connection with the age at which children should commence labour. We all know that 14 years is generally considered a favourable age for beginning an apprenticeship to most, if not all trades. The name of Mr. Sheriff Mechi, of Tiptree Hall, is probably well known to most persons present. He has for many years been connected with agricultural pursuits, and his opinion on a subject with which he is so intimately acquainted, ought to carry with it considerable weight. A short time ago I proposed a question to that gentleman, which seemed to me to be of much importance. It was this : " At what age do you consider a boy ought to be sent to work on a farm in order that he may become a good agricultural labourer?" His answer was, "11 or 12 years would be a sufficiently early age for an agricultural training." Now as we have the choice of the one or the other of these ages, and as the moral and intellectual training must be provided for as much as the industrial, let us select the age of "twelve" as a condition of future success in at least agricultural pursuits. But how painful is the consideration to which this assumption gives rise! For what are the facts of the case? Barely one-fourth of the aggregate number of children under instruction continue their school-life up to the age of 12; nearly two-fourths complete their education at an age somewhere between 10 and 11; probably 30 per cent., certainly more than one-fourth, are altogether lost to the schools at the age of 9; and the small number of scholars who do remain under instruction up to the age of 12 (that named by Mr. Mechi for commencing labour), are the children, not of the working classes, but of the small farmer, the bailiff, the shopkeeper, and the respectable artisan. Now, if by commencing work at the age of 12 sufficient time may be secured to the young for industrial training, and if, moreover, it be of the utmost importance that every child should attend school five years instead of two (for making a deduction on account of irregular attendance the school-life of a poor child seldom exceeds two years), it certainly appears to be absolutely necessary that something should be done at once to bring us past the present educational crisis, and bridge over the gulf which now separates us from some firmer resting-place for our whole social fabric. The genius and spirit of the Conference have a basis in one direction, and, therefore, I shall not allude to a remedy which has often suggested itself to me, simply because it may meet with your disapprobation. To discuss remedies does not appertain to the business of this section; but I trust I may be excused for alluding to a plan, in strict accordance with voluntary agency, which, as far as I know, has not received the notice of educationists. I would submit for the consideration of the Conference, the propriety of forming a Central Committee of distinguished persons, who should keep a sort of register, in which employers should be invited to enter their names as having engaged to employ the services of no child under the age say of 13, who could not produce a certificate of his attendance at some school for two days in the preceding week. This registration of names voluntarily made should be considered an honorary mark of distinction, one entitled to the respect of the highest and noblest in the country.

But I pass on to the last point for the consideration of the section — the "Results" of the early removal of children from school. The complaints which are made in this respect by school-managers are most deplorable. They state that the children have scarcely attained an age favourable to the work which the teacher has to perform — to a period of life when the reasoning faculties begin to expand and the appetite for knowledge grows keen — than they are snatched, as it were, out of the circle of all the salutary associations and restraints that belong to school life, with an abruptness which appears merciless, and a disregard for their future well-being most reckless in its kind and degree. They state, also, that when thus withdrawn, the children, feeble in moral control over themselves, because defrauded of due moral training, are plunged at once into the vortex of daily business and experience — a collision with all that is bad — long before they have acquired sufficient culture to enable them to resist it. I am of course attributing a *moral* as well as an intellectual influence to education. It must be confessed that the prevailing tendency of the age in regard to the rising generation has too exact a resemblance to the act of exposing a poor unfledged bird of a tropical clime to the rigor of an Arctic winter. With such a system in operation amongst us, we cannot wonder that there should be found persons who are asking for more satisfactory proofs of the value of national education, and who altogether doubt its benefits.

To say nothing of the rapidity with which the children, who are soon removed from school, lose the little knowledge they once possessed (and this is too easily proved by the experience gained in our night schools), there is another result which must not be overlooked. The physical strength and energies of the young children of both sexes are overtasked by the heavy demands made upon them by constant labour. The depression and languor which they consequently endure are too great for strength already subject to excessive exactions. For relief, they turn to the aid afforded by unlawful excitement, and thus influences are at work which strike into the root of our moral and social economy.

I cannot refrain from expressing a hope, that this great Educational Conference of 1857 may be the means of drawing the attention of employers of labour, of parents, and of the nation at large, to the difficulties under which we are labouring; and that it may tend to excite a widespread desire to diminish, and eventually remove them. Those who are in the habit of engaging the services of the young have an immense leverage at hand for raising the opinion of the classes beneath them to a level with the importance of education. By giving the preference to those who have attended school the longest, and by insisting on certain intellectual qualifications for labour, they may effect a grand improvement in this country. But they must not forget that in thus dealing with the evils which hedge us round about, there is great need that they should distinguish between a parent's *inability* to educate his child, and his *indifference* in the matter.

On the Educational Statistics of the last Census, in so far
as they bear on Children at School, Work, and Neither,
with the practical Conclusions to which they lead. By
W. H. HYETT, Esq., F.R.S.

THE purport of the present Paper is—by condensing into
a short abstract the Educational Returns of the last
Census, which indicate the relative numbers of children at
school, at work, and at neither,—to bring them under
the attention of those who have not time for an investigation requiring some trouble and thought, and to notice
briefly the causes and remedies to which they seem to
point.

The Population Returns of the Census of 1851 gave
4,908,696 children between the ages of 3 and 15, out of
the total population for England and Wales of all ages of
17,927,609.

The official report of Mr. Horace Mann to the Registrar-
General in 1854 gives a Table based on the Returns under
the compulsory powers of the Census indicating that of
these 4,908,696, 2,046,848 [taken from the Returns to
the Schedule of Questions on Education issued at the time
of the Census] had their names on the books of some day
school on March 31, 1851, while 599,829, employed for
wages, were not at any day school, leaving a remainder of
2,262,019, who, not being stated in the compulsory
Returns of the Householders to be at school or work,
were not positively described. A large proportion of
these must have been at the same time under no process
of instruction or employment—in fact, loitering about

the streets and fields in idleness and mischief, destined to
lives of destitution, drunkenness, and crime, to which a
youth of idleness is the door of entrance.

The point I propose first to ascertain is, what that
proportion was?

The Table in the Census distinguishes the classes
above referred to under four columns, headed respectively
" Scholars," " Employed," " Undescribed," and the
" Total ;" showing also the centesimal proportions to be
42 scholars, 12 employed, and 46 undescribed.

Up to the publication of Mr. Mann's Report in 1854,
it was the almost universal opinion that the *chief* reason
why popular schools did not fill was that parents were
tempted by the small earnings of their children to send
them to work.

But if this Table be correct, or anything like it, it will
at once be seen that it involves important practical conclusions calling for some other explanation. If only 12
per cent. of those of school age are not at school because
they are at work, while 46 per cent. are not at work nor
at school, we must seek for other reasons, more comprehensive than work and wages, to account for the absence
of this far larger proportion who are not at work.

The degree of credit, then, to which these Tables are
entitled, is the chief question which I propose to consider.

That their accuracy has been somewhat vehemently
attacked must be known to many of you — as indeed was
to be expected — for the inquiry was not only met in
advance, and embarrassed from the beginning by an opposition which seems to be the common fate of statistical
inquiries, but its results, when published, being at variance
with preconceived opinions, were naturally enough dis-
trusted and discredited.

The Table referred to is based on the general compulsory returns made by the householders under the Census. It is true the number of the " scholars" is taken in preference from the Educational Returns, which being actual returns from only 44,836 of the 46,042 schools on the lists of the enumerators, were calculated by analogy for the difference, *i. e.* for the 1206 schools from which no returns were obtained. But the returns received, though given voluntarily, bear, as I am informed, many indications of being carefully prepared by the authorities of the various schools [in very many cases by the clergy], underwent the searching investigation of a year's correspondence between the Registrar-General's Office and the enumerators, and on the important point, which is our present object, viz., the proportion of those at school to those not at school through the country, they agree so closely with the intimations of the compulsory returns*, and the opinions of the most competent educational statisticians, that the conclusions on this point are not to be hastily discredited on mere suspicion.

The Registrar-General, in his preface to the Report states, " Great pains have been taken to obtain as complete returns as possible. Still they cannot be stated to be entirely perfect," . . . . " but I believe that in considering the question of providing education for the people, these *returns may be relied on for all practical purposes.*" And, indeed, when attentively and impartially considered, the inquiry seems to have been conducted by Mr. Mann under considerable difficulties, with a perseverance, ability, accuracy, fairness, and success, well calculated to help us in our search for the causes of those ills, which we are all of us striving to cure.

---

* The difference of the total number of the scholars derived from the compulsory returns of the householders, and of that obtained from the voluntary returns to the educational questions being a little more than $1\frac{1}{2}$ per cent.

The chief complaint against the returns is that the amount of education in the country must have been over-stated; inasmuch as they were only voluntarily made by parties interested in exaggerating the numbers of their own schools. Yet the result of these returns was that only 42 per cent. were actually at school, leaving it to be inferred that the whole difference, viz., 58 per cent., *were not at school*—a showing surely bad enough ; but, if it be true that the numbers of scholars are thus exaggerated, exactly in the same proportion matters are so much the worse, and all argument based on defective Education is strength-ened.

To adopt the numbers in the Report is to err on the safe side. It is not then necessary to meet these objec-tions, though, in passing, it may be noticed that I am told the numbers of scholars obtained from the voluntary re-turns are actually rather less than those from the compul-sory schedule ; the former giving only 2,144,000, and the latter 2,182,000, or 33,000 more. Still, be this as it may, the position that those at school are only 42 per cent. of the whole is strong enough.

But there are objections on the other side which must be dealt with. It is urged that to infer from the figures of the table " *that children who are neither at work nor school are uneducated is a fallacy, for numbers are educated at home;*" and certainly the objection, if urged to the bare table, as it stands printed, is a valid one, and it must at once be admitted that the column headed "undescribed," comprises not only the educated at home, but also the employed at home, who, if we are fairly to estimate the proportions under education and employment ought to come under the columns of the " scholars" and the " em-ployed ;" and that many whose health precludes schooling or work should be struck from the account altogether; but it must be observed that these are all points noticed in the text by Mr. Mann himself, for which he affords the best means in his power to calculate the necessary deductions.

That Mr. Mann has printed his table without making these allowances could scarcely be otherwise. In an official report he was bound to give the results of the returns in the form in which they were made; the allowances required are more or less of an arbitrary character, and it was only right to leave his readers to judge of their value, and to make them for themselves. Still such objections as these, when made to the tables generally, without full explanation, damage their credibility, and create an impression that, if the corrections suggested were in fact introduced, the general results might be so changed that the conclusions to be legitimately drawn from them would be the very reverse of what they are now.

How far the true results are so disturbed can only be ascertained by recalculating the table, subject to the several allowances for these disturbing causes. This I have done, and, as few ever follow the details of such calculations stated *vivâ voce*, I have had corrected tables printed *, that any one who thinks the figures in detail are worth attention may refer to them. You will see that for each separate correction the table is re-calculated, with a note explanatory of the process, so that you may at once estimate its accuracy, and the degree in which the results and the deductions to be drawn from them are modified.

At present I confine myself to stating the general result.

Pursuing, then, the corrections through the first four tables, you will see that while No. I., which is the Table of the Census condensed, gives 42 per cent. as " scholars," 12 per cent. as " employed," and 46 per cent. as " unde-

* These Tables (see Appendix) were handed round when the paper was read.

scribed," No. IV., the last table but one of the series, after the several corrections are made seriatim, gives 45 per cent. of those in health as under daily tuition, 16 per cent. as at work, either for wages or at home ; and 39 per cent. neither under instruction nor employment ; — a difference so inconsiderable that it proves at once that these defects, which were thought to impair confidence in these tables, when actually supplied, leave the proportions very little altered.

Still, having observed for years past the numbers who are taken and kept from school by early employment, and being strongly of opinion, in common with others, that it was the chief cause of our unfilled schools, I have been reluctant to admit the truth of a position so different; and, to test it, as far as a single instance is worth anything, in January last I had a house-to-house visitation made in Painswick, the parish where I reside, by a very intelligent parish officer, who, on one of his rounds to collect a rate, entered at every house the numbers of all the children between 3 and 15 — distinguishing those at " school," at "work," and at "neither." His return, which I have reason to believe is strictly accurate, is printed in Table V. in your hands.

You will see that the proportions are 56 per cent. at school, 16 at work, and 28 at neither.   The 16 per cent. at work is exactly the same as that of the average for all England given in the previous table.   But it should be observed that, if the allowances had been made, this proportion, as well as the others, would have been somewhat altered.   It is true that the 56 per cent. at school, compared with the 45, the average of all England, is large; and the 28 per cent. at neither, as compared with the 39 for England, is consequently small; but this is explained by the fact that both education and work in this place are pushed to some extent, which, thus coming into the strongest contrast, offer a fit subject of comparison.

While, *on the one hand*, as it contains more than 7000 acres, many boys are employed in agriculture, and, having a silk mill, a pin mill, and two woollen mills, many girls also are employed in them ; *on the other*, there are two private and six public schools within its precincts, none of them full, and one free. So that for collating the conflicting influence of school and work, it would not be easy to find a better criterion; and yet the results confirm the position that work is insufficient to account for so many school absences.

It must be admitted that single instances are not of much value when general averages are considered; but local returns are at least useful to teach school managers how far their own district is in accordance with general conditions, and enable them to adapt their educational schemes to its peculiar wants. I allude to this return the rather to show how easily valuable local information of this sort may be attained, and to throw out the hint, that if the present Conference were to adopt and recommend a uniform scheme for such inquiries (the simpler the better), their usefulness would be much enhanced. Varying forms of returns, not admitting of general comparison, are limited to narrow and local objects.

I am aware that similar inquiries have been made in other places, and with somewhat different results, especially in Birmingham, where, I hear, they indicate that rather larger proportions of children are kept from school by work; but in such places as Birmingham, Sheffield, the Potteries, and especially where silk and lace mills prevail, such a state of things was to be expected; nor does it by any means follow that they are anything more than exceptions to *the general rule, which, with these tables for all England before me, I must still hold to be that* WORK AND WAGES *are not the chief cause of absence from school.*

If not, what is ? Is it poverty and inability to pay the small school fee ? On this point the official report states that " The condition of many of the *free* schools, where *no* payment is demanded of the scholar, seems to show that ' poverty ' is not an adequate explanation of the children's absence ; for in many *free* schools, though located in the midst of populous neighbourhoods, the attendance of scholars is less numerous and much less constant than in schools which require a fee. The fact that free schools, well conducted, may be found half empty, while a multitude of uninstructed children who might enter them remain outside, seems inconsistent with the theory that *poverty* of the parents is the chief impediment to a sufficient school attendance ; " a position which the experience of the parish of which you have the return before you tends to confirm ; for its free school, though open to twenty-six " poor boys," and though a public quarterly notice is regularly given that candidates will be admitted, is seldom more than half full. At present there are fifteen free boys—a larger number than there has been for some years before.

Or is it that want of schools sufficiently accounts for the multitudes not returned as at any school ? Partially, though only partially, it may. But with the admitted fact before us all, of so many schools in every direction not nearly full, as well as localities where schools and absentees not at work abound together, we can scarcely conclude that paucity of schools is the main cause of paucity of scholars, at least not till individual and official inquiry in various parts of the country shall have shown the positive numbers who actually have no school within reach, and enable us to distinguish between general and exceptional conditions.

And here I hope I may be permitted to press the vast advantages which such inquiries, methodically and impartially made, must confer on the country,—indeed, their *necessity*, while any doubts rest on the subject.

But to pursue the argument to its conclusion.

Assuming that this general absence from school is not sufficiently accounted for by want of schools, nor by wages, nor by poverty, what can we conclude but that parents undervalue Education? Even in the case of either of the two latter causes, though different in degree, the same ultimate motive, a preference for something else, is at the bottom of it all; for none are so poor that, if they esteemed Education, they could not forego what a weekly penny procures, to pay for it.

If, then, the foregoing premises are at all correct, we must at last fall back on the indifference of parents as the true explanation of our difficulty. Nor let us be surprised that it is so. They have never realised the benefits of school in their own persons. In their youth the only schooling within their reach was a little reading, writing, and, but rarely, a little ciphering, taught by some old dame, so imperfectly that it was forgotten as soon as learnt, or, if remembered, never sufficient to be of any real use in after life; nor have they as yet found out that within the last few years the education of the people is of a much higher class; or, if they have, they hear at the same time that history, geography, and music form part of the modern scheme, and, naturally enough, do not as yet understand how a knowledge of such subjects is, as they express it, to put bread in their mouths. Indeed, it must be admitted, however desirable it might be that all these branches of learning should be taught to all who wish to learn them, that they are not exactly calculated to awaken the poor and the ignorant to the real worth of education. The question is not whether they ought to be taught, but whether those whom we have to teach will come to learn them. In the hard and earnest struggle for daily bread, the poor are thinking of what leads to better wages and more physical comforts.

It is in vain to hold out to the destitute and the ignorant the pleasures and advantages of intellectual cultivation; they turn upon you and say they ask for bread and you give them a stone.

What, then, is the remedy for such a state of things? What inducement can we lay before the people, to tempt them to regard education with more favour?

Of course we are only now treating of remedies which schools offer. I am well aware that, to raise the social condition of the poor till they can appreciate the full value of education, many other concurrent agencies must be at work. But I may perhaps be permitted, in passing, to quote a general answer, which has been so well given by Mr. Mann to the question—" What is wanted to ensure a greater measure of success to our present efforts?" " Surely," he says, " the creation of a more benignant atmosphere. However carefully the tree of Knowledge may be planted, and however diligently tended, it can never grow to fruitfulness and beauty in an uncongenial air. Concurrently with all direct attempts to cultivate the popular intelligence there needs to be a vigorous endeavour to alleviate, if not remove, that social wretchedness which blights all educational promise, and to shed around the growing popular mind an influence of wholesome light on which the half-developed plant may feed and thrive. . . . The movements on behalf of temperance, health, cleanliness, and better dwellings; or, for public lectures, libraries, and cheap and wholesome literature, must, by raising the condition of the people, and by bringing within their reach the *fruits* of intellectual toil, inevitably tend to render education much more valued, and, therefore, much more sought after."

But to revert to the question as it especially regards education.

What can we DO to render it more valued, and therefore more sought after? How can we enlist the sympathies of the masses, without which all other remedies are inadequate?

Assuredly by better adapting our schools to what the people *feel* they want. By selling the article they want to buy. It is in vain to offer broad cloth to the navvy and satins to his wife, they must have the strong and the warm to stand work and weather — fustian jackets and stuff gowns. The industry of which these are part and parcel leads to better things eventually. So with schools. First, let us offer what fits for the future struggle of life. The poor will not be slow to find out its purpose and its use. Schools will become more popular. Scholars will remain longer; and the majority may then attain, concurrently with a more practical scheme of instruction, a prolonged education in higher and nobler subjects, which so few now remain long enough to enjoy. To begin with these is to begin at the wrong end.

It was well observed, a year or two ago, in an able article in the *Times*, that "in the village there is a very general distrust of the education given in parochial schools, as of an unreal, formal, and useless character." The object I propose would be to make a direct effort to remove that distrust, by modifying what seems to be unreal, formal, and useless; and it was added, "that children should be taught to use their senses and understandings upon all that passes around them;" — " that while the studies of the university are reformed, why should not the humbler course of the village school be adapted a little to the outer world, and rendered a school for the observation, judgment, and active powers, as well as the faculties usually summed up in the word *Scholarship*."

But to be more precise. Let us infuse into our schools a little more of the practical, which, notwithstanding what Canon Moseley said yesterday, I still venture to call the *industrial* principle, and to press on your consideration, not that I expect children of $10\frac{1}{2}$ to profit by it (and this I beg to be distinctly observed); but what I do expect is, that it will teach parents to look at our schools more favourably, and to leave their children longer under our care than till 10 or 11.

Let us then, I say, infuse a little more of the practical — a little gardening, or carpentry, or mechanical drawing, or printing, or any other manual dexterity suited to peculiar localities or the abilities of particular masters; — let us educate the hand as well as the head,—and so interest both children and their parents; and let us add, whenever we can keep them long enough, some of the elements of those sciences on which the practical arts of every day life depend.   Let us allot the afternoons, or one or two in the week, to some instructive recreation of this sort. The mornings are quite sufficient for head-work. I assure you I am not theorising; I only recommend what I know from some years' experience to have been easily carried out, and what I believe, under the most unpromising circumstances, keeps schools fuller and scholars longer than where such attempts are not made.

When I speak of the Industrial Principle, I am not meaning what is sometimes meant by Industrial Schools, the chief object of which is to enable scholars to earn small wages, so as to retain them longer. What I am pressing especially, is the moral effect on parents and children of a more practical teaching. Still, there are instances where wages are systematically worked out with more ease and success than is generally thought possible, of which, in passing, I may, perhaps, be permitted to notice one of the most remarkable. Although under our eyes, its details up to the present time, are probably unknown to many of you.

The late William Davis, Esq., of Leytonstone, Essex, built and endowed, in 1807, the Free School in Gower's Walk, Whitechapel. "He introduced the Industrial Principle," (I quote from a notice of his death in 1854,) " he introduced the Industrial Principle, be it observed, near half a century before many who now treat it as a recent invention. Printing suited his locality. In 1808 he acquired his first types. In 1818, the year's profits on the printing account had gradually risen to 518*l.* 18*s.* 10*d.*, about which sum they continued steadily till the last Report, which the writer has seen,—that for 1849,—when the total value of the school property, including the original endowment of 2000*l.* and premises, had risen by outlay chiefly drawn from profits to 9726*l.* 17*s.* 2*d.*

" But the mere profits of the school, except as the criterion of its prosperity, are nothing, when compared with its effects on the children. The scheme of management is this. Some of the more diligent and proficient are allowed, as a reward, to work two hours a day at the printing. The eagerness to gain this indulgence is a stimulus to the diligence of all. The industrious receive a share of the profits of their industry—half in money, and half placed in a Savings' Bank, in their respective names, to be paid to each on condition of his remaining at school till the age of fourteen. Of course they remain, for they are started on an apprentice fee or a small fund, with which, and the habits of useful and provident industry, acquired at the school, to begin a life of comparative comfort and happiness, which they owe, for the most part, to William Davis."

The management of the school, on the death of Mr.

Davis in 1854, passed to trustees, under a trust deed appointing the Bishop of London for the time the Visitor. In 1855 they report that the school " is in the same state of complete *efficiency* which has characterised its condition during the last forty-seven years ; and the experience of nearly half a century having fully tested the value of the principles on which it was founded, they desire strictly to adhere to the system, so wisely adopted by the late most excellent founder, as defined in the deed of endowment — ' THE TRAINING UP CHILDREN IN THE PRINCIPLES OF THE CHRISTIAN RELIGION, AND IN HABITS OF USEFUL INDUSTRY.' "

What that efficiency has been may be judged from the following facts : —

The boys' school, though exposed to the competition of a district where, out of a population of 16,000, there are at the different schools, as I am informed, 2200 children, or 1 in 7¼, is always more than full ; and the monthly admission days, from the commencement to the present day, seldom pass without many being rejected.

The average of absences, including sick, rarely exceeds 8 per cent. ; while in good inspected schools it often ranges from 20 to 30.

With very few exceptions, the scholars remain till the age of 14.

Several subsequently pass very satisfactorily a course of three months' instruction for confirmation under the rector of the parish, the Rev. Weldon Champneys ; and several become steady teachers in his excellent Sunday school.

Many old scholars, originally drawn from the very poorest, are now scattered over London in respectable situations, some of whom have lately, at their own expense, put up in Whitechapel Church a monument recording the worth of their benefactor, in terms which, for modest truth and beautiful simplicity, can scarcely be surpassed.

While the boys' school, under the influence of the industrial element, has thus thriven, the girls' school, on the other hand, which from the commencement had adopted needlework, as their industrial branch, continued as popular and full as the boys, till needlework, either taken up by neighbouring schools, or from other causes, fell off; when numbers decreased, and now for many years the girls' school has never been full; the attendance is less regular, and they leave at an earlier age than the boys.

But a scheme for a small kitchen, at another girls' school in Whitechapel, is under the consideration of Mr. Champneys, who has done so much for Ragged Schools. Should it succeed, Mr. John Davis, the son of the founder of Gower's Walk, who worthily follows in the steps of his father, proposes to introduce one there; and should the numbers again increase under such a stimulant, it will afford a still stronger illustration of the advantages of industrial training.

For this digression I should apologise, did I not feel that no one can well judge of those advantages, whose attention has not been directed to Gower's Walk, and that, in citing it, to omit to name its founder, would be to fail in giving honour where honour is due.

Were the effects which the boys' school at Gower's Walk is, and has been, producing for nearly half a century, common to all schools, popular education would be in a far sounder state than it is. Indeed, the scheme seems to obviate most of the defects of which we now complain, so fatal to general educational advancement. It is true, that while the founder professed, as he states in his trust deed, "To promote habits of industry as well as of religion, being persuaded that the former object may be auxiliary to the latter," in secular learning he did not strive to teach more than reading, writing, and arithmetic; but his object was *to teach them well.* Higher branches of learning, now common to most schools, he did not attempt. In the days of Dr. Bell he began by excluding them, and persisted to the last, " continuing " (I quote from his epitaph) " to watch over these institutions with tenacious simplicity of purpose, and full energy of mind, to the advanced age of 88." Nevertheless, in spite of such exclusion, the scholars prosper in life, and the school is popular and full. That its extraordinary popularity and success is chiefly due to its industrial principle, cannot be doubted; but it must at once be admitted that the chief attraction is probably to be found in the wages earned, though the weekly payment rarely exceeds from 3*d.* to 6*d.*

As an example for other schools, no doubt, so profitable a business can seldom be worked out; still, much more may often be done with ease than is at first supposed. When it is, our end is gained. A school may be kept full to overflowing for fifty years, and the poorest children remain at it till 14 years old. When the industrial branch falls off, we fail; the school sinks into the half-empty condition so common elsewhere, and the children leave at the early age of which we complain. But examples are by no means wanting to show that industrial and practical training introduced into a school, even without wages, goes far to satisfy parents that their children are being fitted for a life of successful industry, and so to fill the school.

I mentioned in the early part of this paper that the proportion at school in Painswick, as shown by the table in your hands, is 56 per cent., while that of all England is only 45. A few years ago the success of Gower's Walk attracted the attention of one of the Managers, and hoping,

but without much expecting to work out wages, he imported such parts of the Gower's Walk plan as were calculated to infuse into the school habits of practical industry,
which, while they interested the children, would satisfy
the parents, and most of the afternoons are now devoted
to teaching the use of the hand in various ways.   The
numbers, regularity of attendance, age to which scholars
remain, and school fees, are all raised.   To venture the
positive opinion that all this is directly due to the practical character of the training would be premature and presumptuous, but it seems probable that it explains the
larger proportion of "scholars" in that parish; and *almost
certain that the retaining scholars to a more advanced age
may be directly traced to it.*

Briefly to recapitulate.

While the tables of the Census place it beyond doubt,
that far the largest proportion of children who ought to
be, but are not, at school are not at work, it seems highly
probable that, seeing that in localities where empty Free
Schools and absentees, though not at work, abound together, neither the deficiency of schools, nor the inability
to pay the school fees, nor the employment of children,
are enough to account for so many absentees, we must
conclude that parental indifference to education is the
root of the evil; and that to meet that indifference the best
remedy is to adapt our schools to the wants of the people
more than we have done—that is, to make them more
practical, though it may, but need not be, at the sacrifice
of some of the higher points of book-learning; and *this,*
especially, be it added, as regards girls' schools and *their*
industrial training.   Many certain indications tell us that
female education is far more neglected than male; particularly that all qualifications for the special duties of the
sex, except needlework, which is often less practical than

it should be, have been heretofore almost universally disregarded.

On this point, however, fortunately, public opinion is beginning to be awakened. Our Gracious Queen's Industrial Girl's School at Windsor, Lady Guernsey's at Offchurch, Miss Martineau's at Norwich, Mr. Armitsted's at Sandbach, in Cheshire, and especially the Model School at Belfast, from all of which very valuable hints may be taken, as well as Miss Burdett Coutts's admirable scheme of prizes for common things at the Whitelands Training College, clearly point to the great want of the day.

If the country is to be prosperous and happy, we must educate, and educate *practically*, the mothers of the people. We have not done it hitherto. Let us teach them the value of practical training, and, be assured, when the mother feels it in her own person, the mother's affection will take care that her children shall enjoy it. The remedy may be slow, but it is certain. To blot out the disgrace of national ignorance, *educate mothers*.

One word more. In maintaining that work and wages are *not* the chief cause of empty schools, pray do not suppose I am arguing against any half-time measure which can be made available. On the contrary, 16 per cent. of all of school age are certainly kept from school by work, some of whom half-time measures will assuredly bring into the fold. Nor that I would slight prize schemes and examinations, which indeed might work admirably with the industrial element, particularly when employers, in want of intelligent and handy boys or girls for good situations, are induced habitually to apply to the school for those who have distinguished themselves by prizes or general good conduct and *industry*, and when such applications, becoming general, shall have satisfied parents that the school itself is the door to future advancement and success in life. But in pressing half-time or prize schemes, let us not expect too much from *them* ALONE ; nor forget, that in our present condition, far the largest proportion of the uneducated will be directly touched by neither ; nor that, if education is to be popular, the people must be led to feel its value.

———•———

APPENDIX.

TABLES referred to by Mr. HYETT at the EDUCATIONAL CONFERENCE, June 23rd, 1857, recalculated from the Census, to show that allowances made to meet certain objections do not affect the results in any considerable degree.

TABLE I.

Condensed from Table 2, in the Official Report of Mr. Horace Mann to the Registrar General on the Census of 1851, EDUCATION.— Showing,— the total number of Children between the ages of 3 and 15 in England and Wales on March 31st, 1851, and the relative proportions of " Scholars " whose names were on the Books of some Day School,— of those, who, being "Employed" for wages, were not on the Books of any such School,— and of the remainder, under the head of the " Undescribed " in the Returns, who, it may be persumed, were neither at School nor at Work.

	Scholars.	Employed.	Undescribed.	Total.	Per Centage of		
					Sch.	Em.	Und.
Males	1,106,528	381,774	978,179	2,466,481	45	15·5	39·5
Females	940,320	218,055	1,283,840	2,442,215	38·5	9	52·5
Total	2,046,848	599,829	2,262,019	4,908,696	41·7	12·2	46·1

TABLE II.

Showing the allowances made in TABLE I. *for those educated at home.*

	Scholars.	Employed.	Undescribed.	Total.	Per Centage of.		
					Sch.	Em.	Und.
Males	1,125,914	381,774	958,793	2,466,481	45·6	15·5	38·9
Females	970,934	218,055	1,253,226	2,442,215	40	9	51
Total	2,096,848	599,829	2,212,019	4,908,696	42·7	12·2	45·1

The correction adopted is this. Mr. H. Mann states the numbers of those returned in the " Householder's Schedule " as " Scholars at Home" to be 17,302 males, and 27,323 females, in all 44,625, but these numbers do not comprise children under 5. He suggests that to meet the difference of those between 3 and 5, 50,000 (preserving the proportions of the sexes, viz., 19,386 males to 30,614, females), may be assumed as the number of "Scholars at Home," an allowance which seems amply sufficient for all between 3 and 15. These latter numbers therefore in the Table above, are deducted from the males and females respectively in the column of the "Undescribed," and added to that of the " Scholars."

TABLE III.

Showing the allowances made for Girls employed at home.

	Scholars.	Employed.	Neither.	Total.	Per Centage of		
					Sch.	Em.	Nei.
Males	1,125,914	381,774	958,793	2,466,481	45·6	15·5	38·9
Females	970,934	378,543	1,092,738	2,442,215	40	15·5	44·5
Total	2,096,848	760,317	2,051,531	4,908,696	42·7	15·5	41·8

In this case the data for correction are neither so apposite nor certain as in the last. It is not so easy to determine how many girls may be legitimately considered as "employed at home." The question is not how many are said to be so employed, or kept from school by idle parents to do nominal or trifling jobs, but strictly how many are required to do the real work of the house, so that their parents, who ought to do it, may be at liberty to earn wages for the family. The proportion of boys shown in these Tables to be employed is 15·5 per cent. of the whole, while that of the girls is only 9. By raising the one to the other and treating the percentage of the girls as 15·5, we at once carry over from the columns of the " Undescribed" to that of the " Employed " 160,488 girls.

How far is this number sufficient to meet the case? Below *ten* none ought to be, and very few are, employed in work. The total number of girls in England and Wales returned as between *ten* and 15 are of

Scholars.	Employed.	Undescribed.	Total.
301,456	198,418	499,488	999,362

Thus there are 499,488 who might be employed at home ; and the 160,488 proposed to be treated as required for such employment, are to the 499,488 as 1 to 2·8 or 10 in every 28, and when it is recollected that the larger number often comprises more children of the same family within the above limits of the working age than would be required for the work, it may not be thought that the proposed correction is understated.

TABLE IV.

Showing the allowances required for the Sick who are permanently unable to attend School.

	At			Total.	Per Centage at		
	School.	Work.	Neither.		Sch.	Work.	Neith.
Males	1,125,914	381,774	835,469	2,343,157	48	16	36
Females	970,934	378,543	970,628	2,320,105	42	16	42
Total	2,096,848	760,317	1,806,097	4,663,262	45	16	39

Mr. Mann considers that, in a sound educational condition

of the country, it might be expected that as many as 3,908,696 children between 3 and 15 would not be prevented by *employment* from attending school. From that number he subtracts 5 per cent., or 195,435, as a fair deduction for the permanently sick. Not to err on the side which favours the argument, I assume 5 per cent. on *all;* that is, 245,434 as sick, out of 4,908,696, the total children between 3 and 15 ; and in the following table deduct that number from the column of the " Undescribed," and of the " Total ;" and submit that, after these corrections, the Table now gives a sufficiently near approximation to accuracy to enable us to form a fair and safe judgment of the numbers of children in health and of school age, actually scholars at school and at home ; of the numbers employed and consequently not scholars, and of the numbers neither scholars nor employed ; *i. e. of those under education, under employment, and under neither.*

TABLE V.

Showing the total numbers of children in the Parish of Painswick, in the County of Gloucester, in Jan. 1857, between the ages of 3 and 15, and the relative numbres of the same " At School," " Work," and " Neither."

	At			Total.	Proportion per Cent. at		
	School.	Work.	Neither.		School.	Work.	Neither.
Boys	209	76	84	369	56·5	20·5	23
Girls	208	44	125	377	55	12	33
Total	417	120	209	746	56	16	28

The returns for this Table were obtained by employing the Parish Rate Collector, on one of his rounds, to register at every house the answer required. Allowances for the corrections under Tables II., III., and IV. are not made. Had attention been directed to the point in time, the actual numbers required to be transposed might have been ascertained. In small districts actual numbers can alone be relied upon. General averages are found to be quite inapplicable. The Table is published in the Annual Report of the School (Groombridge and Sons, Paternoster-row), and suggests to others the usefulness for local purposes of an inquiry which can be so easily and satisfactorily answered, and removes all doubts how far the locality may be an exception to general rules.

So easy is the above process through the Rate Collector, that an Annual Census of all of school age, " at school," " at work," and " at neither," might be obtained at the expense of a few shillings in each parish. Were the Conference to adopt and recommend a uniform scheme for such returns, their value would be greatly increased to all.

On our past Educational Improvement and the Means of Future Progress, especially in lengthening the Term of Education. By MR. EDWARD BAINES.

THE number of children in this country entirely without education is believed to be very small; the real evil being that their education is too short, and terminates at too early an age.

Although the total number of children in England and Wales, between the ages of 3 and 15 years, is 4,908,696, and of that number only 2,046,848 were found in school at the Census of 1851, it does not follow that those who were not at school at that date never had attended, or would attend school. From the 3rd to the 15th year includes 12 years of life; and it cannot be supposed that the children of the working classes can attend school 12 years. Some of them attend school at one age, and some at another age; comparatively few go to school before they are 5 years old, or continue at school after they are 12. Some are prevented from attending school by sickness or physical defect,—some by the illness or death of parents,—some by the care of younger children,—some by insufficient clothing or want of work, —some by the intemperance, improvidence, or criminality of parents.

The facts are correctly stated by Mr. Horace Mann in his preface to the Educational Census, when he says,—

" The *average* school-time of ALL the children in England and Wales between their 3rd and 15th years, is as nearly as possible *five years;* and between their 5th and 15th years it is 4⅔ *years.*"

It is right to add that there are at least two sources of defect in the educational returns—namely, 1st, that some schools were probably overlooked — a probability confirmed by the fact that the Householders' Returns give 135,893 more children at school under 15 years of age than the School Returns ; and 2nd, that many children receiving education at home are not included in the returns. The Census informs us that there were 44,625 children receiving education at home " from tutors or governesses not members of the family ;" and probably there is a greater number educated by mothers, sisters, or other relatives.

Further, the day-school education is supplemented in England by two most important agencies very little known on the Continent, namely, 1st, by the Sunday schools, 23,514 in number, taught by 318,135 teachers, and containing no less than 2,407,642 scholars,—which gives an average of about *eight years* of Sunday school instruction for every child of the working classes; and 2nd, by the Mechanics' Institutions and Mental Improvement Societies, of which above a thousand were enumerated in the Census, and which are daily increasing in number and efficiency. There is also a third supplemental means of education, namely, the evening schools : those for children were not enumerated in the Census, and those for adults included 39,783 students.

It is encouraging to know from the evidence of the Census, that the educational deficiencies of the country, so far from being on the increase, have, throughout the whole of the present century, been in course of steady and rapid diminution. Our authentic statistics do not extend further back than the year 1818 ; but between that year and the year 1851, whilst the population increased 54 per cent., the number of day scholars increased 218 per cent., and the number of Sunday scholars 404 per cent. Nearly the whole of this extraordinary increase must have been in the children of the working classes, brought for the first time under education. The unendowed public schools, which have been created almost wholly by the zeal and benevolence of religious associations for the express benefit of the labouring classes, numbered only 861 in the returns of 1818, and number 11,390 in the Census of 1851.

If we can ascertain the causes which originated or have carried forward this great work of popular education, we may be enabled to judge whether it is reasonable to expect continued progress from the same causes. In general terms we may ascribe this work to the spirit of the age. But we may more particularly specify, first, the growth of enlightened views on the advantages of education among all the educated classes, spreading gradually and naturally to the classes formerly uneducated; second, the newly discovered power of association, by which many important educational institutions have been formed; third, the zeal of the Established Church and all the other religious communities, each quickening the rest, in providing an education for the young, combining religious knowledge and influence with secular instruction; fourth, the activity of benevolent men, who regarded chiefly the social benefits of education; fifth, the agency of the press, not merely in recommending education, but in cheapening and multiplying books, magazines, newspapers, and tracts, which at once stimulate and gratify the desire for knowledge; sixth, the penny postage, in increasing the inducements to possess the art of writing; seventh, improved systems of education, by which the school has been made more attractive and more obviously useful; eighth, the great advances in science and the mechanical arts, and especially railways and the telegraph; ninth, the increased prosperity of the country, and especially the better wages of the labouring classes; tenth, the stimulus given by our free institutions to the popular intellect; and eleventh, the improvement in the morals and habits of the people, caused by Temperance Societies, Sanitary Reform, City and Town Missions, and all the means of religious and moral instruction.

As all these causes continue in full operation, we may anticipate a continuance of the effects.

But it is our duty to endeavour to remove the evils which still exist; and the principal evil which impedes the success of popular education is the early age at which children are removed from school.

Probably the most efficient means will be found in a systematic visitation of parents, either by the teacher or by members of the school-committee, for the purpose of explaining the advantages of continuing their children longer at school, and the danger of their forgetting what has been learnt if they are removed at too early an age. Such a visitation would be attended with many incidental benefits to the families visited.

Secondly, the distribution to all parents of plain and familiar tracts, showing the credit and practical uses of education, and the disgrace of ignorance, and defining the smallest amount of attainments which ought to satisfy them.

Thirdly, meetings of parents half-yearly at the schools to witness examinations, and to hear addresses on the subject.

Fourthly, practical addresses by the ministers of religion from the pulpit on the value of education and the duty of making it efficient.

Fifthly, associations in every town and district for the promotion of an extended term of education,—their means being public meetings, the press, and personal visits, so as to influence parents, teachers, school-committees, and employers.

Sixthly, honorary certificates on leaving school,—half-time schooling where the nature of the employment makes it practicable,—examinations with prizes, like those recently adopted by the Society of Arts,—a gratuitous introduction to Benefit or Sick Societies, and other means yet to be devised by philanthropic ingenuity, may combine to influence parents and children in favour of extended education.

On the Results of Returns from Birmingham, showing the degree in which Labour and Idleness respectively interfere with Education. By J. D. GOODMAN, Esq., of the Birmingham Education Association.

AT the close of last year an association was formed in Birmingham, the main object of which, at the outset, was the removal of the existing obstacles to education. The opinion was general that the first great obstacle was the ready employment afforded to our children in the workshop, and it was proposed to inquire how far it would be desirable to call in the aid of legislative enactment to moderate this great impediment to the social improvement of the children of our working classes.

The Association at once turned its attention to ascertaining, as far as lay in its power, the real facts of the case, and with this view a Statistical Committee was appointed. The results of the inquiries of this Committee I propose to lay before you in this paper.

The Educational Returns of the Census accompanying the Report of Mr. Horace Mann were first referred to. Much valuable information was there found; but owing to its general character, it did not give such detailed facts as were required by an association having for its object an inquiry into the condition of the children of a locality subject to peculiar influences. It was determined to institute a special inquiry, directed particularly to those facts which would enable the Association to ascertain not only what number of children were receiving the benefits of education, but what description of education they were receiving, and how far the workshop was a barrier to attendance at school.

With this view the assistance of the clergy was called into requisition. A form of return was addressed to the clergyman of each parish and district within the borough. As it would be impossible for the clergy to obtain returns from every house, prepared with that accuracy which the nature of our inquiry rendered necessary, we aimed at obtaining full returns from small numbers scattered over every part of the town. Each clergyman was therefore requested to select in different parts of his district groups of about twenty-five contiguous houses, such parts being chosen as would give fair indications of the state of the working classes, both among the respectable artisans and those resident in our lowest courts. It was requested that returns might be obtained from two such groups in each district. This course has been adopted as far as practicable ; but in the centre of the town the groups are more subdivided, as many streets do not supply more than five or six houses of the class under investigation. The map I now exhibit is marked on each locality from which returns are made with a figure indicating the number of houses in the group. We have returns from fourteen districts. Had we received them from all, we should have had twenty-one. The absent returns account for the blank spaces in the map, which are to be regretted ; at the same time, the fifty-five groups from which we have obtained returns, are so very fairly scattered over almost every part of the map that the information received may be accepted as affording average examples of the entire mass.

It may be well that I should describe the nature of the information asked for in the form of return which we issued. The name of the family is first given, followed by the nature of employment of both father and mother.

From this information respecting the latter, it was hoped to ascertain the effect upon the management of the family caused by the employment of the mother in factory work, or, on the other hand, in attention to her domestic duties. The column has not been filled up with that regularity which has enabled us to arrive at any result.

Then follows a list of the children in each family, including only those between the ages of 7 and 13, this being regarded as the educational age. The age of each child is given in years and months. They are classified under three heads. " At school," " Employed," and " Unemployed." The School column is subdivided into " Day," " Evening," and " Sunday school," so that we may ascertain what description of school each child attends. Under the " Employed " head we have the nature of employment in which the child is engaged, with the age at which he first went to work. The " Unemployed" column receives only those who are neither at day school nor at work; we therefore ask the reason why? The last column in the return calls for remarks on the cases. In this column we frequently learn that drunkenness, neglect, or illness interferes with the good management of the family.

The 55 groups from which the returns have been received include 1043 families, in which were found 1373 children between 7 and 13 years of age, viz., 753 males and 620 females.

Of these 1373 children, 1050, or $76\frac{1}{2}$ per cent., are receiving some kind of education. 42 per cent are at day school, and of these 3-4ths, or $30\frac{1}{2}$ per cent., attend both day and Sunday school.

The next class are those who are employed and also attend such schools as their employment will permit; $22\frac{1}{2}$ per cent. of the children come under this class. They are subdivided into $19\frac{1}{4}$ per cent. who go to Sunday school, $2\frac{1}{3}$ per cent. both evening and Sunday school, and

$\frac{1}{2}$ per cent. evening school only. We thus see that a very few of the employed children resort to evening school; and those who do go to evening school attend Sunday school also, as $\frac{1}{2}$ per cent. only of the children resort to the evening, and neglect the Sunday school.

Having thus found $76\frac{1}{2}$ per cent. of the children at some kind of school, we have $23\frac{1}{2}$ per cent. at none. Of these $10\frac{1}{2}$ per cent. are employed in workshops during the week, and 13 per cent are neither employed nor at school. After deducting the sick out of this 13 per cent., we have here a class in which great improvement may be effected; and indeed, as Sunday school education can do but little when the rest of the week is passed in idleness, we have 25 per cent. of the children of whom the same may be said.

Brought under the three great heads, we have

> 42 per cent. at school; that is at day school.
> 33   ,,   employed.
> 25   ,,   unemployed.

When we compare boys with girls, we find

> At school $41\frac{1}{2}$ per cent., boys.
>   ,, $42\frac{1}{2}$,,   girls.
> Employed $38\frac{1}{2}$,,   boys.
>   ,,   26   ,,   girls.
> Unemployed 20   ,,   boys.
>   ,, $31\frac{1}{2}$,,   girls.

If we trace the children at the several ages, we find that, between

7 and 8 — 58 per cent. are at school, and $4\frac{3}{4}$ per cent. employed.
8 ,, 9 — $61\frac{3}{4}$,,   ,, $11\frac{1}{4}$,,   ,,
9 ,, 10 — $45\frac{3}{4}$,,   ,, $24\frac{1}{4}$,,   ,,
10 ,, 11 — 38   ,,   ,, $37\frac{1}{2}$,,   ,,
11 ,, 12 — 26   ,,   ,,   61   ,,   ,,
12 ,, 13 — $13\frac{3}{4}$,,   ,, $71\frac{1}{2}$,,   ,,

On again comparing boys at school with girls, we find

AT SCHOOL.

	7 & 8	8 & 9	9 & 10	10 & 11	11 & 12	12 & 13
Boys	62	61	$45\frac{1}{2}$	$41\frac{1}{2}$	$17\frac{1}{2}$	$10\frac{1}{2}$ per cent.
Girls	$53\frac{1}{2}$	$63\frac{1}{2}$	46	$33\frac{1}{2}$	36	17 ,,

And on making the same comparison between boys and girls employed, we find

EMPLOYED.

	7 & 8	8 & 9	9 & 10	10 & 11	11 & 12	12 & 13
Boys	6	13	$28\frac{1}{2}$	$44\frac{1}{2}$	$73\frac{1}{2}$	$82\frac{1}{2}$ per cent.
Girls	3	9	$18\frac{1}{2}$	$27\frac{1}{2}$	46	$60\frac{1}{2}$,,

The average gives 41 boys employed in every hundred to 27 girls.

From these figures we gather that the day-school life of 1-4th of these children who attend school ceases at 9 years of age; 2-4ths remain at school till 11; and the remaining 4th only are found to have prolonged their education to between the ages of 12 and 13.

It is satisfactory to observe the large number of the employed who attend Sunday school; and it is worthy of remark that the following figures taken from Table I., Males, show that the proportion of those between 10 and 13 who attend Sunday school is larger than of those under 10, showing that the desire for education increases as they advance in age.

The following figures show the relative proportions at each age :—

EMPLOYED AND AT SUNDAY SCHOOL.

	7 to 8	8 to 9	9 to 10	10 to 11	11 to 12	12 to 13
Boys	6	13	$28\frac{1}{2}$	$44\frac{1}{2}$	$73\frac{1}{2}$	$82\frac{1}{2}$ per cent.
Girls	4	8	21	$31\frac{1}{2}$	$54\frac{1}{2}$	$55\frac{1}{2}$,,

Of the girls not quite so large a proportion of those employed go to Sunday school; but still we find that more than one half do so. The exact difference is shown by the following figures.

70 per cent. of the employed boys go to Sunday school.
61　 „ 　　　 „ 　　 girls 　 „ 　　 „

The evening school is shown to have but little influence. The numbers are—

AT EVENING SCHOOL.

	7 & 8	8 & 9	9 & 10	10 & 11	11 & 12	12 & 13
Boys	$\frac{1}{2}$	$\frac{1}{2}$	4	$2\frac{1}{2}$	$7\frac{1}{2}$	$11\frac{1}{2}$ per cent.
Girls	0	1	0	$3\frac{1}{2}$	$4\frac{1}{2}$	4　 „

If we compare the boys unemployed with the girls, we find that while the per centage of boys steadily decreases as they advance in age, it is not so with the girls; this is doubtless to be explained by the fact that the girls are retained at home to assist in nursing younger children, and otherwise to make themselves useful, while the mother is at work at the factory.

UNEMPLOYED.

	7 & 8	8 & 9	9 & 10	10 & 11	11 & 12	12 & 13
Boys	32	26	26	14	9	7 per cent.
Girls	$43\frac{1}{2}$	$27\frac{1}{2}$	$35\frac{1}{2}$	39	18	$22\frac{1}{2}$　 „

We will now inquire into the nature of the employments which draw these children from the school. The returns show 77 different employments in which the boys are engaged, and 32 for the girls. The list is too long to read, but we find that 10 out of the 77 employments take 159 out of 267 boys, or 6-10ths of the whole number; these 10 are —

Brassfoundry, employing 16 per cent.

Errands	,,	12	,,
Button making	,,	$8\frac{1}{2}$	,,
Gun making	,,	4	,,
Jewellery	,,	4	,,
Glass cutting	,,	4	,,
Shoe making	,,	$3\frac{1}{4}$	,,
Spoon making	,,	$2\frac{3}{4}$	,,
Filing	,,	$2\frac{3}{4}$	,,
Blacksmiths	,,	$2\frac{1}{4}$	,,

The remaining 47 per cent. of the boys are distributed among 67 different employments. From the column in our returns, showing the age at which the children *first* go to work, we find the ages to be as follows:—

Button making	9	years	1	month.
Gun	,,	9	,,	1	,,
Errands	9	,,	5	,,
Brassfoundry	9	,,	7	,,
Jewellery	9	,,	10	,,
Glass cutting	10	,,	1	,,

The average age at which the boys commence work is $9\frac{1}{2}$ years.

The information on this head which we have with reference to the girls shows that they are distributed among 32 different employments; but, as in the case of the boys, a few employments take the large majority. Six only absorb 7-10ths of the whole, or 80 out of 100. They are —

Button making, employing	31	per cent.
Service	23	,,
Warehouse girls	7	,,
Paper-box making	$5\frac{1}{2}$	,,
Guard chain making	$3\frac{1}{2}$	,,
Pin making	$2\frac{1}{2}$	,,

26 other employments take the remaining $27\frac{1}{2}$ per cent.

The ages at which the girls first go to work are as follows : —

Button making -	9 years	2	months.
Guard chain making	9 „	10	„
Service - -	10 „	3	„
Paper-box making	10 „	7	„
Pin making -	11 „	3	„
Warehouse girls -	11 „	6	„

The average age at which the girls commence work is 10 years.

It is important to follow up the inquiries which have given the foregoing results by ascertaining as far as we can what are the inducements offered by the factory to children of the tender age at which we find them employed. What is the nature of the employment offered to them? What remuneration do they obtain? Our returns show us that the button trade employs 31 per cent. of the girls and $8\frac{1}{2}$ per cent. of the boys, a proportion far exceeding that of any other employment. They also show that the average age at which the children commence the employment in this trade is—

Boys 9 years and 1 month.
Girls 9 „ 2 months.

A few days ago I visited one of our largest button manufactories, where I was kindly permitted by the proprietors to make any inquiries I thought proper. In the several establishments connected with this manufactory there are at times as many as one thousand persons employed, chiefly women and children.

I was first taken into the carding-room, where I found girls from 9 years and upwards engaged at that work. The duty consists in arranging buttons on cards, previously perforated to receive the shanks.

They commence at weekly wages of 1s. per week.

Several girls of 10 years of age, of whom I made the inquiry, were earning 1s. 3d.; one of 11 years earned 1s. 9d.; one of 12, 2s. 3d. When they become proficient they are paid by the piece.

Girls of 14 and 15, when very expert, can card 100 gross of buttons per day, or nearly 15,000 buttons.

The hours during which these children work extend from 8 in the morning till 7 and 8 at night, with intervals for meals of an hour and three quarters during the day — an hour and a quarter for dinner, and half an hour for tea.

No distinction is made in favour of the very young ones. The same hours prevail throughout the factory.

The putting-in department employs the youngest children; the work consists in placing together the parts of a button which is made up, for instance, of a metal back, with a glass front, and a piece of foil between the two; the child arranges the parts for a woman at a lathe, who fastens them together. Here I found many children of 7 years of age, all earning 1s. per week. At this work they do not rise higher than 15 or 16 pence. When arrived at an age when they should earn more money, they leave for another department.

A large number of girls of all ages are employed in working hand-presses. A great variety of work is done by these presses; the required forms are given by them to the metal blanks; the shanks are fastened in, and the buttons are finished as far as structure goes. I found children of 11 years at this work, earning their 2s. per week; at 12 earning 3s.; 13 and 14, 4s. to 5s. The great majority of the *women* are engaged in this description of work, their earnings vary from 6s. to 11s.; but all to whom I addressed myself agreed that the latter sum could be earned only by hard work and overtime.

A large number of the press-women employ children to

arrange the parts of the buttons for them, as in the case of those who execute the putting-in work. All these children are employed by the women and paid by them. It was mentioned to me that two or three women in the establishment could earn 15s. to 20s. per week, but they were quite exceptional cases; their earnings depended on the possession of high skill in colouring buttons, or other such work.

I have spoken hitherto only of females; boys are much less numerous; 8½ per cent. only as compared with 31 per cent. I found one of 8 years placing the button blank right side up for the man who stamped it into form; he was paid 1s. per week. One of 9 was shaking buttons in a bag, and earned 1s. 6d. Several of 9 and 10 were turning the wheels of burnishing lathes; they earn 2s. per week. This is heavy work, when we consider that it is steadily pursued during 10 working hours in a day.

In the casting shop boys of 12 to 14 were assisting the moulder in arranging his moulds and removing the ingots of metal; and their earnings varied from 3s. to 4s. A boy of 8 was blacking japanned buttons for 1s. per week, another of 11 earned 2s. at the same employment.

The pearl button trade employs a large number of boys in cutting out and drilling the pearl buttons. I usually found, in the case of the boys, that, in addition to the weekly wages, there was " a penny or sometimes twopence for himself," according to good behaviour.

In a branch of the establishment devoted to the manufacture of cloth-covered buttons I found a large number of *very young children.*

The labour is nearly all performed in presses worked by women, every press requiring an attendant child. This work demands close application, as the child places the button in the press to be stamped, and must promptly follow every blow; their earnings varied from 1s. to 1s. 4d. per week.

The youngest child I found in the factory was a pretty rosy faced girl of 5 years only; she assisted her mother by placing the wire shanks in paper buttons, which the mother fastened in the press. This little thing had been two months thus engaged, and was sufficiently adept to do 20 gross per day, as many as the mother could press. This woman had three children, all in the factory, and an idle husband, who left to her the task of supporting them. I should mention that with this exception I found no child in the factory who was under 7 years of age.

In answer to my inquiries about attendance at school, I found many who went to Sunday school; but of these a large number were unable to read, as but very few of them had ever attended a day-school, having entered the factory at so early an age. A few, but very few, attended evening school, and these only two nights in the week. The late hours at the factory prevented their attendance. I inquired particularly among the older girls and young women. Many who had once attended evening school had left off in consequence of the frequent necessity for working overtime breaking in upon their regular attendance.

I was assured by the young women that they would gladly avail themselves of the evening school, if the hours at the factory would permit it. An opportunity of attending school from 7 to 9 o'clock would be gladly made use of, if practicable; but while they work from 8 in the morning until 8 in the evening in the factory, they cannot attend the evening school.

I should apologise for so long a digression; but while our inquiry is, What is the influence of the factory upon the school, it is highly important that we should know what the factory is that exercises this influence.

We are naturally led to inquire how it is that so small an inducement as a weekly remuneration of one shilling should induce parents to send their children to labour. The solution of this inquiry is doubtless to be found in the indifference of parents to the value of education on the one hand, and on the other, that it is a far less evil that a child should be steadily engaged under the care, perhaps, of a mother, sister, or neighbour, at some light employment, rather than be running about the street in dirt and idleness. What has been the training of many of the mothers of these children? Brought up, like themselves, in the workshop, which they may have entered at an age precluding the possibility of their obtaining any education whatever, they marry young, and, as may be expected, after such training, they find themselves unfitted for the duties of domestic life. If they leave the factory when the cares of a young family first keep them at home, they afterwards find home lonely. Their inability to make their homes comfortable probably drives the husband to the tavern; their old factory habits cling to them, and they naturally, in many cases, return to it and to their old companions. The care of their children is not allowed to be an obstacle to their leaving home. The younger ones they place under the charge of a neighbour; and, when arrived at a sufficient age, they send them to work. They might at very little sacrifice send these latter to school; but in addition to the pecuniary profit of the workshop, it offers to them the further advantage of occupying their children more hours than the school; indeed, until they are themselves at liberty to attend to them at home.

I do not wish it, however, to be understood, that a large majority of the mothers of these young children are to be found in the factory.

The partial returns that we have received with reference to the employment of the mothers, enable us to show how 411 mothers out of the 1043 families are engaged: 132 out of 411, or one third, are attending to their domestic duties; 79 are laundresses; 33 keep a shop; and 27 are needlewomen. These three employments absorb another third; the remaining third are employed in 44 different occupations, manufacturing and otherwise.

Can legislative interference in any degree lessen the evils which I have described, is an inquiry which has lately received much anxious attention in Birmingham.

The feeling is general in Birmingham that any law restricting the employment of children in factories would, with us, be found to be inoperative. The question, however, is one of deep importance, and will doubtless immediately be brought under the consideration of the Birmingham Association. A fact which has an important bearing on the case, and which is one well known among us, is, that one-half the productions of Birmingham are manufactured in what may be called home workshops, or in small establishments, which no officer of the law could by any possibility inspect.

The large manufacturers, in many trades, employ " outworkers," who may be regarded as little masters, employing a few assistants under them. It is very questionable whether the law could regulate the age at which those assistants should be employed. Even in such a factory as I have described, the law would be a dead letter—the children, instead of working in one large establishment, would be employed at the homes of the workmen or in small shops, where the processes could be carried on quite as conveniently as in the large establishment of the master manufacturer.

The carding of buttons, hooks, and eyes, and other small articles is already carried on to a large extent in the homes of the workpeople.

In those trades where machinery is employed, and where the work is necessarily carried on in large establishments, it will be found that there is but an inconsiderable demand for the labour of children of the ages which would come under the operation of any modified form of the Factory Act.

I wish it to be understood that the opinions which I have expressed on this subject, are opinions for which I alone am responsible, and that they must in no degree be received as an authoritative exposition of the Association for which the statistics were prepared. It was not generally supposed in Birmingham, prior to the publication of the facts which I have laid before you, that the education of our children was so general as the returns prove it to be; they still, however, show a vast field for improvement, and the lamentable fact remains, that of those who go to school one fourth leave before they attain 9 years of age: and further, although 42 per cent. of our children are receiving a day-school education, we still have 25 per cent., the great majority of whom, during six days of the week, are wasting their time in idleness. Among the 33 per cent. that are employed we find that evening-school education is but little resorted to; we have reason at the same time to believe that a disposition exists, among both children and adults, to make use of such schools, if the opportunity were afforded to them. As a first step, in Birmingham, a Prize scheme has been adopted. It is hoped that this will tend to reduce the numbers which we now find in the " employed" and " unemployed" classes, and that it will retain the children at school beyond the average ages of $9\frac{1}{2}$ and 10. A movement is also on foot for an extension of evening-school education; to this we may look for improvement in that class that will retain under the head of " employed."

J. D. GOODMAN.

Upon the State of Education among the Working Classes of the Parish of Sheffield. By Rev. S. EARNSHAW.

THE chief manufactures in Sheffield are knives, scissors, razors, files, edge-tools, joiners' tools, scythes, sickles, shears, saws, steel, railway springs, anvils, vices, stove-grates, fenders, fire-irons, silver, plated and Britannia metal goods; and it is in these that the children are chiefly employed when they leave school. Great numbers are, however, on first leaving school, employed in running errands and carrying out parcels.

According to the unanimous testimony of the school-masters, the majority of boys leave school between the ages of 8 and 10.

According to the information obtained at the manu-factories, the majority of boys are taken into employment between the ages of 8 and 11.

But the average duration of a boy's stay at any one school is under *six months;* and the average age at which boys leave any one school is 9 years. On an average, the highest boys in a school began to go to school $5\frac{1}{2}$ years ago. About one third of the children educated in day schools began their education in infants' schools.

In any one school, the average amount of knowledge at the entrance of the children into that school is—an ability to read words of two syllables, but with difficulty; and at leaving the school the average amount of knowledge is—ability to read the Bible, but imperfectly.

The schoolmasters believe that the majority of children leave school without having received any *permanent* moral impression for good; and this belief is borne out by their observation of the children that have left school some years.

The children who leave school most imperfectly educated are found to be afterwards *most unwilling* to attend Sunday schools and night schools.

As long as boys do remain at school the regularity of their attendance is increased by raising the school wages which they pay for instruction to a sufficient sum for that purpose.

Great numbers of children begin to work in manufactories under 7 years of age, but there are some trades at which a boy cannot be employed before 13 or 14 years of age, according to his strength.

The schoolmasters are of opinion that most parents care but little about their children being educated; and in workshops it is found that the idle and dissolute workmen are opposed to any scheme of compulsory education; while the steady and diligent workmen are decidedly in its favour, as a means of preparing the way for universal suffrage.

Many causes conduce to the early removal of children from school to work; but there are some of a more general character than others.   Ex. gr.—

It is found to be a fact in this town, that children attend most regularly at school, and are not so early removed to workshops, in the time of *moderate trade,* i. e., when trade is neither very good nor very bad.

When trade is very bad, parents cannot afford to pay school wages; and when trade is very good, the temptation to profit by their children's earnings overcomes their desire (generally a feeble one) to have them educated.

The profit which parents derive from taking a child to

work is much greater than the mere earnings of the child. For, in this town boys are generally apprenticed to their father or to a workman ; and a boy takes off his master's hands errands and those portions of the work which require but little skill and strength, and occupy much time; and by so doing the master by applying the time thus saved to him by his apprentice to those portions of the work which require skill and strength, is enabled himself to earn several shillings a week more wages than he could do without an apprentice to assist him.

The wages which a boy can earn on commencing work vary in the majority of cases from 2s. to 4s. per week; and the master of the boy earns from 18s. to 21s. a week.

It is found to be a fact, that parents, whose income ranges from 18s. to 25s. a week, educate their children much better than those whose income is either much higher or lower. And another fact allied to this is, that parents whose wages are *fixed* and *moderate*, or (according to the phrase by which it is expressed here) who work at *daytal wages* (i. e., at so much per day), are far the most steady and respectable men. The families of such men are far better brought up; their homes present more comforts ; their children are better educated ; and they themselves set better examples to them.

High wages must therefore be set down as one of the most prevalent antecedents of the early removal of children from school in this town.

Working by the piece must be set down as another ; and this, both because of its action on the master, and also on his apprentice. For by multiplying apprentices a workman can himself waste several days at the beginning of the week in dissipation at the public house, expecting by increased exertion in the few remaining days of the week, and by exacting a certain amount of earnings from each apprentice, to secure enough for next week's dissipation, and for such demands of his family as he cannot put off. Thus, working by the piece leads the master into habits of drunkenness, and the neglect of home and his family's wants. With regard to apprentices, whatever they can earn, over and above what their master has fixed as their quota of earnings, they are allowed to appropriate to their own use ; and the sums thus placed in their hands they spend in following the example of their master. And thus piece-work is in this town the origin of much profligacy, corruption of manners, and ignorance.

In many cases also the money earned by the children is all the mother can lay her hands on for providing for her family, her husband squandering in betting, card-playing, and drunkenness all his own earnings; this therefore acts with the mother as a strong reason for removing the children from school to work at the earliest possible age.

An American notion of liberty is also another reason for children's early beginning to work. On this ground many parents, after a boy begins work, exert no parental restraint upon him. If only he earn his appointed quota, he is left to consider himself in other respects his own master, and to follow the bent of his own inclinations. For this liberty children naturally long ; and are themselves anxious to leave school and begin work that they may at once " *become men,*" and imitate the vices and follies of those that are grown up. Such children often lodge with their parents, at per week when apprenticed elsewhere — and upon any restraint, will remove to other lodgings.

Early removal from school causes the children to shun night schools and Sunday schools. For having left school when imperfectly educated, reading is remembered only as a task ; and the pleasure of being able to read and write with facility being unknown to them, school and learning are therefore in after life remembered only as disagreeables, which they are not willing to encounter again.

Young men, thus imperfectly educated, have much spare time on their hands, which they will not fill up by attendance upon any means of better instructing themselves; but fall into sensual habits, get connected with young women as ignorant as themselves, employed also in workshops*, and form early marriages, which lead to all the well-known consequences of children becoming the parents of children, without the knowledge or ability to bring them up properly. In this town the number of juvenile marriages is very surprising. Children of 15 to 21 get married without ever asking themselves how they are to support themselves and a family. The young wife, having been taken early from school to nurse her mother's or a neighbour's baby, and to run errands, and afterwards into a workshop, is utterly ignorant of household management; and the necessary consequence is, the wages of her boy-husband are not employed to the best advantage, and *want* follows *waste*, home becomes miserable, and he seeks among his former companions in smoking, drinking, dog-fighting, betting, casinos, theatres, and the public-house, that enjoyment and happiness which he cannot have at home. The evils produced by these early marriages can hardly be exaggerated.

Another obvious result of the early removal from school is, that the impression sought to be made upon their minds, whether moral or religious, has not had time to become permanent, but is quickly removed by influence of companions. The lessons learned at school are presently forgotten, and learning is remembered only in connection with tasks and restraints. Children who continued at

---

* Hair-seating weavers, spoon and comb buffers, and silver polishers, and warehouse women, and nailmakers.

school till 13 years show, in general, signs, in their after-course, of good received from school training; — and so manifest is this fact, that the schoolmasters are of opinion, if compulsory education were had recourse to, it would not be necessary to extend it beyond 13 years of age. In a school in this town for the maintenance and education of 100 orphan boys, they are dismissed from school at 13 *years* of age, having been, on an average, about 4 years in the school. And it is a known fact to all the town that these boys almost universally turn out well; and in many instances rise in society to a higher position.

From this it appears that not much moral good can be produced on the children of the working classes unless they can be retained longer than at present in the hands of the schoolmaster; and that if a compulsory law be passed, it will not effect much real good unless it keep a child at school till he can read and write so well —that is with such facility—as to have lost the impression of reading and writing being tasks.

In consequence of the children of this town being apprenticed not to the *manufacturers*, but to the *workmen*, the Factory Act cannot be applied here. After much thought, no other mode of enforcing the education of children has seemed feasible here but this one: —

To make apprenticeship illegal until a certificate has been obtained of ATTENDANCE at an approved school a certain number of days (say 500 *whole* days, *rejecting halves*) after the age of 6 years. There are insuperable objections to the certificate being for MERIT.

The above information has been obtained by the Sheffield Clerical Committee on Education with great care from every available and reliable source; and has been confirmed by both masters and workmen.

S. EARNSHAW,
Secretary of the Committee.

PART II.

——◆——

On the Comparative Condition of Children in English and Foreign Towns. By JOSEPH KAY, Esq.

THE object of the paper which I am to have the honour of reading is to show, for what period of their lives and by what means the children are kept under the influence of education in some of the continental countries.

I shall venture to state very briefly the facts, which render this subject so worthy of consideration, and which, as it seems to me, offer a justification of the foreign systems.

One of the most startling features of our times is the growth of our provincial towns. The days in which we live have been fitly designated " the age of great cities." The growth of this vast metropolis has been extraordinary, but even this has been far surpassed by the comparative growth of many of the centres of our provincial industry. Allow me to give you one example to explain the significance of this statement.

Take what is called the " Manchester District." It is a circle, having Manchester for its centre, and a radius of about 14 miles. This small area contains 16 towns and their suburbs. In 1801 it contained a population of only 311,544. The London District at the same date contained 958,863. In 1851 the population of the Manchester District had increased to 1,044,816, while that of the London District had increased to 2,362,236; so that between 1801 and 1851, for every 100 persons, 146 were added in the London District, but 236 to that of Manchester.

I have said there are 16 towns within the little area of the Manchester District. Allow me to remind you what the separate growth of some of them has been between 1801 and 1851.

	Population.		Increase per cent.
	1801.	1851.	
1. *Manchester* - - - -	94,409	404,808	**329**
2. *Oldham* - - - -	9,024	46,820	**419**
3. *Stockport* - - - -	18,880	53,610	184
4. *Bolton* - - - - -	17,429	60,711	**248**
5. *Ashton-under-Lyne* - -	4,837	40,723	**742**
6. *Bury* - - - - -	6,852	27,762	**305**
7. *Stalybridge* - - - -	1,500	23,877	**1,492**
8. Rochdale - - - -	8,500	29,195	243
9. Heywood - - - -	2,800	12,194	335
10. *Hyde* - - - - -	863	10,050	**1,065**
11. Middleton - - - -	1,765	5,740	225
12. *Leigh* - - - - -	700	5,206	**644**
13. Radcliffe - - - -	1,847	5,002	171
14. Eccles - - - -	2,000	4,108	105
15. Tyldesley - - - -	1,809	3,608	99
16. Atherton - - - -	2,109	2,780	32

This is only an example of what is going on in a greater or less degree all over the kingdom. Look at the rest of Lancashire, at Yorkshire and its towns, at the Glasgow District, at Staffordshire, Birmingham, the mining districts, and other great centres. It has been justly said, " we are doing the town-population work of more than one-half the world in addition to that of our own country. We are finding the capital and labour and taking the profits of this town-industry. We are wielding the power, social and political, and incurring the responsibilities of this position. Our towns for any merely British purpose are already immensely in excess." Each year they increase faster than before.

The steam-engine; improved machinery; increasing facilities of communication; our great natural advantages; our island situation; our vast colonial empire, which we are opening up more and more every day by railways and steamboats; the discovery and development of new markets in distant lands, and many other causes, are rapidly transforming our villages into towns and our towns into cities.

Who can say what the end will be?

The causes which are stimulating the growth of our villages and towns with this hot-bed vitality, give them at the same time a very peculiar character.

In these towns of labour, the vast bulk of the inhabitants are workmen depending upon weekly wages.

Unlike capitals, except in size and population, they contain scarcely any of the houses of the wealthy and educated. Railways enable the rich to separate themselves from the poor, and dwell in distant suburbs or villages. These great towns are therefore wanting in many of those civilising influences which exist where the Court, the government, or the wealthy have their residences; while in all of them, multitudes of the poorer classes are densely crowded together.

Scarcely any rich people live in Manchester; few even of the richer shopkeepers. Each year it is becoming a vaster city of the poor, who dwell crowded together round the palaces of mills and warehouses, which at night are all untenanted, except by the solitary watchmen.

Such a state of things no doubt offers vast opportunities for civilisation, if its attendant evils are counteracted; but it creates great moral and political dangers in the midst of a community, if its peculiar necessities are not wisely provided for. A great city may be made the school of Christian civilisation; but it may easily become the nursery of degradation and of crime.

In these towns, the greatest part of our children are reared to manhood; and, in my opinion, the very worst feature of our English towns is the condition of a great part of their juvenile population. Certainly, there is nothing like it throughout the countries I am going to mention.

I venture to remind you of it, because I believe that this result of our system is an ample justification for the policy which is pursued by the Swiss, the Dutch, the Germans, and the Danes.

I fear, however, to offer a sketch of it, lest those who may not have examined this subject for themselves should think me guilty of exaggeration. Yet remember, that in 1851 and 1852, a committee of gentlemen spent several thousands of pounds in examining the state of the children in Manchester and Salford. The most careful and elaborate inquiries were made. Time and money were lavished upon the examination. What was the result? They found that in 1852, in Manchester and Salford alone, in that city of well-paid labour, 17,177 children between the ages of 3 and 15, were neither attending any school NOR AT WORK! What, then, were they doing? Where were they spending their time? Under what influences were their minds and habits being formed?

Take another fact, which makes what I wish to refer to more credible. Mr. Horace Mann, in his report on education, founded upon the Census returns, states that in 1851 there were in England and Wales alone, 2,764,318 children between the ages of 3 and 12 who were not attending any school, and that of these there were upwards of 800,000 whose absence could not be explained either by illness, occupation, professional home instruction, or any legitimate excuse.*

But, independently of any statistics, if you go at any hour into any of the crowded back streets of London, Liverpool, Manchester, Newcastle, Birmingham, or any other great town, you will see numbers of young children of both sexes, from 4 to 15 years of age, filthy, wretchedly clothed, rude in manners and language, and exhibiting all the signs of poverty, neglect, and degradation.

Seen from this point of view, there is no more painful spectacle than the back street of a great English town.

Most of these children are unemployed; many are locked out of the houses while the parents are occupied from home; all are idling about, indulging in unclean habits, and learning mischief from teachers brought up in a similar school.

Many are sent out to beg; some have no parents and no fixed home; many live by pilfering, many have been

---

* His Royal Highness Prince Albert, at the Educational meeting yesterday (June 23, 1857), put the statistics in the following striking point of view. He said, "We are told that the total population in *England and Wales* of children between the age of 3 and 15, being estimated at 4,908,696, only 2,046,848 attend school at all, WHILE 2,861,848 RECEIVE NO INSTRUCTION WHATEVER. At the same time, an analysis of the scholars with reference to the length of time allowed for their school tuition shows, that 42 per cent. of them have been at school LESS THAN ONE YEAR, 22 per cent. during one year, 15 per cent. during 2 years, 9 per cent. during 3 years, 5 per cent. during 4 years, and 4 per cent. during 5 years. Therefore, out of the *two millions of scholars alluded to more than one million and a half remain only two years* at school. I leave it to you to judge what the results of such an education can be. I find further that of these 2,000,000 of children attending school, only about 600,000 are above the age of 9."

in gaol, while others are the neglected offspring of parents who began life in a similar manner.

All these children, during that part of their lives when their minds are most susceptible and retentive, hear hourly the foulest language of the worst part of our towns, and see hourly the most immoral of their spectacles. The gin palaces, beershops, penny singing rooms, and penny theatres, are all open to them, and offer them stimulants suited to their tastes.

In 1851 11,617 of these young creatures were convicted! What a population of such characters we have, this fact may enable us to imagine, when we reflect how small a proportion the convicted bear to the offenders. Such are the companions among whom many of even those children who go to school in the mornings spend their evenings. It seems to me that an association of this kind must undermine much of the influence of the healthier life in the schools.

The larger our towns grow, the more these evils must become, unless we remove the children from the streets.

What is the cause of all this? Is it the want of school room? In some districts this is no doubt one cause among others; but it is by no means the principal cause. However many schools we build, we cannot, with our present regulations, get these children into school, or keep them long there, even if we were able to induce them to commence attending.

True it is that really good schools will sometimes draw all the children of one district into them. I have seen first-rate schools founded in some of the roughest districts of Lancashire, where nothing but miserable dame schools had existed before. I have seen the new schools provided with libraries, reading rooms, well-educated teachers, forms and desks, apparatus and excellent playgrounds; and I know instances where every parent of the district round such schools is sending his children and paying the weekly pence, although even in these instances few children remain after the completion of their 7th year.

I know many other schools in Lancashire where the teachers are men of the old system, where there are neither desks, libraries, or playground attached to the schools, where education is dreary, punishment of daily occurrence, and where the schools are thinly attended, as they deserve to be. Many such instances exist in all the towns. Some of our newest and most costly schools are of this character. I was in one a few weeks since. It was a large stone building, with several great class-rooms. It had only just been finished. It must have cost nearly 2000*l*. The teacher was a dirty and ignorant man. The great rooms were filthy. There were no desks, no apparatus, no playground. The school was not nearly half full, though in a populous town. But still the absence of the children is by no means to be attributed always, or even in the majority of cases, to such causes as these. The real cause, as I believe, why we cannot get the children to school, and why we cannot keep them there long when we have got them, are :—

1. The degraded and selfish character of many of the parents.

2. The great poverty of many others, which renders it impossible for them to pay the school pence, or to provide decent clothing.

3. The absence of any local organisation, by means of which poor parents might be assisted to pay the school pence and to provide decent clothes.

4. The fact that the law does not require vicious or selfish parents to do their duty towards their children with respect to their physical or moral training.

5. The miserable character of so many of our town

schools, many of which have neither library, desks, intelligent teachers, or playgrounds.

I have ventured to make these remarks to enable me the better to explain how the children are saved from street life throughout Central and Northern Europe, and how long they are kept under the influence of respectable and well educated teachers. Throughout Switzerland, Prussia, Holland, Denmark, Saxony, Baden, Wirtemberg, Bavaria, and, in fact, throughout nearly the whole of Germany, all the children who are between 5 and 15 years of age are saved from the moral and physical evils of this street training. Throughout nearly the whole of the countries I have mentioned, all the children of the towns and nearly all the children of the country districts spend their days in schools, which have clean, well-ventilated, and well-furnished rooms, roomy and dry playgrounds, and an ample supply of useful school books and apparatus, and which are managed by intelligent and well-trained men.

I scarcely need remind you of the character of the Swiss and German town-schools. Many of those I have seen contained as many as ten large and comfortable class-rooms, each of which was under the care of a separate trained teacher. Some were still larger, and contained still more class-rooms, and afforded therefore still greater facilities for classification and management.

I saw one in Leipsic with fourteen class-rooms, and a similar number of teachers. Nearly all the children commence their education in these schools. The children of the poor, nearly all the children of the small shopkeepers, and many of the children of professional men, of merchants, and even of the nobles, sit there at the same desks side by side. I have seen this mingling of the children of all classes in all parts of Germany and Switzerland. I don't say it is desirable, but as it is the result of the free choice of the parents, it will show you how excellent the schools must be to induce the richer parents to consent to it.

I remember particularly that I asked each of the children in one class-room in Munich in what positions in life their parents were—one was the son of a lawyer, another of a physician, two were the sons of nobles, one was the son of an officer of the court, while many were the children of parents who were too poor to pay the school pence, and who were assisted out of the city rates. The father of one of these poor children took me to the school. There were ten admirable class-rooms in that school, ten teachers and about seventy children in each class; all were equally neat and clean in person.

Much has been said against Prussian centralisation and the tyrannical character of the educational regulations, but it has been forgotten that the Swiss educational laws are more stringent than the Prussian, and that there is less centralization and a purer democracy in Switzerland than in any other country in the world.

In Switzerland, *one-fifth* of all the people are in regular daily attendance at these schools. In Prussia, in nearly the whole of Germany, and in Denmark, one-sixth, and in Holland one-eighth, of the people attend the schools regularly.

There are large and populous manufacturing towns both in the western and in the eastern provinces of Prussia; and there are also thriving manufacturing districts in Switzerland. I visited them, and saw a good deal of the progress of education in these parts. I spent some time in Elberfeld, a great manufacturing town of Prussia, living with the teachers. There is nothing in any of these districts at all similar to the state of many of the children in our English towns. All the children are clean and decently clothed, and spend their mornings and afternoons in excellent class-rooms or in playgrounds, under the care of intelligent teachers. If anyone will go and examine the state of the small streets of these towns, he will see the difference between their back streets and ours in a moment.

During the school hours he would see no children there at all. In the early mornings and in the evenings, he would see clean and healthy-looking children going to or returning from the schools, carrying their knapsacks of books which belong to them, and which they take home with them as their own property.

Now put aside all thought of what the children learn in the schools. Suppose they only learn to read or write. How untrue such a supposition is, those who know what the daily instruction in a Swiss, Dutch, German, or Danish school comprises, will understand. But suppose they only learn to read and write. Is not a healthy, a moral life in clean homes, such as the Swiss, Dutch, or German school premises are, a good sanatory and moral regulation, if it is nothing else? Is it not worth all the expenditure if it has no better result than this?

Surely such an institution is better than either prisons or reformatories. They have chosen the one; we have preferred the other.

And yet, no one could have attended the criminal courts of this country for nine years, as I have done, and have seen the tens of thousands whom I have seen, tried and sent to the gaols from the great towns of Lancashire and Yorkshire, without feeling too well assured that nearly all our crime is to be traced directly to the street training of the children, and to their early initiation to the beerhouses, and to still worse scenes than these.

Throughout all the foreign countries I have mentioned, and I believe throughout Sweden and Norway also, every parent, whether he be rich or poor, is obliged to provide for the education of each of his children, either at home, or at some school of his own selection, from its 5th to the completion of its 14th year; and in several cantons of Switzerland, the law obliges the children to attend the evening classes to the completion of their 16th year.

If the parent is too poor to pay the school pence, or to clothe his children, his town or parish is obliged to supply him with the means; for the law will not allow a parent to neglect his child's moral and physical training, any more than our law will allow him to inflict immoderate chastisement. There is no country in which the law does not to some extent regulate the parent's duties towards his child. The only question is a question of degree. In our country a parent may not neglect to provide his child with food. In Switzerland, Germany, and Denmark, he may not neglect to provide his child with a good physical and moral training.

Except in the manufacturing districts of Germany and Switzerland, all the children are attending the schools from their 5th to the end of their 14th year. In the manufacturing districts of Germany, the law allows the parent to send his children to work when they are 9 years of age, but not before; and even then only on condition that they continue to attend the evening-classes and the Sunday-schools till the completion of their 15th year. In some of the manufacturing districts of Switzerland, the law does not allow the children to begin to work in the mills before the completion of their 13th year; and not even then unless they have obtained certificates from the inspectors that they can read and write, or unless they continue to attend the evening-classes until they are 15 or 16 years of age. In the country parishes a similar period of school attendance is required; but during the busy time of harvest the older children are generally allowed to assist their parents.

In Holland the attendance of the children is insured by making the right to public relief conditional on the parents having sent their children to school regularly.

But even if these compulsory laws were not in force, the measures which have been adopted would ensure the attendance of most of the children. The children are cared for so well, both mentally and physically, that the value of the schools is thoroughly understood by the poorest of the people. Their pride is stimulated by seeing the children of richer people attending in the same class-room. Their interest in their children is appealed to by providing the latter with neat and comfortable clothing for school attendance, and by keeping them clean and orderly in appearance.

All these causes have now been in operation for nearly forty years, throughout the countries I have named. The present generation of parents have nearly all in some degree experienced themselves the blessings of a good education. The homes have already been reformed, and the teachers are generally so much looked up to and respected, that even if the compulsory regulations were done away with, the school attendance would not, as is generally believed, be materially affected. Not however that there is the slightest chance of their ever being repealed, for, as in Switzerland, the most rigorous enforcers of them are the people themselves.

Time does not permit me to enter into any of the minuter details of the foreign educational system. But as I have told you that the law obliges a parent to send his child to some school or other, if it is not educated at home, I will state to you in a few words how the law provides for each locality being furnished with good schools.

In each town or parish a school committee is elected according to certain legal regulations.

This committee, when formed, is empowered to levy an educational rate in its own district.

Out of the proceeds of the rate, the committee is obliged

To provide healthily situated and sufficient school-room for all the children of the district:

To elect a sufficient number of trained teachers for all the district schools:

To provide houses and the legal amount of salaries for the teachers:

To supply all necessary school apparatus, books, &c., for each district school:

To keep all the class-rooms and teachers' rooms in good repair, well whitewashed, and well warmed.

To provide each school-house with a roomy and dry playground:

To personally inspect each school a certain number of times in the year:

To see that every parent in the district provides for the education of his children either at home, or in some public or private school:

To see that the teachers give the children sufficient exercise every morning and afternoon in the play-grounds:

To pay the school fees, and provide decent and comfortable clothing for the children of parents too poor to do this for themselves.

One of the most curious features of the school system of Prussia is the great neatness and cleanliness of the children.

There is one other fact I would mention to you, and then I have done.

You must not suppose there are no schools founded by societies and by private individuals in Germany and Switzerland. There are many such.

Anyone may found a school if he will comply with the following conditions : —

1. He must allow it to be visited by the inspectors, who have, however, no right to interfere with the management of the school.

2. He must provide the school with a playground, and he must let the children have regular exercise there every morning and afternoon.

3. He must teach reading, writing, arithmetic, geography, history, singing, and the rudiments of the physical sciences in the school.

4. He must provide a sufficient number of teachers, generally about one to every seventy children.

5. He must keep his rooms clean, warm, and ventilated.

6. He must not employ anyone as a teacher, except a person who has obtained certificates of health, of competence, and of good character, at some one of the numerous normal colleges.

How many of our schools would be closed to-morrow if they were asked to comply with such terms as these ?

In conclusion, I venture to repeat, that the system for which we have to legislate is a new and untried one ; that we see around us a phenomenon different to all that has preceded it ; that it is one of extraordinary growth ; that it is generating at present evils very dangerous to our future ; and that it requires to be met by a legislation designed expressly for its necessities.

The future of our great provincial towns is one of indefinite development.

It is clear that we are — with the vast markets of the East, and the enormous agricultural districts of the West opening to us — only on the threshold of their history.

Are we prepared for the consequences?

The more these towns increase in magnitude, the

greater will be the number of their juvenile population ; and the greater also, unless we interfere, will be the multitude of children exposed to the influences I have described.

To leave them thus neglected is to deteriorate the moral and physical condition of a great part of our people and our race ; to injure the physical character of our town populations ; to breed moral disease and political danger in England, the heart of our vast Anglo-Saxon empire ; to fill our gaols and penal settlements ; to prepare audiences for the demagogues in times of gluts and depression of trade ; to render such times times of grave political danger, and to make our cities, instead of being the schools of Christian civilisation, the nurseries of disaffection and of crime.

We have two futures for our country before us. It is for us to choose.

L'École Primaire et le Travail Professionnel.   By
M. EUGÈNE RENDU, Paris.

MESSIEURS,—En ouvrant un Congrès *d'Education popu-
laire*, en plaçant ce Congrès sous son auguste patronage,
l'Angleterre donne aux autres nations de l'Europe un
grand exemple et une grande leçon.   Elle prouve que ses
hommes d'état n'attachent pas moins de prix aux intérêts
moraux et intellectuels des masses qu'à la grandeur indus-
trielle et commerciale du pays.   Elle fait comprendre que,
chez un peuple chrétien, le respect des droits de l'intelligence et le culte des âmes sont la loi du progrès; que,
chez un peuple libre, ce qu'il faut développer ce n'est pas
seulement l'aptitude professionnelle qui fait de l'individu
un instrument de richesse, mais les qualités de l'esprit et
du caractère qui font de l'homme un citoyen.
   La question que vous avez proposée, Messieurs, est de
première importance.   Elle témoigne, une fois de plus, de
cet esprit pratique qui dirige la nation anglaise dans l'é-
tude des intérêts sociaux; car il s'agit de savoir si, en con-
tinuant l'influence de l'école au-delà de cet âge auquel
commence pour l'enfant la vie de l'homme, on veut réellement faire une œuvre durable, et si l'on posera le cou-
ronnement sans lequel l'édifice de l'instruction primaire est
presque fatalement condamné à la ruine.

I.—LES FAITS.

   Rechercher à quel âge, dans les districts agricoles et
industriels, les enfants abandonnent l'école, quels sont les

causes et les résultats de cet abandon, c'est toucher nécessairement à cette seconde question qui se confond, jusqu'à un certain point, avec la première : " Combien d'enfants dans ces mêmes districts restent étrangers à toute instruction?" Un même intérêt prescrit de rapprocher deux faits dont l'un n'est que l'exagération de l'autre, et dont les causes ainsi que les résultats sont nécessairement identiques.

En France, plus de 3,500,000 enfants de sept à treize ans, —sans compter les très-jeunes enfants admis dans les *salles d'asile*,—fréquentent les écoles primaires. En dépit des efforts persévérants des communes et de l'état, le nombre de ceux qui ne les fréquentent point, et ne reçoivent aucune instruction dans la maison paternelle, est encore très-considérable ; il s'élève au moins à 400,000 jeunes garçons, et à 450,000 jeunes filles.

A ce nombre des abstentions totales il convient d'ajouter celui des enfants qui ne fréquentent l'école que très-irrégulièrement ; qui, par exemple, ne s'y rendent que deux ou trois fois par semaine ; ou qui, après trois ou quatre mois d'assiduité, pendant l'hiver, la désertent lorsque revient la saison des travaux des champs, c'est-à-dire depuis le mois de mai jusqu'au mois de septembre, ou même, dans les contrées vinicoles, jusqu'au mois d'octobre ou de novembre.

Quelle qu'ait été la régularité ou l'irrégularité de la fréquentation, l'âge auquel les enfants abandonnent l'école varie de la douzième à la quatorzième année ; presque partout, en France, la première communion marque la fin du cours d'études. Ce cours est prolongé ou abrégé, selon que le curé a pu retarder ou a dû avancer l'acte religieux qui est la sanction de la première éducation religieuse. Malheureusement, il n'est pas rare de voir les instances intéressées des familles contraindre en quelque sorte le chef spirituel d'une paroisse à ne pas différer la première communion au-delà de douze et même de onze ans. Alors commence pour les enfants la vie d'apprentissage; alors aussi trop souvent a lieu la rupture avec les traditions religieuses et les exercises intellectuels de l'école.

II.—CAUSES.

Ce triple fait qui, à vrai dire, n'est qu'un même fait envisagé sous trois faces différentes : défaut absolu de fréquentation, fréquentation irrégulière, abandon prématuré, s'expliquent par des causes multiples, et qui pourtant sont étroitement liées entre elles.

En première ligne il faut placer *l'indifférence* qui naît de l'ignorance et de l'incurie. Des familles qui n'ont jamais goûté les avantages de l'instruction, et qu'une routine traditionnelle attache à une besogne machinale, ne sentent point le prix de l'enseignement pour leurs enfants : "Nous avons vécu ainsi, nos enfants vivront bien de même ! "

Cette première cause agit particulièrement dans les départements du Centre, de l'Ouest, et même du Midi de la France.

Ainsi, dans l'Allier, sur 43,660 enfants de sept à treize ans, 12,220 jeunes garçons et 12,395 jeunes filles ne reçoivent pas d'instruction; dans la Creuze, 9,000 jeunes garçons et 11,490 jeunes filles, sur 34,734 enfants; dans le Puy-de-Dôme, 10,545 jeunes garçons et 10,000 jeunes filles, sur 73,028 enfants; dans l'Ariége, 7,936 jeunes garçons et 10,493 jeunes filles, sur 32,450 enfants. Cette même cause est heureusement beaucoup moins puissante dans les départements du Nord et de l'Est. Ainsi le Bas-Rhin, sur 88,000 enfants de sept à treize ans, ne compte hors des écoles que 542 garçons et 235 jeunes filles; les Vosges, 597 garçons et 669 jeunes filles, sur 52,945 enfants; dans la Meuse, sur 31,448 enfants, 466 garçons et

346 jeunes filles seulement grandissent sans instruction ; &c. &c.

On doit remarquer que les départements du Nord et de l'Est comptent beaucoup plus d'usines et de manufactures que ceux du Centre et de l'Ouest. Ce n'est donc pas seulement sur l'industrie exclusivement, tant s'en faut! qu'il convient de faire peser la responsabilité de la désertion des classes primaires.

Dans quelques départements de l'Ouest, l'éloignement des familles pour l'école a pour cause, jusqu'à un certain point, un sentiment plus élevé que celui d'une grossière indifférence. L'académie composée des départements qui forment l'ancienne Bretagne compte à elle seule 169,263 enfants de sept à treize ans ne sachant ni lire ni écrire. Une sorte de patriotisme local, dont une langue reste la vivante expression, y résiste à un enseignement qui est le véhicule d'idées et de mœurs accueillies aujourd'hui encore avec une certaine défiance.

La seconde cause qui explique les faits dont nous cherchons à nous rendre compte, est le désir dont sont animés les parents de *tirer parti* le plus tôt possible du travail de leurs enfants.

Ce dèsir lui-même repose sur deux mobiles très-différents.

On peut regretter, à certains égards, mais on ne saurait trouver coupable que le chef d'une famille pauvre prétende associer, dans une mesure raisonnable, ses enfants, jeunes encore, à des travaux qui l'aideront à soutenir des charges écrasantes. Confisquer la journée entière des enfants de onze, douze et treize ans au profit de l'enseignement spéculatif de l'école, et au détriment de tout travail professionnel, cela peut être séduisant, en principe ; mais les douloureuses exigences de la vie d'ouvrier ne s'accommodent guère des théories sur lesquelles peut reposer un plan d'études. Ainsi, dans ces deux dernières années de récoltes insuffisantes et de cherté extraordinaire de subsistances, le nombre des élèves des écoles avait partout notablement diminué. Il y a donc ici, pour les familles d'ouvriers, un droit né de la nécessité, celui d'attendre du travail de chacun de leurs membres une portion du salaire qui leur permet de vivre ; et toute législation scolaire qui ne veut pas rester lettre morte doit s'efforcer, dans la distribution des heures d'étude, de mettre cette nécessité et ce droit en harmonie avec les faits.

Mais autant il peut être convenable de réserver, chaque jour, une portion de l'activité de l'enfant pour le travail professionnel, autant il importe de le mettre à l'abri de cet abus de la force qu'on appelle *l'exploitation*, et qui est l'œuvre des passions cupides.

Cette exploitation, il est inutile de la décrire dans la variété de ses formes. Mieux que d'autres pays, l'Angleterre la connaît ; autant et plus que d'autres elle lutte contre elle ; et le Congrès lui-même n'en est-il pas la condamnation solennelle et authentique ?

Or, qu'on le remarque, il ne s'agit pas seulement ici de cette grande industrie qui vit des mouvements fiévreux au sein des villes populeuses ; nous voulons parler de ces industries paisibles, si l'on peut dire, qui sembleraient pouvoir se concilier facilement avec le travail de l'école. Telle est, dans plusieurs de nos départements de l'Est, l'industrie de la broderie et de la dentelle. Là, on trouve des enfants de huit, sept et six ans attachés douze heures durant à une pièce de broderie. Les parents considèrent comme préjudice personnel et comme une sorte de vol qui leur est fait toute occupation de nature à distraire ces malheureuses créatures de la tâche imposée. Dans les communes où règne ce fléau, l'école elle-même se tranforme en atelier ; on voit des parents ne consentir à y envoyer leurs enfants qu'à *la condition expresse qu'on ne leur apprendra ni à lire ni à écrire.*

Si l'institutrice résiste, si elle veut accomplir sa mission vis-à-vis de ces pauvres êtres, l'école est abandonnée, et les enfants sont envoyés alors dans les ateliers privés, loin de toute surveillance, et dans un état de promiscuité qui corrompt à la fois leur cœur et leur intelligence.

Nous sommes ici en présence d'abus qu'il ne faut pas laisser à la conscience publique seule le droit de flétrir. Quand la cupidité des parents prend le masque de la misère ; quand le salaire gagné par les enfants au prix de la vie de l'âme, et souvent même au prix de celle du corps, vient alimenter les grossières jouissances d'un père, qui n'impose à de pauvres créatures un travail sans proportion avec leurs forces que pour s'en dispenser lui-même ; il faut bien se demander si la société n'a pas le droit de protéger le faible contre le fort, et d'élever un rempart légal entre la famille et l'enfant.

La troisième cause se trouve dans les nécessités même de l'industrie. Il est des usines et des manufactures dans lesquelles le travail des adultes ne peut s'accomplir sans le travail des enfants. Dans ce cas, pourquoi ne partage-rait-on pas les jeunes travailleurs en groupes que le chef d'usine appellerait alternativement à l'atelier et à l'école ? Plusieurs directeurs ont déjà donné à cet égard un exemple très-profitable ; et la loi de 1841 a mis d'ailleurs à la disposition de l'autorité une arme qui pour être puissante ne demanderait qu'à être confiée à des mains énergiques.

Une quatrième cause, c'est le défaut d'action suffisante de la part des pouvoirs publics. Il faut traiter chaque peuple selon son tempérament particulier. En France, on attend tout de l'état. Qu'on profite donc de cette disposition ; et que les agents directs de l'administration, préfets, sous-préfets, et maires, sachent employer non-seulement les conseils, mais les négociations et les mille moyens d'influence dont ils disposent pour assurer la fréquentation de l'école. Dans les communes où les maires comprennent leurs devoirs à cet égard, bien peu d'enfants restent en dehors des écoles.

La cinquième cause de l'abandon absolu ou prématuré de l'école, ce n'est pas hors de l'école, c'est dans l'école même qu'il convient de la chercher. Les parents ne tiennent pas à l'instruction, les enfants eux-mêmes la prennent en dégoût, parce que trop souvent encore elle est donnée de telle façon que ni les uns ni les autres n'en aperçoivent les résultats pratiques. Si les familles croient que les enfants perdent leur temps à l'école, si les résultats ne leur présentent pas une compensation suffisante des sacrifices pécuniaires qu'elle entraîne, comment s'étonner qu'il y ait hâte de l'abandonner le plus tôt possible? Le père dont le fils suit l'école depuis des années et qui, regrettant l'argent dépensé pour lui acheter des livres, voit que l'enfant ne peut pas même lui rendre compte de ce qu'il lit, a de la peine à croire que la lecture doive faire de son fils un laboureur ou un artisan plus habile; lorsqu'il le voit barbouiller tous les jours de longues pages en conjuguant des verbes, analyser machinalement tous les mots d'une phrase, parler à tort et à travers de conjonctions et de prépositions, de transitifs et d'intransitifs, sans être en état de lui rédiger une lettre, un mémoire, un devis, le compte-rendu d'une affaire ; que la pratique de la division ou la multiplication ne l'a pas même conduit à pouvoir résoudre le plus simple problème emprunté à la vie quotidienne, le père n'est-il pas tenté avec quelque raison de se demander : "à quoi bon?"

Ignorance et incurie des familles, désir d'exploiter le travail des enfants, caractère vague et abstrait de l'enseignement, telles sont les causes auxquelles il faut attribuer l'abandon absolu ou l'abandon prématuré de l'école.

III.—RÉSULTATS.

Les résultats de l'abandon prématuré de l'école ne sont que trop faciles à constater; en Angleterre comme en France ils éclatent à tous les yeux.

Il y a quelques jours seulement, une des plus hautes autorités religieuses de ce royaume, l'archevêque de Canterbury, s'adressant à la Reine au nom des prélats et de tout le clergé de sa province ecclésiastique, déplorait hautement le fait que " les enfants quittaient les écoles avant d'avoir pu recueillir les avantages d'une bonne éducation, et d'avoir été instruits dans leurs devoirs envers Dieu et envers l'homme." *

En effet, une fréquentation si peu assidue et si peu prolongée de l'école laisse à peine quelques traces. En de telles conditions l'enseignement est à l'esprit et à l'âme de l'enfant ce que serait une goutte d'eau à un champ desséché. Au point de vue *moral,* les élèves n'ont pas eu le temps de se pénétrer des croyances religieuses et des idées qui constituent la vie traditionnelle des peuples chrétiens. Le but que poursuivait la société au prix de tant d'efforts est manqué; la barbarie grandit au sein de la civilisation, pour lui livrer un jour peut-être de redoutables combats.

Au point de vue *intellectuel,* deux ou trois années après la sortie prématurée de l'école un grand nombre d'enfants ne savent même plus ni lire ni écrire. Pour eux, l'œuvre de l'école se trouve nulle et non avenue. En ce qui regarde la France, je citerai un fait aussi curieux que triste. Le nombre des jeunes gens qui, au moment du tirage au sort, c'est-à-dire à l'âge de vingt ans, sont désignés comme ne sachant ni lire ni écrire est, sur plusieurs

---

* Adresse présentée le 20 juin pour l'ouverture de ses nouvelles *Convocations.*

points du territoire, resté stationnaire dans les quinze dernières années.

Par exemple, dans la Dordogne, le nombre des jeunes
conscrits ne sachant ni lire ni écrire, en 1840, était de
2,933; en 1853, il était descendu seulement à 2,675.
Pour le département de l'Allier, on trouve, en 1840, le
chiffre de 2,560; en 1853, ce chiffre était encore de 2,382.
Dans le Nord, il n'y avait eu d'autre progrès, de 1840 à
1853, que celui qui est marqué par la différence entre
3,714 et 3,444. A plus forte raison en est-il ainsi dans
l'Arriége, dans le Morbihan, dans le Finistère.

Certes, il n'en est pas ainsi, je n'ai pas besoin de le dire,
dans l'immense majorité des départements français. Si l'on
envisage le résultat général, on trouve que le chiffre des
jeunes gens tout-à-fait illettrés au moment du tirage au
sort, qui était de 125,760, en 1840, était tombé, en 1853,
à 99,684. Mais les exemples que je viens de citer sont
les conséquences regrettables des faits dont il vient d'être
parlé.

Il serait facile, je pense, en regard de ces faits, de citer
pour l'Angleterre des phénomènes analogues : ce n'est pas
à moi de rappeler qu'en 1850 une adresse présentée au
Parlement par *l'Union des Ecoles* de Lancashire déplorait
"que la moitié de cette grande nation ne sut ni lire ni
écrire, et que, de l'autre moitié, une grande partie ne pos-
sédait que la plus misérable instruction." On n'a pas
oublié qu'il y a quelques années, un homme investi d'une
haute autorité, et dont les conseils sont pour vous, Messieurs, une lumière et une force, M. Moseley, constatait,
dans un rapport où ses observations portaient sur 112 localités, que les enfants ne profitaient des écoles que dans
la proportion de 2 sur 39; que sur 11,872 enfants sortant
des écoles, 5,805 pouvaient à peine épeler; que 1 sur 5
n'avait pas la moindre notion d'arithmétique.

Ainsi, en Angleterre comme en France, la plaie est

sondée et mise à nu. Dans les deux pays, il reste à chercher les remèdes et à les appliquer d'une main ferme et résolue.

Je m'arrête ici, Messieurs, car si j'entrais dans l'examen de ces remèdes ; si je vous exposais les détails de la législation des différents états de l'Allemagne, au point de vue de l'enseignement obligatoire ; si je vous parlais des *écoles de répétition* (*Wiederholungsschulen*), où, à la sortie de l'école primaire proprement dite, les enfants doivent se rendre jusqu'à l'âge de quinze ans ; si j'essayais de déterminer le partage du temps qu'il serait possible de faire entre le travail de l'école et le travail professionnel, selon les exigences des temps et des lieux ; si j'abordais la question de l'union intime de l'instituteur et du ministre de la religion dans l'œuvre des *Ecoles du Dimanche* ; si j'entreprenais d'énumérer les conditions dans lesquelles je concevrais que pussent être délivrés les *certificats d'études*, et accordés les *prix* ou *récompenses*, je sortirais des limites tracées par votre programme à la section devant laquelle vous m'avez fait l'honneur de m'engager à porter la parole.

De l'Education des enfants des classes ouvrières, et spéciale-
ment de leur retrait prématuré de l'école. Note sur l'état
de cette question en France ; par le Dr. MATTER, in-
specteur général et honoraire de l'instruction publique.

Je suivrai, dans ma Notice, l'ordre si parfaitement in-
diqué par le programme des Conférences : j'aborderai suc-
cessivement le fait, les causes, les effets, les moyens ou le
remède au mal spécial qu'il importe avant tout de combattre.

I.—LE FAIT.

Malgré tout ce qu'on a fait en France, depuis 1830 et an-
térieurement, pour combattre l'éloignement prématuré de
ces enfants de leurs écoles, ce fait y est encore plus général
que dans ceux des états d'Allemagne où l'école est demeu-
rée dans des rapports plus intimes avec la religion et ses
ministres.   Toutefois, le fait varie selon les provinces, les
mœurs et les influences locales, comme il varie selon les
trois grandes catégories de travail : les mines, l'agriculture,
et l'industrie.

Nous avons peu de mines où les enfants soient appelés
prématurément au travail.

En revanche, ils s'engagent trop tôt dans le travail des
champs sur la presque totalité de la France.

Mais ils sont surtout poussés par les familles, ou entraî-
nés par l'appât du gain vers le travail des fabriques, partout où celles-ci s'établissent, ce qui, chaque jour, se fait
de plus en plus, même dans les districts autrefois pure-

ment agricoles. L'Angleterre peut donc se persuader que ce qu'elle fera de bon et de nouveau sous ce rapport, pourra tourner comme un exemple au profit même de ses plus proches voisins.

La fréquentation défectueuse ou incomplète des écoles par l'enfant du pauvre et de l'ouvrier, varie cependant beaucoup suivant les circonstances que j'ai indiquées; et c'est un fait à signaler, que, dans toutes les communes, et surtout dans les écoles rurales, où l'influence de l'instituteur est complète, où elle est aidée de celle du maire et de celle du ministre de la religion, les enfants suivent, à peu près tous, l'enseignement public jusqu'à l'âge de quatorze ans.

Il y avait autrefois des paroisses catholiques où l'on était admis à la première communion dès la onzième année; s'il en est encore, elles sont rares, et dans les autres on les ajourne à la treizième et à la quatorzième année. Encore, les *frères* et les *sœurs* qui dirigent les écoles s'efforcent généralement de retenir leurs élèves jusqu'à l'âge de quatorze et de quinze ans, ainsi que font les maîtres et les institutrices laïques. J'ai vu des enfants plus âgés encore dans les écoles.

La cessation ou la continuation des études tient donc à des influences locales et personnelles, scolastiques et religieuses surtout, mais non pas à des influences de confession ou de communion religieuse. Dans les cinq communes agricoles, qui se trouvent à une lieue, ou à moins, de ma résidence, se montre ce fait, que la fréquentation de l'école par tous les enfants, été comme hiver, est complète dans deux (sauf les congés autorisés par les maîtres pour les cas extraordinaires); tandis que, dans les trois autres, le chiffre des élèves, qui est de 80 à 90 en hiver, se réduit à 15 et à 12 en été. Ces communes sont dans les mêmes conditions, sous la direction de la même autorité académique et préfectorale, sous l'inspection des mêmes délé-

gués, étant du même canton. Il est des paroisses protes-
tantes où le ministre n'obtient l'autorisation d'admettre les
enfants à la première communion, ou à la confirmation,
qu'à cette double condition : 1. qu'ils soient âgés de quatorze ans ; 2. qu'ils sachent lire et écrire et répondre sur
le catéchisme ; preuve évidente que ce sont les habitudes
locales et les influences personnelles qui l'emportent sur
les circonstances communes et générales. C'est là, à mon
avis, une indication décisive pour la question du remède
au mal.

Dans les communes manufacturières l'éloignement de
l'école commence généralement, plus ou moins complet,
dès l'âge de huit ans, et n'est plus que stérilement com-
battu dès l'âge de douze ans.

II.—CAUSES.

La première, selon l'opinion commune en France, c'est
le besoin, c'est la pauvreté, qui dans quelques localités
va jusqu'à la souffrance, jusqu'à la misère. Il faut su-
bir nécessairement les conséquences, les effets inévitables
de cette cause, car, pour la faire disparaître, il faudrait
faire évanouir d'abord la misère et les circonstances qui la
produisent. Mais, tout en acceptant ces conséquences, il
faut les circonscrire dans leurs véritables limites et lutter
contre l'habitude générale, d'attribuer au besoin qu'on a
de tirer parti du travail des enfants toutes sortes de fautes
et de négligences, qui se glissent dans les familles sous ce
pavillon de détresse. En effet, une fois que les parents
ont commencé à retirer les enfants de l'école et à goûter
le fruit de leur travail, ne fût-ce que par voie d'exception,
ils prennent aisément l'habitude de faire de l'exception la
règle, et une fois ce pli pris, il y a difficulté extrême à l'ef-
facer de leurs mœurs : tout prétexte devient motif. Le
vice lui-même prend, pour s'en couvrir, le voile de la mi-

sère. On a vu des parents contracter des goûts de dissipation et d'ivrognerie avec l'argent gagné par les enfants. Par exemple, ce fait que dans un établissement qui occupe 600 ouvriers, on compte de 80 à 100 enfants, noueurs, rattacheurs, tisserands, ne s'explique point par la souffrance, par la misère des familles : il s'explique par le goût qu'elles ont pris aux jouissances qu'on se procure avec le salaire des enfants ajouté au salaire des parents.

La deuxième cause du fait, cause très-légitime aussi en son principe, c'est donc le simple désir d'ajouter au bien-être, à l'aisance de la famille; et il n'y aurait que demi-mal si ce désir était contenu dans de justes limites. Mais ce désir dégénère facilement et procure non-seulement des jouissances qui sont de luxe et payées trop cher, mais le gain donne aux enfants, qui apprécient promptement ce qu'ils valent, avec des sentiments d'indépendance, ces goûts de toilette, et ces penchants pour la dépense qui sont la ruine d'un trop grand nombre de jeunes gens et de jeunes filles.

La troisième cause du fait, et la plus inexcusable de toutes, c'est le goût prématuré des enfants pour l'apparente distraction ou pour le charme réel qu'offrent le travail des champs et le grand air, ou le travail des fabriques et ses attraits sociaux, attraits bien funestes et bien trompeurs, sans doute, mais bien puissants pour l'imagination du jeune paresseux, du jeune étourdi, qui aime mieux flaner aux abords d'une grande manufacture, ou dans les prairies d'une vaste plaine, que de rester sur les bancs de l'école. En effet, notre imagination française, qui a des complices dans tous les pays, n'est pas une des moindres sources, et elle est une des plus incurables causes, du fait que nous déplorons.

La quatrième cause, qui est réellement aussi impérieuse que le besoin d'argent des familles, c'est le besoin d'ouvriers des fabriques, c'est-à-dire que ce sont là, en France, les deux causes les plus décisives et qui s'entendent le

mieux, pour escompter prématurément les forces, les ressources physiques et morales de la jeunesse des classes
ouvrières. Il est certain que les intérêts les plus essen-
tiels de l'industrie, et en partie ceux de l'agriculture, ré-
clament l'intervention des enfants et se trouvent en collision permanente avec les intérêts sacrés de l'éducation; et
la collision ne s'arrête pas là. Elle est plus intime, et
par conséquent plus difficile à combattre. Il faut, pour
l'atteindre, pénétrer dans la famille et disputer l'enfant à
l'autorité paternelle. " Dans nos environs," m'écrit un
des industriels les plus honorables et les plus zélés pour la
moralisation des classes ouvrières, un véritable apôtre de
l'Evangile, " les enfants sont généralement employés par
leurs parents au dévidage et au tissage en couleur, travail
qui se fait en famille. Il y a lutte constante entre les
ministres de la religion ou les instituteurs, qui veulent retenir les enfants le plus longtemps possible à l'école, et les
parents qui, pressés par le besoin, veulent profiter du travail de leurs enfants."

C'est donc entre les parents et les protecteurs moraux
de l'enfance qu'a lieu le conflit. Les maîtres n'y figurent
point en apparence, et le fait est qu'ils n'y entrent en réa-
lité que par l'attrait du salaire qu'on trouve dans leurs
maisons. Mais ce salaire, ils le proportionnent, l'élèvent
ou l'abaissent naturellement, selon les fluctuations de leur
industrie, et là gît un tel attrait que le conflit réel est bien
entre la fabrique et l'école. Les variations du salaire sont
tempérées par les maîtres, par leur philanthropie, leur charité, leurs mœurs, et leurs convictions religieuses; et il en
est qui s'empressent, dans l'intérêt de l'école, de les rendre
sensibles pour le travail que les enfants font en fabrique,
celui des rattacheurs, par exemple, pour lequel il faut des
enfants; mais ils ne peuvent se passer entièrement du con-
cours de ces derniers, et ils n'ont aucune influence tuté-
laire quant au travail qui se fait en famille.

En général, si ce mode de travail est moins funeste pour l'enfance, en revanche il est plus difficile à réglementer par une autorité externe que le travail qui se fait en fabrique et en commun. L'autorité externe mérite ici une mention spéciale.

La cinquième cause du mal, la cause la moins signalée et la plus facile à modifier, c'est l'intervention insuffisante de l'autorité publique. Nous, en France, dans l'éducation comme dans l'instruction, nous aimons l'intervention du pouvoir dans toute son étendue. D'habitude, nous comptons même trop sur le gouvernement; jamais nous ne lui demandons trop peu, au contraire, nous en faisons volontiers la providence sociale, et quand il nous dit: *aide-toi et le Ciel t'aidera*, nous recevons ces mots comme une gracieuse défaite de sa part. Il est donc établi pour nous, puisque le mal existe encore, que l'état n'a pas encore rempli tous ses devoirs, et il n'y a dans cette idée aucune espèce d'opposition. J'ai cité plus haut l'exemple de cinq communes toutes également placées sous l'action de l'autorité publique, et dont trois y échappent par l'incurie de ses agents, ou par l'insuffisance de leurs moyens. Cet exemple se reproduit partout, et partout l'opinion désintéressée, l'opinion de tous ceux qui n'ont aucun intérêt à la continuation du mal, se reporte vers l'autorité publique avec le vœu qu'elle y mette fin et avec l'offre de lui livrer tous les pouvoirs, et tous les moyens qui lui seront nécessaires.

III.—EFFETS OU RÉSULTATS DE L'ABANDON PRÉMATURÉ DE L'ÉCOLE POUR LA FRÉQUENTATION PRÉMATURÉE DE LA FABRIQUE.

Je serai bien bref sur ce point, convaincu, non pas que tout est dit, car tout n'est pas dit quand il s'agit d'un état de choses qui prend chaque jour des formes nouvelles, et des formes autres dans chaque canton; mais convaincu qu'il faut peu de mots pour constater ce qui est incontestable et partout analogue.

Le premier résultat du travail prématuré des enfants hors l'école, est d'ordinaire celui qu'on recherche par ce travail, plus d'argent. Cela est vrai, mais, si cela veut dire plus de jouissances de nourriture et d'habillement, plus d'apparences d'aisance, cela ne veut pas dire plus d'aisance réelle, une nourriture plus saine, des habillements mieux entendus. Ce résultat se voit quelquefois, mais il est rare, et le contraire ne l'est pas; c'est-à-dire, qu'on voit naître des goûts de dissipation et de frivolité, des prétentions d'élégance, qui prennent la place des anciennes habitudes de modeste réserve et de sage économie, et surgir des aspirations de bien-être et de comfort, qui sont des tourments plus forts que ceux de la pauvreté sous ses formes anciennes.

Le second effet de ce passage trop rapide au travail est ce degré de développement intellectuel que donnent des rapports sociaux trop multipliés et plus intimes. Ce développement est incontestable et son action dispose maint enfant à son rôle futur d'heureux industriel ou de contre-maître bien payé, et, en ce sens, c'est un bien. Mais ces succès inspirent à une foule d'autres des rêves et des ambitions dont l'évanouissement jette dans l'âme de profondes amertumes. Le développement en question est d'ailleurs très-borné, et même borné il n'est pas général; il n'est pas même commun à tous les enfants heureusement doués sous le rapport de l'intelligence. Il n'y a donc pas lieu d'en faire grand cas, ou de le porter en ligne de compte comme un avantage propre à balancer bien des inconvénients.

Le troisième effet est cette ignorance dans les choses morales et religieuses, et même dans les sciences populaires, qui va souvent au-delà de toute conception. On voit des garçons de dix-huit ans qui ne savent pas lire.

Ce sont des exceptions; mais le même fabricant que j'ai déjà cité m'écrit ces lignes : " *Généralement* les enfants de ma localité (elle est petite et chargée de fabriques qui attirent des enfants de plusieurs lieues à la ronde) fréquentent l'école irrégulièrement, y restent trop peu de temps. Il en résulte une instruction très-insuffisante, et qui *ordinairement* se perd quand, après la première communion, tout le temps des enfants est consacré au travail."

Le quatrième effet, ce n'est plus seulement l'absence de bonnes habitudes, et de mœurs pures, c'est une véritable démoralisation, qui ne se borne pas à un seul genre d'aberration, mais qui envahit toute l'âme du jeune homme, et qui ne circonscrit pas dans les districts manufacturiers, mais se communique aux cantons agricoles. Or, elle y enfante, sinon une corruption plus profonde qu'aux mauvais jours du passé, du moins des faits nouveaux, quant à l'amour des plaisirs et quant aux moyens de se procurer les deniers nécessaires pour s'y livrer. On voit des enfants, et mêmes de faibles et coupables mères de famille, vendre les provisions les plus indispensables du ménage afin de se procurer l'argent nécessaire pour figurer dans les fêtes du village.

Le cinquième effet, c'est cet évident appauvrissement de la constitution physique qui éclate partout sous la même forme, et qui va très-loin.

Et ces deux derniers effets ne sont pas concentrés dans les localités à grands ateliers; ils se produisent là même où le travail prématuré se fait en famille. Il me serait aisé, si cela m'était possible, d'appuyer cette assertion sur mon expérience personnelle et sur des observations faites dans une région des Vosges, dont l'éducation religieuse a été dirigée et est devenue un objet de respectueuse admiration pour toute l'Europe, grâce à la piété apostolique et au dévouement admirable d'un pasteur devenu célèbre dans le monde chrétien tout entier.

Ce qui doit surtout être signalé, c'est qu'en compensation de tout cela n'est pas même venue l'aisance. La pauvreté est la même, et elle est devenue plus sensible par les idées qui sont survenues comme par les sentiments qui s'en sont allés.

IV.—LES MOYENS OU LE REMÈDE AU MAL.

1. Le premier qu'on emploie en France c'est la loi, c'est la limitation d'âge et l'obligation de suivre une école, inscrites dans la loi relative au travail des enfants employés dans les manufactures, usines et ateliers. Cette loi, rendue le 20 mars 1841, prescrit que, dans tout établissement qui occupe plus de vingt ouvriers réunis, les enfants, pour être admis, devront avoir au moins huit ans, et qu'ils n'y pourront être occupés, jusqu'à douze ans, que pendant huit heures sur vingt-quatre. Interdisant tout travail de nuit avant treize ans, elle oblige tout enfant jusqu'à douze ans à fréquenter une école.

Complétée par divers réglements d'administration, qui offrent des moyens précieux à la philanthropie évangélique, cette loi est rigoureusement surveillée par l'autorité. Elle produit encore plus de bien en faisant entrer de précieuses idées de protection et d'humanité dans les esprits, et l'on ne saurait trop apprécier l'influence de toute bonne loi, de toute mesure philanthropique, de toute démonstration publique de cette nature.

De précieuses, de généreuses instructions ont été données aux inspecteurs des écoles pour la parfaite observation de cette loi, et pour assurer la plus grande extension possible de ses bienfaits, directs ou indirects. Il y a des maîtres qui se plaignent un peu de la gêne que leur cause la rigueur des surveillants, mais qui admirent et bénissent le zèle avec lequel ils remplissent leur devoir.

2. Le second moyen qu'on emploie pour arrêter le pas-

sage prématuré de l'étude au travail, c'est le *livret* délivré
à l'enfant, non pas qui fréquente l'école, mais qui travaille
dans une fabrique. Ce livret se donne dans le but de faci-
liter aux inspecteurs la vérification des abus, car il porte
l'âge de l'enfant certifié par le maire, et fournit aux surveillants le moyen de forcer le jeune ouvrier, l'ouvrier
prématuré, à continuer de fréquenter l'école.

Sous ce point de vue, le *livret* diffère complétement du
certificat que le programme des Conférences met en avant.
Le livret et le certificat se touchent cependant en ceci, que
le livret aussi, revêtu d'attestations de la part du maire et
de l'*employeur*, peut devenir un titre de recommandation
et une source d'avantages pour son jeune possesseur.

3. Le certificat. J'ai consulté des fabricants sur les
effets qu'on pourrait obtenir par ce moyen en France.
" Les certificats qui attesteront une fréquentation complète et une instruction même supérieure, auraient parmi
nous peu de valeur, car le travail dans les manufactures
exige rarement de l'instruction : la force musculaire, l'intelligence, la bonne conduite, qui peuvent se rencontrer
sans l'instruction, y sont mieux appréciées." Cela paraît
assez évident, et cela est un peu décourageant au premier
abord. Toutefois, cette appréciation, qui n'est pas tout-à-
fait la mienne, n'est pas celle de tout le monde, je pense.

Chacun peut voir, au contraire, que ceux de nos domes-
tiques qui ont de beaux certificats, de quelque apprentissage que ce soit, en sont extrêmement jaloux et fiers ;
quoique dans notre pays les maîtres se dispensent volontiers de consulter des certificats en engageant leurs servi-
teurs.

4. Les *primes.* " Les primes seront mieux appréciées,"
m'écrit-on, " mais pour équivaloir au salaire de l'enfant,
qui varie de 40 c. à 1 fr. par jour, il faudrait un beau
fonds." Je partage cet avis en ce qui concerne la France.
Parmi nous le budget de l'état serait nécessaire, sinon

pour fournir ce beau fonds tout entier, du moins pour le rendre suffisant. Il faut pourtant considérer la valeur du mot attribué à M. de Talleyrand: *Dans les grandes choses, le matériel n'est rien, le moral est tout.* Il s'agit ici d'une des plus grandes choses du monde, et, pour mon compte, je crois à la puissance morale du certificat dans quelque pays que ce soit; je ne crois pas à sa puissance universelle, mais à sa puissance dans les circonstances données. Il ne faut pas non plus s'attendre à son efficacité immédiate, mais on doit compter sur celle que lui donneront le temps et les mœurs qu'il forme.

Des primes en vêtements, livres et outils, on n'apprécierait en France que les premières, et encore n'auraient-elles pas d'influence déterminante en l'état actuel de nos mœurs, mais tout change les mœurs, toute idée, toute institution, toute pratique.

5. Le *demi-temps.* " Il ne peut être question," m'écrit-on (parmi nous bien entendu), " de faire travailler les enfants moitié de temps, soit la moitié du jour, soit la moitié de la semaine, à moins d'avoir double série d'ouvriers-enfants, par la raison que le travail de l'enfant est presque toujours lié à celui d'un adulte." Mais d'abord, le système de deux corps *d'enfants-ouvriers* est très-praticable. En second lieu, le système du demi-temps ou d'une fraction de temps, est dès maintenant pratiqué dans plusieurs de nos établissements. Un instituteur est attaché à la fabrique. Il est engagé d'ordinaire aux appointements de 1000 à 1200 francs et le logement. Cet instituteur réunit deux fois par jour les enfants-ouvriers dans ses classes, aux heures les plus favorables, et sans qu'il en manque un seul de ceux qui doivent fréquenter les leçons. Nous avons encore de ces écoles qui comptent de 30 à 100 élèves. Dans nos jours classiques de libéralisme, au temps que nous appelons l'opposition de quinze ans, et où nous étions sous le charme de l'enseignement mutuel, tout fa-

bricant qui visait au conseil municipal, au conseil général, ou à la députation, rattachait une école mutuelle à sa maison. Ce que la politique d'opposition nous faisait faire quand le gouvernement faisait peu ou mal la religion ou la charité évangélique, nous le ferait faire encore, surtout le gouvernement y aidant.

Ce que l'Angleterre projette dans sa situation, au nom de ses mœurs et de ses lois, en vue de ses ressources et avec ses sentiments, trouverait donc, soit des éléments d'analogie, soit l'autorité de l'exemple même dans nos mœurs et dans notre situation si essentiellement différente. L'analogie ne saurait surprendre quand il s'agit d'un intérêt de moralité et d'humanité.

Telles sont les premières observations que j'ai pu tracer d'une plume rapide sur la belle question, sur l'œuvre évangélique dont se préoccupe l'Association pour l'Education des Enfants de la classe ouvrière. Je demande pour ces indications toute l'indulgence que peut mériter la promptitude avec laquelle j'ai dû les rédiger, et je fais des vœux bien sincères pour que les résultats de la Conférence du 22-24 juin, si peu positifs et tout directement applicables qu'ils puissent paraître, reçoivent la divulgation la plus étendue. La lumière éclaire tout; la charité féconde tout.

The Educational System in Germany and its Advantages.
By Captain Boscawen Ibbotson, F. R. S.

By the method of education pursued in Germany, the pupils, besides receiving instruction, are stimulated by emulation into a system of good conduct and strict moral observances. The general object of education is, that all persons should have the opportunity of gaining, and be encouraged to seek, such instruction as will enable them to become useful members of all communities, and to adapt themselves, by their education and by the development of their talents, to their after pursuits in life.

It is proved by experience, that children, when good encouragement and opportunity is afforded them, are found to possess unknown talents of great utility to the commonwealth, although their commencement has been the most unpromising. I could quote numerous instances of this fact; but I will merely state, that it depends greatly on their early associations as a groundwork for their future advancement. I do not mean to say that cases have not occurred where persons, without such advantages, have made themselves notable by their talents and their discoveries; but I mean to say, that if such persons had received at first a good " elementary education," and afterwards followed it up from class to class, as far as their time and occupations would permit, that instruction so gained would decidedly have raised them much higher, and with greater ease and security, than their talents alone, without such instruction, could have procured them.

The German rule of forced public examinations has great advantages. If the pupils at these examinations get a good certificate, they are certain of being employed, either by the state or the town, or that certificate will greatly facilitate any other private employment. This is not the only good result of a public examination: it also enables the parents to find out what pursuits are best adapted to their childrens' talents; as most children have latent talents, little known even to themselves, which require study and example to develope. Public examinations also avoid, in a great measure, favouritism, which is the bane of all moral advancement. In Prussia, and in some other states in Germany, no persons can be appointed to any state offices, and, in some places, to any employment as apprentice, or to any trade, without passing a well-defined examination, to show their fitness to enter into such employment. Each examination is made in different gradations, according to the education necessary for their various pursuits. These examinations were introduced by Herman Franke, in Halle, in the year 1696.

Money prizes are also given in many states. In 1853 Munich gave altogether twenty-nine prizes, varying from 120 guldens. The first prize was awarded to a postilion's son, a mechanic 16 years of age. Owing to the cheapness of the country, this sum has enabled him, with the aid of the town, to settle in business. The second prize to a watchmaker's apprentice; and the third to a type-setter.

It is by this liberality on the part of Government, that parents are encouraged to let their children remain at school; for if they leave before an examination, they cannot reap any of these benefits. And the "principle" that is most detrimental to the progress of education in

England is, that the parents take their children too early from school, but which could be in a great measure remedied by liberal encouragement from Government, who would themselves reap the benefit of it.

The system of education in Germany is a progressive one, and in most places the pupils cannot enter into a higher class or school without passing an examination of their qualifications on leaving a lower class or school.

A Latin or Greek education is only employed by those students entering into higher professions—as surgeons, chemists, &c., not tradesmen and artisans; but it is considered necessary that they should possess a sound knowledge of mathematics, physics, and mechanics in their lower branches. It has been said in England that without that system of education, the English workmen bring their work to greater perfection than the Germans; but this is not the fact. The English mechanic works rapidly only at the occupation he is trained to, and does that effectually; but he is, from deficient education, incapable of working any new branch of his business; and high class labour is scarcer in England than elsewhere; whereas a German, who understands the principle of mechanics and physics, can set to work to produce any instrument or machine the principle of which he can understand. This is found to be the case, particularly by philosophical instrument makers.

The Prussians were the first in Germany to find out the necessity of a national education to the poorer classes, not only for their own good, but for the good of the state. We see in Mrs. Austin's " Germany," that the leaders of that movement were Wm. von Humboldt, Schleiermacher, Niebuhr, and Count Dohna, and the new system of education was commenced when the country was in a most deplorable condition, viz. in 1808, just after the treaty of Tilsit. It was such a year, says Mrs. Austin, that gave birth to the system of National Education which has since obtained so much notice and admiration. Pestalozzi's method was introduced, and a pupil of his engaged to teach at Berlin, and although the country was in a state of poverty, the Government gave 150,000 thalers for educational purposes. The king also presented to the university the palace of Prince Henry. " It was the highest example," says Ficht, " of a practical respect for science ever afforded by a state ; for the measure was entered upon during a period of the direst oppression, and under the greatest financial difficulties. It was not a matter of display that was sought for, but an instrument to give new health and vigour to the nation."

In all lands, you find from the earliest periods of civilisation, that those states wherein education has been made the standard of all advancement in worldly pursuits have raised themselves to the greatest pre-eminence.

The great increase of pupils in all the industrial schools in Germany is worthy of notice, showing that the people begin to see the practical necessity of industrial education to enable them to keep pace with the rapid strides that science and manufactures are now making in all parts of the globe, and that the country that does not encourage this system of a solid education for their youths must lose caste both morally and financially.

Industrial education has been much neglected in England, and it is very rare to find artisans well instructed in the lower branches of mathematics, physics, and mechanics, whereas in Germany it is very uncommon to find any who are not well instructed in all these branches of knowledge. I know from experience that many old hands in the English factories know nothing of the rationale of their business, and fancy, through want of education, that their work cannot be surpassed. Their labour is all chance, and they always follow up the same routine, without any likelihood of improvement, the why and the wherefore being never thought about. The Exhibition of 1851 has done much good in undermining this state of ignorant prejudice, as it has opened the eyes of many foremen and workmen, who were before that bigoted to their own opinions. The establishment essential for this country, and which would be highly popular, would be a large industrial school in London, copied from the Polytechnic schools of Vienna, Hanover, Dresden, the (Gewerbe)Industrial School of Berlin, Carlsruhe, &c., and take the best plan from each of them, with branch schools belonging to it in all parts of the country, as in Prussia.

In some towns in Germany they have large gardens in which only the students are employed and paid for their labour ; there is a house in the garden in which they make nets for walls, matting, straw hats, &c., so that they are always employed. If the custom of organising such institutions were established in many towns in England, it would be another encouragement for parents to allow their children to remain at school ; and it would, I am convinced, be found to be a profitable speculation.

The progressive classes of schools in Germany are as follows :—

1st. *Krippe or Klein kinder anstalten* institutions for the reception of infants.

2nd. " *Elementary Schools,*" from which they branch out to either the

(A.) *Gymnasium* or Latin school, and from thence to the University for the learned professions ;

(B.) Or to the *High School,* and from that to either of the following classes or schools.

a. *Fach Schule,* or an industrial, or mechanical and physical school for artisans, &c.

b. Or to the *normal or teachers'* schools ;

c. Or to the *Polytecnische Schule,* which is in fact in

some places, as for example, in Berlin, called a *Gewerbe* or industrial school; but this term *gewerbe* varies, as the *Gewerbe* School of Carlsruhe is in fact a journeyman and apprentice school (Fortbildungs Anstalt).

The general opinion in Germany is, that the infant's education is one of the principal points to be seen after; therefore, the infant schools are particularly attended to. Their regulations are various; some are free, and supported by voluntary contributions; to others the parents pay a small sum for their maintenance, according to their means. In some places, as at Dresden, babies are admitted of a few months old; in others, they are admitted from 3 years of age to 6. This appears to be the general system. In some towns, as in Munich, for example, they are not allowed to have any instruction, the supposition being that early instruction weakens the intellect. In other towns,—as, for example, Augsburg,—I have seen a child 6 years of age make a very tolerable pencil drawing, and also show a proficiency in reading and spelling. Their childish amusements are always instructive, accompanied with cheerful singing, with which they take great pains. Everything is done to please them. The system throughout seems to be to make school a pleasure to them from their earliest infancy, and to make it a grief to them to leave it.

Professor W. Eisenlohr, who was the first to introduce Gewerbe or Industrial schools into Manheim, told me that at first he had some difficulty to get the children to attend; but after 2 or 3 years, by giving prizes and insuring them employment, if deserving, the pupils became so numerous, that the state was obliged to buy the schools, and establish them on a large scale.

In some places they have " Fortbildungs Anstalten," or schools always warm in winter, for workmen, journeymen, and apprentices to enter when their leisure will allow them.   The Handwerk Schule of Hanover is one of this sort.

In some parts of Germany, particularly in Bavaria, they have practical agricultural schools, forming a part of the Polytechnic and industrial schools, and under Government.   The best is at Hohenheim, near Munich.   It is in a royal castle, with plenty of land, and admirably conducted.   One great advantage of these progressive schools being linked together, is, that the pupils of both agricultural and industrial pursuits get acquainted with each other at the high school, and thereby is avoided that jealous feeling which unhappily exists in general between the agriculturist and the mechanic.

There is a gymnastic ground attached to each school. Singing forms also a part of the national education, and particular attention is paid to free hand, lineal and geometric drawing.

In Germany, the Government always tries to keep up a spirit of emulation, by getting novelties, in the ways of teaching, into their schools, which prevents them from remaining the least in the background.   For this purpose, they have, in addition to their home inspectors of schools, a travelling inspector of schools, who visits all the educational establishments in foreign countries, and reports, not only on any new method of education, new school books, &c., but also new methods of diagrams, explanatory mechanical apparatus, &c.   The advantage of this plan is too self-evident to need any further explanation.

As a great part of the plan of education in Germany was derived from one source, I will briefly explain to you the rise and progress of one of their largest and oldest establishments, and show what the energy of one man can do when well applied.   It is the Orphan School in Halle.

The Orphan School in Halle.—This institution was established by August Herman Franke, from 1694 to 1721, at which period it was the custom of the poorer classes to congregate near the houses of the rich to receive food, &c. Franke also, as clergyman of the town of Glauca, gave his bread to them, but he took the opportunity, at the same time, to try to give them instruction. He allowed also the parents and the children to enter his house, and he asked questions of the children relating to their catechism, and allowed the parents to listen ; kept them a quarter of an hour, and finished with a prayer, and then gave them food. This took place every Thursday. The ignorance he found was astounding, and he hardly knew in what manner he should begin to ameliorate it. He began by giving money to the children for their schooling, but that did not answer, as he found that the money was sometimes spent for other purposes, and if applied for schooling that they still gained but little instruction. He then bought a begging-box, and put it in the hands of some well thinking students, and that produced about 1s. 6d. per week. In the year 1695 he placed a similar box in his room, with an appropriate inscription under it. It had this good effect, that a Madame C. S. Knorrin left about 13s. 6d. in the box. When Franke saw that sum he said from this I will establish a poor school. I will not follow up in detail all the progress he had made, step by step, in his laudable exertions, but will merely state that in twenty-seven years, viz. in 1721, that he not only founded his poor school, but also founded the following institutions :—

1. An Orphan Asylum, to which belonged 55 boys ; in a Gymnasium or Latin school, for professions, 45 ditto ; in Gewerbe, an Industrial School for Artisans, 25 girls. With 17 teachers. This was a free school.

2. Seeing the necessity for a particular and separate education for teachers in schools, he established what is here called a normal or training school. Both

their education and board was free. He had 75 scholars.

3. An extra free table or dinner, partly for very poor scholars, and partly for such as later in life might become teachers. He fed 64 persons daily.

4. Eight school classes. The Latin school had, besides the 55 orphans before-mentioned, 103 scholars. In the other German school, a boys' and girls' school, besides the 70 orphans, he had 418 scholars out of the town, and he had altogether, besides the inspectors, 67 teachers.

5. The Royal Pädogogium, for boys of the middle and higher classes. He had 70 scholars, 12 upper teachers, and 5 under ones.

6. A book and publishing trade, in which was employed one principal, one servant, and one apprentice.

7. A chemical laboratory, with a bookkeeper, 4 laboratory assistants, 2 journeymen, and 2 apprentices.

8. A widow's asylum for 4 widows.

9. Also an asylum for the poor of his parish (Glauca), and for travelling beggars.

10. The Gynäceum, or female seminary.

Herman Franke died in 1727, in his 65th year.

At the time of my visit to this institution, then under the direction of Dr. G. Kramer, there were 3140 students.

The renowned Rauhenhaus, or reformatory school, at Horn, near Hamburgh, owned its existence to similar circumstances as the latter. It was established in 1832—1833.

It was first started by a society called the Mänliche Besuchs Verein, a society still existing, whose object was to seek out persons and families in distress, and afford them relief. The idea struck them of the necessity of a reformatory school for juvenile offenders; but as this

society was composed of persons with very small pecuniary means, the difficulty was to procure the necessary
funds to establish it. Shortly after they had met together, and started this subject among themselves, a person,
almost a stranger, entered into the office of one of the
associates of this Society, and said he wished to place in
his hands a sum of about £15 (100 thalers) for charitable
purposes, but that he was desirous that it should be employed in the forming of some religious institution for the
benefit of mankind. The associate was astounded, as it
seemed that a kind Providence had sent this sum on
purpose to forward their good work. They then thought
of making their plan public, and for that purpose laid
their scheme before a man well known for his zeal in all
matters relating to the poor of Hamburg. He published
the receipt of the above sum, and the name of the Rettungs
Haus, or Reformatory School, was for the first time
published.

A citizen of Hamburg died, and amongst many other
legacies left about £1060 (17,500 marks) to forward this
new institution. The Society then thought of hiring a
house to start their plan, and an article in a country
journal (" Bergdorfer Boten ") gained many subscriptions;
one lady sent about £6 (100 marks); a servant girl and
a shoemaker's apprentice sent all their savings. Dr.
Wiegern, the present director of the establishment, called
on the late Syndicus Lieveking to ask his advice on the
subject, and he gave to the Society an acre of land in
Horn on which to form their school, and a house which
from time immemorable had been called the "Rauhe
Haus;" thus is derived the name of the institution.
Dr. Wiegern and his mother entered upon the premises
in 1833, and directly received their first three boys. At
the end of the first year they had twelve boys. Their
plan is to put no perceptible restraint upon the boys, and

no locks and keys are allowed. Each twelve form what they call a family. Each began to learn a trade. They built their own houses, made their furniture, clothes, &c. The establishment so increased by good management that in 1853 they had 20 houses, 41 acres of land, 26 acres of which was their own freehold. Each family is governed by a so-called brother, representing the elder brother of a family. They are all young men of exemplary character, and all get good situations. Out of 158 that have been educated there, 113 have been well placed. Taking the average of 200 children, the boys take a little more than 4 years to reclaim them; the girls 5 years and a half. And the result of the amendment is as follows, 200 placed in situations : 23, viz. 17 boys and 16 girls, irreclaimable ; 22, viz. 11 boys and 11 girls, served badly ; 10, viz. 9 boys and 1 girl, were tolerable ; and 145, viz. 124 boys and 21 girls, turned out good. There are about 24 of these establishments in Germany.

Our Noble President, H. R. H. Prince Albert, has, in conjunction with his brother, the Reigning Duke of Cobourg and Gotha, established and endowed a normal school for elementary teachers at Cobourg. The scholars remain 3 years. They enter at from 16 to 21 years of age ; and, on their leaving, they all receive stipends, according to their merit, to aid their establishment in life.

PART III.

———+——

*A consideration of the expedients which have been proposed
for keeping the Children of the " Working Classes"
longer at School, and an Examination into the Nature
and Administrative Machinery of Prize Schemes.* By
Rev. NASH STEPHENSON, M.A., Incumbent of Shirley
near Birmingham, and one of the Examiners of the
Birmingham and of the Coventry Archidiaconal Prize
Schemes.

IN compliance with the request of the Committee of the
Educational Conference, conveyed to me through Mr.
Lonsdale, I have ventured to accept the office of Secretary
to this Sectional Committee, and to prepare some few remarks, which I will now read, on the expedients proposed
for keeping the children of the " working classes" longer
at school; dwelling, however, more at large on the nature
and administrative machinery of·educational prize schemes,
one of the subjects specially delegated to our consideration to-day.

It is matter for gratulation to the friends of popular
education that the Certificate Scheme, the Prize Scheme,
and the Halftime Scheme, should be selected by the able
and eminent men convening this conference, as the most

prominent, and well nigh the sole subjects for deliberation by the Association. The very selection proves that much has already been effected, even though it also shows that much remains to be accomplished. Had we been called together ten years since, our thoughts would have been directed to the ways and means of erecting school buildings, of supplying an efficient staff of teachers to fill them, and of children to occupy them. These difficulties have to a considerable degree been considered, met, and overcome. Money, public and private, has been sown broadcast over the country; schools, elementary and normal, have risen on all sides, and, by means of their districts, as with a network, have covered the land*; registered and certificated masters are fast superseding the former incompetent teachers; a trained band of 9000 pupil teachers are aiding them in their labours; upwards of 2,000,000 children, between 3 and 15, have their names on the school books; and a sufficient number of government inspectors, whose labours are beyond all praise, are ever watching over the expenditure of public grants; stimulating the efforts of managers and masters; comparing results; placing before the public the newest and most suitable means and appliances of carrying on the scholastic work; and publishing, in their most valuable Reports, the experience of their annual labours in the several districts assigned to them.

But, notwithstanding these encouraging marks of progress of late years, there obtrudes itself on our notice the indisputable fact that the vast mass of children that leave our parochial schools receive but an imperfect and result-

---

* In the year 1853-54 the number of children in attendance at schools liable to inspection was 461,445 ; whilst accommodation was provided for 558,073. That is, there was room for 20 per cent. more. In the year 1854-55, the attendance at schools under inspection was 537,583, whilst the accommodation was 811,794 ; leaving an absolute waste of accommodation of over 50 per cent.

less education. And how, with the advantages alluded to, is this evil to be accounted for? If we turn to the Census of 1851, we shall find that although very few children are in the present day completely uninstructed *, yet that out of the two millions then at school, the average number of those who would remain at school over ten years of age would be as follows: viz. that 49 out of every 100 would remain till 11 years of age, and that 28 per cent. only would remain till they were 13.† We also learn from the Report that, "practically, there are very few labourer's children at school after 11."‡ This disheartening statement I am compelled to indorse by facts within my own experience. On the last anniversary meeting of the Birmingham Church of England Schoolmasters' Association, attended by about forty of the principal masters and mistresses of the town, it was given, as well nigh an unanimous opinion, that 9 or 9½ was the average age in the town at which children left, and that year by year the average was becoming lower. In a most valuable statistical report, recently published by the "Birmingham Educational Association," it appears that 45 per cent. are receiving daily education between 9 and 10; and 38 per cent. between 10 and 11; that between 11 and 12 the school attendance diminishes to 26 per cent., and between 12 and 13 to 13¾ per cent. § In my own school, in a purely agricultural district, the average age at which the children leave is between 9½ and 10½, and perhaps a little over. Within

---

* Educational Census Report, by Horace Mann, Esq., p. 26.

† Census Report, p. 23.

‡ In the Report of the Brooke Deanery Association (Norfolk), of the present year, it is stated (p. 13) that, "throughout the Deanery, the average age of boys receiving daily instruction, is as low as *seven*. They are removed as soon as they can be employed to earn a few pence in farm work of the simplest kind.

§ Statistics of Education in Birmingham, by Birmingham Educational Association, p. 3. Simpkin and Marshall.

the last five years the average with me has certainly been on the increase ; but, in regard to the labouring class, the increase is apparent, but not real. By the instrumentality of superior teachers, and the advantages of pupil teachers and government aid, I am in a position to hold out to my parishioners a course of instruction far in advance of bygone years, and of the ordinary boarding and commercial school, and at a rate of payment that would speedily ruin a private adventure school. The result has been the introduction of a superior class of children who, while paying a higher rate than the rest, remain to a more advanced age, and thus raise the average. But the labourer's child, driven by poverty into the labour-market, remains under the improved system a shorter rather than a longer time. The termination of his school-life is the attainment of the imperfect standard of his parent's acquirements, and not the attainment of a certain age. But as this standard is now reached more quickly than heretofore, the period of continuance at school is shortened rather than prolonged.

And what must be looked for as the inevitable and legitimate results of such a state of things ? Who amongst us would deem a child of the middle or upper classes to have completed its instruction at the age of eleven, and to be qualified to go forth into life to cope with its difficulties, and resist its temptations? And yet, in this instance, the schooling would probably have been uninterrupted, and there would be superadded the influence, and example, and instruction of home. What then must be the imperfect standard attained by the labourer's child, and how utterly ineffective must be his primary instruction, when he leaves the walls of our schools at the immature age of 11 at the outside, and when we know that the modicum of schooling received has been desultory and interrupted, and that the teaching and example of the cottage in too many instances, have more than kept pace in undermining and undoing the training of the school.

The extremely early age at which children are removed from school is the difficulty of the day, the master obstacle that must be surmounted or ever a national education can be accomplished. Next in importance, I would classify the indifference of parents of the lowest grade to education at all*; the remedy for which is to be found in compulsory attendance at school. It is much to be feared that voluntary efforts, and the influence of public grants have well nigh reached, in the descending scale of society, the utmost they can effect, and that the period has now arrived when legislative interference is imperatively called for to meet both these difficulties. In this opinion I have been much strengthened by the evidence of large manufacturers, that I have taken while recently engaged on a committee of an " Association for the Removal of Obstacles to Education in Birmingham and its neighbourhood." The points on which legislation should be based, appear to be as follows : —

I. The prohibition of juvenile labour under 8 years of age.

II. The extension of the Half Time Act to boroughs

---

* In the Birmingham Statistical Returns (p. 12), the following skilfully tabulated results will indicate the various causes that operate against the attendance of children at school :—

Age.	Per centage at day school.	Per centage employed.	Per centage unemployed.
7 to 8	58	$4\frac{3}{4}$	$37\frac{1}{4}$
8 „ 9	$61\frac{3}{4}$	$11\frac{1}{4}$	27
9 „ 10	$45\frac{3}{4}$	$24\frac{1}{4}$	30
10 „ 11	38	$37\frac{1}{2}$	$24\frac{1}{2}$
11 „ 12	26	61	13
12 „ 13	$13\frac{3}{4}$	$71\frac{1}{2}$	$14\frac{3}{4}$
Total	42	33	25

and towns, and a modification of the Print Works Act to rural districts.*

III. The substitution of in-door for out-door relief to all paupers who decline or neglect the sending of their children to school. The Guardians must be compelled to make good the school payments in cases of necessity.†

IV. The multiplication of Industrial Schools where out-door pauper children may attend, and be supplied with food on the workhouse dietary scale, at the expense of the Board of Guardians.

V. The extension to England of the provisions of Dunlop's Act, which has been productive of so much good in Scotland.‡

* Under the Factory or Half-time Act every child between 8 and 13 years of age, employed in the factories, must attend a school for three hours daily, for five days every week, or for five hours daily during three days of the week. Under the Print Works Act, an attendance at school for 150 hours (or 30 days) in each half year, is a necessary condition of employment. The valuable regularity of the Half-time Act really affords all that, under the circumstances of the case, could be desired ; and I know of no insuperable difficulties in the way of its extension to towns. In rural districts the case is different. The farming operations requiring juvenile labour (such for instance as bean dropping, bird tending, potato setting, potato clearing and getting,) require at certain seasons the continuous attendance of the children, and could not be accomplished were a Half-time system in active operation. The provisions of a Print Works Act would obviate this difficulty and work beneficially, provided the half-yearly attendance was increased to 220 hours in each half-year, or, in other words, to 88 days in the year, the minimum term allowed by the Committee of Council as the condition of a Capitation Grant.

† The Guardians are empowered, under Mr. Evelyn Denison's Act, to make good the school fees. Unfortunately the power is permissive, and not compulsory.

‡ Dunlop's Act (17 and 18 Vict., cap. 74) : — "By this Act a magistrate may send to any institution in Scotland sanctioned by the Secretary of State any child found begging or without a home, or wandering, unless security is given for a year's good behaviour. The child may be detained long enough for education and training, but not beyond the age of fifteen, unless with his or her consent. The managers of the institution may refuse to admit the child, and the magistrate is directed to have due regard to the religious belief of the child, or the wishes of his or her relatives as to the particular institution to

The substance of this Act is embodied in a bill brought in by Mr. Adderley, and now under the consideration of the House with every prospect of success.

VI. The extension of the franchise to all young men above 21 years of age who could pass a certain examination, and could show that they had for four or five years attended a school under government inspection. The vote should be registered in the usual way, but should not be allowed to be exercised until the person claiming it had become a householder, and paid rates for the period of two years. The machinery by which it is proposed to work Mr. Temple's scheme of a middle class examination, will provide a ready and most economical method for carrying out this suggestion in every part of the country.

It would be useless to occupy time in the discussion of all or either of these heads, because it must be acknowledge that, in regard to some, any attempt at legislation

which the child is sent. Punishment may be inflicted for absconding from the institution, and for inducing a child to do so. The treasurer of the institution may sue the parents or step-parents of the child for the expenses of his or her support (at a rate to be fixed by the sheriff). Expenses not thus secured may be charged to the parish fund. The Privy Council is empowered to grant aid, the institution being open to their inspectors." The cost of support would be about 1s. 7d. per head per week.

" The following tables exhibit the number of juvenile vagrants apprehended by the Aberdeen rural police during the four years prior to 1845," the year in which the industrial schools were established, " and the four years subsequent to that date:"—

1841 -	- 328	1844 -	- 345	1847 -	- 6
1842 -	- 294	1845 -	- 105	1848 -	- 6
1843 -	- 397	1846 -	- 14	1849 -	- 1

And the number of juvenile delinquents, under 12 years, committed to prison during the same period :—

1841 -	- 61	1844 -	- 41	1847 -	- 27
1842 -	- 22	1845 -	- 49	1848 -	- 19
1843 -	- 53	1846 -	- 28	1849 -	- 16

For further details see a pamphlet on Industrial Schools by Mr. Alfred Hill (Cash, London), and Minutes of Evidence before House of Commons on Manchester, &c. Bill, pp. 174, 32, &c.

in the matter would at the present be unsuccessful; and, moreover, the subjects to which our attention is limited are the consideration of such educational schemes as can be carried out by voluntary efforts.

I will therefore proceed to enumerate, without comment, the different plans that have from time to time been put forth and been adopted, within my knowledge, with more or less of varying success.

I. Prizes in money and books purchased out of the Capitation Grant : in one case taking a moiety ; in another a third ; in another three-fourths ; in another three-tenths of the sum granted by Government.

The prizes are awarded in different proportions, and on different grounds in different schools.   1. Equal prizes to all who had attended the minimum of 176 days.   2. Prizes of 1*l.* to all who had attended every time the school was opened ; 15*s.* to all who had attended 176 days, and 10*s.* to such as had attended some less number.

II. The establishment of penny clubs with an addition to as many as had completed a year.

III. The weekly issue of cards with the master's signature, containing a report of " Days present, Times late, School Fees, General appearance, Home lessons, General conduct."   The cards are given to the children on the Friday evening, and returned on the Monday morning, signed by the parents.

The annual issue of certificate cards of attendance for each of the three years after the age of 9, dating also all years of attendance prior to 9.

IV. The giving instruction on special subjects, such as algebra, chemistry, drawing, &c., to such children as were most advanced.

V. Annual examinations and prizes for attendance and attainments to be paid for out of the Capitation Grant or the school funds, or both combined.

VI. The offer, by manufacturers, of employment in their works to a certain number of children nominated by the managers.

VII. The constant attendance, supervision, and co-operation, of the clergyman of the parish in his school. I am gratified in finding a hearty concurrence in this opinion, and a general feeling that a school languishes or prospers mainly in proportion to the care and trouble bestowed upon it by the clergyman.

VIII. The establishment of an extensive and well-digested prize scheme.

As it is this last plan that has proved most effective in retaining children at school, and as it forms one of the two schemes on which it will be the duty of this Sectional Committee to report to-day, it will be needful to consider it at length and in detail. I will therefore proceed to examine :

1. How the Prize Fund should be raised.

2. The conditions under which the prizes should be awarded.

3. The nature of the prizes.

4. The results that, from past experience, may be looked for.

If it can be proved, as will be attempted, that prize schemes have hitherto been powerfully effective in stimulating the efforts of masters, and in retaining children at school, the funds needful for carrying them out should certainly be supplied out of the public purse, and the management and direction of the whole might fairly be entrusted to the Committee of Council on Education. At the present time a Capitation Grant of 6s. per head is paid for every child that attends 176 days in the year, irrespective of its attainments. The vote under this head amounted, last year, to no less a sum than 40,000l. One-fourth of this sum would be sufficient for every expense connected with a scheme for England and Wales. Such an addition would readily be sanctioned, when it could be shown that every candidate had attended 176 days, and that the successful candidates had, moreover, exhibited a degree of proficiency adequate to their future station in life. The grants could be given either on a percentage of candidates, or on the attainment of a prescribed number of marks, or in proportion to what might be raised by voluntary local efforts.

Inconsiderable as would be the sum required, when regarded as a national subsidy, it is nevertheless in excess of what could be raised by any single central society. The utmost that could be effected by a metropolitan society would be to stimulate local efforts by small grants in aid; to publish, from time to time, suggestions and improvements, and to furnish, when solicited, efficient examiners, who would take the conduct of examinations and decide on the claims of the candidates.

But there can be little doubt that, where the merits of the scheme were properly ventilated and placed before the public, individual efforts would amply supply the sum needful for the locality. The *religio loci* would furnish what the *amor patriæ* would fail to elicit. Hitherto, wherever the appeal has been made, the response has been most satisfactory; and, in one or two instances, the unwonted error has been committed of subscribing too much instead of too little.

It would be difficult, or rather impossible, to lay down any general rule as to the parties who should be invited to subscribe to the funds. Each district will supply a law to itself. In some, any admixture with dissent would inevitably ruin the scheme. In others, any attempt on the part of churchmen to exclude nonconformists would signally fail. As a broad statement, it may be affirmed, that in rural districts churchmen would do well to act alone, and in towns and mining and manufacturing districts they should amalgamate with other religious communities.

In considering the conditions under which the prizes should be awarded, the authority by which they shall be determined is the first question. Should Government supply the funds either in whole or in part, Her Majesty's inspectors would of course be the examiners. In any other case, the policy of soliciting their services is questionable. A continuous interest in the scheme is more likely to be sustained where the whole machinery is worked by the parties furnishing the funds, than where there is introduced the enervating and deadening influence that too frequently accompanies government interference. Where churchmen alone are concerned, the selection of examiners may be vested in the Bishop or Archdeacon. Where various denominations unite, examiners should be appointed yearly by the general committee of the Association.

In respect to the qualifications of candidates, the balance of advantages would appear to be against any limitation of age. "Palmam qui meruit ferat," is the maxim we adopt in our parochial, our private and public schools, and our universities ; and, with these examples for guidance, it would be unwise to adopt a different course. If children above a certain age are excluded, it should be remembered that advanced years are more frequently the proof of neglected early education than of matured intellect or superior proficiency. If children under a certain age are excluded, it should be borne in mind that there is something akin to injustice in depriving talent and industry of their due rewards, on the ground of their existence in an earlier age than what has been marked out. Judging from the results of two years' experience as an examiner of a prize scheme that is nearly co-extensive with the

Archdeaconry of Coventry, it is evident that no allowance or limitation need be made for age ; that efficient country schools are enabled, number for number, to compete with town schools; girls with boys; and schools not under inspection with such as are. To prevent the intrusion of children from private schools, a certificate of attendance for a year of 176 days, in a public school for the industrial classes, should be made *a sine quâ non*. To promote good behaviour, a testimonial of character and conduct, signed by the teacher, and countersigned by the minister or manager of the school, should also be required of every candidate.

In order to avoid desultory teaching, and in fact with the view of limiting the masters to such teaching that may most benefit the children, a programme of the different subjects, and the exact amount required in the examination, should be drawn up and published. The programme should include a three years' progressive course, corresponding with the gradations of prizes, which should proportionately increase in value. The advantages of a defined over an undefined examination are very great. The full energy of neither master nor scholar will be put forth, so long as their labours seem objectless and interminable, and after all may be ill-directed, and no goal appears within their view. Her Majesty's inspectors are now permitting masters to present to them a schedule of subjects on which they would wish their children to be examined. I believe that in so doing the inspectors will double the efficiency of the schools committed to their care. The subjects of the general examination should comprise all that are mastered in an efficient school, with the exception of the art of reading. Where the candidates are numerous, the possibility of giving marks for proportionate excellence in reading is questionable. The principal and sole difficulty under this head consists in dealing with the religious element in the case of societies including members of different denominations.   Religion must not be made the covert instrument of proselytism, nor must it be emasculated of its best qualities, nor must it be eliminated altogether.*   The most feasible mode of dealing with the difficulty would be as follows : A short time prior to the public examination, let each denomination assemble their candidates together, and subject them to an examination in distinctive points of faith, as strict and as searching as they may deem proper.   Prizes may or may not be awarded to those who excel ; but to all who fall short of a prescribed number of marks, the required signature of the minister and manager, needful for admission to the public examination of the Association, ought at once to be peremptorily refused.   While the Christian, moral, and historical portions of the religious subject, unconnected with party or sectarian views, would be dealt with by the examiners of the Association, the apprehension of latitudinarianism would thus be removed ; the feelings of the public would not be outraged by an annual conflict of parties ; and the end to be obtained would be fully and certainly gained.

The examination should be conducted entirely on paper. By this means the same printed questions can be used for any number of children on the same day at different

---

* The pressure of the Prize scheme is so great for some months prior to the examination, and to a certain degree throughout the year, that no subjects are taught in the schools except such as directly bear on the examination.   The exclusion of religion, therefore, from the scheme is to a great extent tantamount to the exclusion of it from the school.   The experiment has been tried in America, of excluding religion from the common schools ; and the result has been most disastrous.   The Treasurer of the National Society has, in the present year, published some " Remarks on the Common School System of the United States," (Rivington, London,) and proves, by the testimony of the American writers, that the promoters of a secular system are beginning " to open their eyes and stand aghast at their own work."

places; the diffident child would be placed on an equal
footing with the forward child; the power of expression of thought, of orthography, of grammar generally, of
neatness in writing, is tested, and the examiners are enabled leisurely and accurately to weigh and estimate the
respective qualifications of the several candidates.

In discussing the question of prizes, it may be remarked, that they should form the exception, and not the
rule. Where the prizes are nearly as numerous as the
candidates, the certainty of success deadens exertion,
undermines the proper feeling of pride at success, and sours
the unsuccessful by the merited disgrace attached to failure.
Any attempt to compete in price with the labour-market
is entirely out of the question; and, therefore, large
sums of money are not needed. In many cases premiums
would be useless, and in others they would be much in
excess of the amount that could be offered. Ornamented
cards of commendation * and handsomely bound books would
appear to be most suitable, as being both economical and
durable. Lists of the successful candidates, with the ages
of the children, and the order in which they stand, should
be printed and circulated; and a copy, together with the
questions, should be presented to all who are named, to the
teachers of all schools within certain limits, and generally
throughout the district. A twofold inducement is thus
held out to the children: first, to secure a prize; and,

---

* A very appropriate design of an ornamented card has been ex-
pressly got up for the use of the Coventry Prize schemes. Messrs.
Underwood, lithographers, Birmingham, can supply any number on
French bank post, *mutatis mutandis*, at the following prices :—

          100 impressions 13s. 6d.
          500   ditto   8s. 6d. per 100.
          1000   ditto   7s. 6d. per 100.

In my own school the children have, at the expense of their parents,
had their cards framed and glazed. The cost was 2s. 6d. each. Very
delighted are the parents at the progress of the children; and very ornamental do the cards look suspended on the walls of the cottage.

secondly, to stand high in the list. Incompetent teachers would thus also be furnished with specimens of the standard that is attained; and employers, willing to further the work of education, would be enabled to accomplish this end by the offer of situations to successful candidates.

Before proceeding to state the results that have followed the institution of Prize schemes, it may, perhaps, be as well to notice an objection that has been urged, though not, within my knowledge, by men of experience or competent authority. Fears have been entertained lest the stimulus of prizes should induce teachers to confine the whole of their attention to a few sharp and intelligent children, to the neglect of the remainder of the school. The evil is theoretical rather than practical. It is reasonable to suppose that, during a few weeks prior to the examination, the candidates would engross an unwonted share of the teacher's time and attention. But it should be borne in mind, that the competitors are children on the eve of closing their school life; and that, with a view to success, they must be subjected to a severe course of study, and be imbued with a knowledge of subjects, useful in their working life, that will be well nigh indelible. If, then, at this important juncture, the teacher should for a brief period bestow a more than ordinary amount of care and trouble on his class of candidates, who would be bold enough to assert that such time could have been better employed, or that the Prize scheme had failed of its object, and worked a greater amount of evil than good? But view the objection in its fullest bearing; and assuming that a teacher, betraying the trust reposed in him, were, for a lengthened period, to devote himself exclusively to a select number of his most forward children, and see to what results such suicidal conduct would inevitably lead. On the first examination of such a school, the wrong done to the remainder of the children would

instantly be discovered, and a damaging report of the
school would be the just reward of the dishonest teacher.
Moreover, such a forcing system would break down
almost at the outset; for there would be wanting, after
the first year or so, a succession of fitting candidates, since
it must be clear that an effective first class can only be
sustained by a due amount of care bestowed throughout a
school on the junior as well as the senior classes.

Besides the objection I have stated, I know not any
that merit comment or remark, or that do not bear on the
face of them their own refutation. Of the unmistakeable
beneficial effects of a well-digested Prize scheme in elementary schools, I am enabled to speak in the most confident and unqualified terms. In a district under its
operation the clergy become interested in the educational
progress of their schools, and are led to take an active,
personal part in instruction; the teachers are encouraged by the presence of their clergy, and stimulated
to greater exertion by the hope of distinction in their
profession; the children become more regular in their
attendance, more willing to get up their home lessons, and
more attentive in school; and the parents, seeing the
interest taken in their children, and gratified where success has followed, forego the advantages of the child's
home labour or weekly earnings, and retain him longer
at school in the expectation of securing the higher rewards.

I am prepared to support and sustain each and all of
these assertions by the testimony of masters of important
schools in the mining districts of Staffordshire and the
agricultural portions of Warwickshire, but refrain from
so doing, partly through fear of trespassing too long on
your time, and partly through the knowledge that the
results of Prize schemes will form the subject of another
paper. I would, however, briefly state, as important general results, that at the Kidderminster Prize-Scheme Ex-

amination, (now three years old), there were 27 boys above 12 the first year, and last year there were 66 ; that there was an increase in attendance from 306 to 407 ; and that the average age had risen from $10\frac{1}{2}$ to $11\frac{1}{4}$ years.* I have been informed by Her Majesty's Assistant-Inspector, Mr. Sandford, that the average of the girl candidates of the South Staffordshire Prize-Scheme is 13 years and 9 months, and that of the boys $12\frac{1}{2}$ years; showing, in respect to the girls, an increase of $\frac{3}{4}$ of a year in their age since the last examination. In the Prize-Scheme Examination for the Archdeaconry of Coventry, (Birmingham excepted), in the first year there were 201 candidates, and in the second year 344 ; the average of the whole of the successful candidates being $12\frac{1}{3}$ years. In the first year 54 candidates received prizes; and in the second year 32 of these 54 again presented themselves for the second year prizes; a proportion that never would have con-

* In the Report of the Worcester Archidiaconal Board of Education of the present year, it is stated that in the three years during which the Prize scheme has been in operation in Kidderminister and Stourport, there has been an increase both in the number of scholars and in the period of their education, as will be seen by the annexed table.

AVERAGE AGE OF FIRST CLASS.

St. Mary, Kidderminster,	Christmas, 1853, 10 yrs.		Christmas, 1856, $10\frac{1}{4}$.	
St. George, ditto	„	1853, $10\frac{3}{4}$ yrs.	„	1856, $12 \cdot 2\frac{1}{2}$.
Stourport -	„	1853, $11\frac{1}{4}$ yrs.	„	1856, 11·11.

NUMBER.

St. Mary, Kidderminster,	Christmas, 1853, 113.		Christmas, 1856, 180.	
St. George, ditto -	„	1853, 97.	„	1856, 127.
Stourport - - -	„	1853, 96.	„	1856, 110.

It is proved from the above tables that the average number of children in attendance has increased from 306 to 417, and the average age from $10\frac{3}{4}$ to $11\frac{1}{4}$. The result shows that many boys have been kept at school a year longer than they would otherwise have been, and that in this way one object aimed at has been obtained. Other advantages, too, have arisen — several boys have become pupil teachers, while situations have been gained by some as the fruit of their prizes.

tinued at school, but for the powerful inducements held out by the Prize scheme.

The establishment of prize schemes by private efforts in so many parts of the country, in the last few years, affords of itself no inconsiderable proof of the estimation these schemes are held in by men of influence and position. Birmingham, the remainder of the Archdeaconry of Coventry, the Archdeaconry of Worcester, and the most considerable of the mining districts of England and Wales, already possess their various associations, their different plans of examination, and their separate tests of excellence. The value attached to prize schemes would be greatly enhanced, could uniformity of action be produced, and a general standard of excellence be established. The present I believe to be the occasion of accomplishing this desirable end; and I trust that this section will conclude its labours, not indeed by affirming the advantages of prize schemes,—a truism which the community have already affirmed for themselves,—but by sending forth, under the sanction of their high authority, a scheme that may serve as a model or guide for existing or future associations. For this purpose, and as a groundwork, I venture to bring before you two schemes that have undergone the most searching examination by two Boards of Education, and that are now, with slight modifications, in active operation — one in the borough of Birmingham, and the other in the remainder of the Archdeaconry of Coventry; and to the consideration of each of these I now respectfully draw your attention.

APPENDIX.

Proposed Details of a Diocesan or Archidiaconal Prize Scheme.

PRIZES.

ONE HUNDRED PRIZES, OF THE VALUE OF EIGHTY-FIVE POUNDS.

Sixty handsomely bound, gilt edged Prayer Books of the Christian Knowledge Society, of the value of ten shillings, for the Third or Lowest Class.

Twenty-five handsomely bound, gilt edged Bibles of the Christian Knowledge Society, of the value of one pound, for the Second or Middle Class.

Fifteen prizes of cash, of two pounds, and ornamental cards, for First Class.

The number of prizes should, of course, vary in proportion to the expected number of candidates. The above prizes are calculated for three hundred. The proportion should not exceed one in three, but ornamental certificate cards may be added, but not so as to make the gross average of successful and commended candidates more than a moiety.

REGULATIONS.

CANDIDATES FOR THE THIRD CLASS OR LOWEST PRIZE.

Candidates to be boys or girls (not being pupil teachers or paid monitors) who can produce certificates : —

I. That they have attended for one year, and are still attending, some parochial school of the Church of England within the diocese or archdeaconry of ——

II. That during this period they have borne a good character, and have been attentive to their religious duties.

The certificates of attendance and of character must be signed by the teacher of the school, and countersigned by the clergyman of the parish to which the school belongs.

If a child removes from one parochial school to another, certificates must be produced from each school attended during the period for which attendance is required.

CANDIDATES FOR THE SECOND CLASS OR MIDDLE PRIZE.

Candidates must have gained the Third Class Prize, and must produce certificates : —

I. That they have attended school for two years.

II. That during this period they have borne a good character, and have been attentive to their religious duties.

N.B.—The successful candidates for the Third and Second Class Prizes will not be permitted to compete for them a second time.

A certain number of candidates who have not obtained prizes will be recommended, and receive ornamental cards of commendation. The commended candidates will be at liberty either to compete again for the prize for which they have failed, or for the next higher prize.

CANDIDATES FOR THE FIRST CLASS PRIZE.

Candidates must have gained the preceding prizes and produce certificates : —

I. That they have attended school for three years.

II. That during this period they have borne good characters, and have been attentive to their religious duties.

N.B.—This prize may be gained by the children in each successive year until they leave the school.

SUBJECTS OF EXAMINATION.

FOR THE THIRD CLASS OR LOWEST PRIZE.

Candidates will be expected to write a good legible hand ; to spell correctly ; to write out any portion of the text of the Church Catechism ; and to answer questions relating to our Blessed Lord's Life, illustrative of the Apostles' Creed ; to work the first four Rules of Arithmetic, Simple and Compound ; and to be able to name the counties and chief towns of England.

Should the religious knowledge not be deemed sufficient, the parables or miracles of our Blessed Lord could be added, and taken in alternate years.

FOR THE SECOND CLASS OR MIDDLE PRIZE.

The meaning of the Church Catechism, with Scriptural proofs, to the end of the Lord's Prayer; the Book of Genesis; the first seven chapters of St. Matthew; Arithmetic, as far as Reduction and Practice; the physical and political map of England.

> The first part of St. Matthew has been selected as containing a brief sketch of our Blessed Lord's early life, as also his Sermon on the Mount.

FOR THE FIRST CLASS PRIZE.

The meaning of the whole of the Church Catechism, with Scriptural proofs; the Old Testament, to the end of the Book of Judges; the Gospel of St. Luke and the Acts of the Apostles; Arithmetic generally; the map of Europe and the British Possessions; parsing a simple sentence.

> St. Luke and the Acts of the Apostles have been selected as containing a continuous history by the same writer of the primitive Christian Church.

THE TIMES OF EXAMINATION.

I.—The examinations will be held annually in the early part of the season of Lent, on some certain day to be named by the Archdeacon, in such places within each Rural Deanery as may seem needful and convenient to the different Rural Deans or Inspectors of each Deanery.

> The early part of Lent has been selected as the best season for finding children at school in agricultural districts. The Prizes may be given in the holiday time of Easter week.

II.—The examination will be on paper, and the questions (drawn up by the Archdeacon, or examiners appointed by him,) will be forwarded to the respective Rural Deans or Inspectors in the week previous to the examination, closed and sealed, and will not be opened until the children have assembled, and the hour of examination has arrived.

III.—The papers of the Candidates will, on the day following the examination, be forwarded to the Archdeacon, or the Examiners appointed by him, in order that they may be examined and the Prizes adjudged.

IV.—The Prizes will be given to the successful Candidates at ——

In order to afford the scheme a fair chance, it would be as well at the outset either to increase the proportion of first year Prizes from sixty to one hundred, or else to permit Candidates to contend for either class without the necessity of having obtained the Prizes in gradation.

SPECIAL PRIZES.

Individuals will be allowed to offer Prizes for Special Subjects, subject to regulation by the Committee. No child shall compete for more than one Special Prize.

EXAMPLES OF SUBJECTS.—(Boys and girls.)—Catechism, Liturgy, Scriptural Knowledge, Arithmetic, Grammar, English History, Composition.—(Girls only.)—Sewing, Knitting, Darning, &c.

CONDITIONS OF PRIZES FOR SEWING, KNITTING, &c.

Girls competing for these Prizes must not compete for any other Special Prize.

FIRST PRIZE.

The children are to work a shirt sleeve of seven inches in length and eight inches in breadth; the sleeve, when doubled, being four inches in width. The gusset must be three inches square. The piece for the wristband must be five inches in width and three in depth, when doubled to be one and a half inches in depth. The material is to be white calico of 6d. per yard, and to be well scalded. The children are to bring the whole ready cut out; the button hole cut, the threads drawn ready for back stitching, and in every respect prepared for sewing.

The shirt sleeve must be commenced at the wristband, which must be finished first.

SECOND PRIZE.

For the running with darning cotton the heel of a woman's cotton stocking of the price of 8d. per pair.

THIRD PRIZE.

For the hemming, whipping, and sewing on a broad tape, half a yard long, one piece of lawn, one yard wide and one and a half inch deep.

FOURTH PRIZE.

For knitting the heel of a worsted sock.

Could all the girls be furnished with the same material, and were they to make a mark on the work, repeating the same outside an envelope, writing their names inside, the task of adjudicating the Prizes would be easier, and the awards could not be subjected to any imputation of partiality.

The time allowed for each of these Prizes will be two hours of the afternoon of the day of the General Examination—from two to four o'clock. No child can compete for more than one prize, and none will be considered eligible who have not attempted, although perhaps unsuccessfully, the Morning's paper of Questions.

Each child must come provided with the materials for work, and with her name legibly worked in full, or written in marking ink on a bit of calico, which must be firmly attached to the work when completed.

A committee of Ladies will adjudicate the Prizes. Quickness and neatness in the work will be the two points of excellence which will decide the awards.

The Examination cannot well extend beyond a single day. The children should be allowed three hours for the General Examination Paper, viz. from ten till one o'clock, and two hours for the Special Prize Paper, viz. from two to four o'clock.

Attendance, &c., Certificate.

(To be folded up with the Candidate's Examination Papers.)

ARCHIDIACONAL EXAMINATION.

MARCH   , 185

This is to certify

I. That   has attended the Parochial School of   in the Archdeaconry of   during the twelve months ending February last, and appears from the

School Register to have been present at least 176 days during that period.

> N.B. In computing the 176 days, two half days, whether morning or afternoon, may be reckoned as a day, and Sunday attendances may also be counted in.

II. That   bears a good character, and has been attentive to h   religious duties.

> N.B. The responsibility of determining whether a candidate deserve this last certificate or not must rest with the clergyman and teacher of the school. No qualified certificate can be accepted. It is the earnest wish of those who give these Prizes that none should be admitted to the examination who have not shown during the past year at least a marked endeavour to merit the approbation of their clergyman and teacher.

Occupation of the Candidate's parents.

Signed,

Teacher.

Countersigned,

$\left\{ \begin{array}{l} \text{Incumbent,} \\ \text{Officiating Minister,} \end{array} \right\}$ of the Parish of

Pupil teachers and paid monitors are not permitted to be Candidates.

No boys or girls will be admitted who fail to bring this paper, on the day of examination, carefully filled up, and signed by their clergyman and teacher.

If a child has removed from one school to another, certificates must be produced from each school attended during the period for which attendance is required.

Each child should bring one or two sheets of ruled foolscap, some scribbling paper, and pens.

The Prizes for the first, second, and third classes must be gained in succession, and the Prizes for the first and second classes cannot be gained twice. The girls that contend for the sewing will not be permitted to compete for any other Special Prize.

Masters and mistresses are not permitted to remain in the room during the period of examination. Should any of the clergy be present they are respectfully requested not to speak to the candidates, or to overlook their papers, until they are finished, and have been placed in the hands of the Clergyman Inspector.

THE EDUCATIONAL BOARD. Rural Deanery of

EDUCATIONAL PRIZE SCHEME.

LENT EXAMINATION, MARCH 18 .

List of Candidates from } { Boys' / Girls' / Mixed } School. Total No. for { General Prize Examination,—1st Class, 2nd Class, 3rd Class, Total, - - - Total / Special Prize Examination, - - - Total

*** The successful Candidates for the First and Second year's Prizes will not be permitted to compete for them a second time. The same Special Prize may be gained by a child in each successive year until he leaves School. Every child must attempt, although perhaps unsuccessfully, the General Examination. No child can compete in one year for more than one of the Special Prizes.

Signed,   Teacher.   Officiating Minister.   Post Town.

☞ This form, if required, must be filled up and returned to the Rural Dean on or before the of February, and will be returned by him on or before the to the Honorary Secretary, so as to allow time for a sufficient number of copies of the Questions of Examination to be struck off.

No.	Name in full.	Age.	General Examination.			Special Prizes.						Special Prizes for Sewing, Darning, Knitting, &c.			
			1st Class.	2nd Class.	3rd Class.	H. Scrip.	P. Book.	Cate-chism.	Hist. of Eng.	Arith-metic.	Gram-mar.	1st Prize.	2nd Prize.	3rd Prize.	4th Prize.

Proposed Details of a General Prize Scheme.

QUALIFICATION OF CANDIDATES.

THIRD CLASS (LOWEST) PRIZE.

1.—Boys or girls, (not being pupil teachers or paid monitors), who can produce certificates that they have attended for one year, and are still attending, any public elementary school within   and who can also produce certificates of good conduct and character, and of efficiency in the knowledge of distinctive points of faith.

This last qualification could best be ascertained by each religious denomination conducting an examination of its own in the week prior to the Public Examination, and rejecting all Candidates that did not reach a certain standard.

2.—These Prizes being intended for the children of the industrious classes, the committee reserve to themselves the right of defining what schools shall be eligible to send Candidates.

SECOND CLASS (MIDDLE) PRIZE.

3.—Candidates for the second class must produce certificates that they are attending school, and have attended for two years; and must produce the same certificates as for the third class.

FIRST CLASS (HIGHEST) PRIZE.

4.—Candidates for the first class must produce certificates that they are attending school, and have attended for three years ; and must produce the same certificates as in the former classes.

5.—No child can compete for the second (or middle) prize without having previously obtained the third (or lowest) prize, or a certificate of commendation ; nor can any child compete for the first (or highest) prize, without having previously obtained the third and second prizes, or corresponding certificates.

6.—For the first and second years the preceding clauses should be modified, so as to allow properly qualified Candidates to compete for Prizes in the three classes.

7.—A year's attendance at school will, throughout this scheme, be understood to mean that the scholar has attended not less than 176 days in the year. In computing the 176 days, two half-days, whether morning or afternoon, may be reckoned as a day, but Sunday attendances will not be counted in.

8.—The certificates must be signed by the teacher of the school, and countersigned by the minister of religion to whose place of worship the school is attached, or by the managers of the school.

9.—If a child moves from one school to another, certificates must be produced from each school attended during the period for which attendance is required. In cases of change of school, the aggregate attendance will be counted as attendance within this rule, provided the committee are satisfied that sufficient reason is shown for such change.

SUBJECTS OF EXAMINATION.

10.—THIRD CLASS (lowest): Candidates must write a good legible hand; spell correctly; work the first four rules of Arithmetic, simple and compound; answer questions on the Map of England.

11.—SECOND CLASS (middle): Candidates must work the first four rules of Arithmetic, Reduction, Proportion, and Practice; answer questions on the Map of Europe; parse an easy sentence.

12.—FIRST CLASS (highest): Candidates must answer questions in Arithmetic generally; in Geography (general outline); in English Grammar; and on the outline of English history.

13.—RELIGIOUS KNOWLEDGE.—Candidates will be examined in various portions of the Holy Scriptures, to be fixed from year to year by the Board of Examiners.

SPECIAL PRIZES.

14.—Individuals will be allowed to offer Special Prizes for the following subjects, subject to regulation by the Committee: Boys and Girls—Arithmetic, Grammar, Geography, Mechanics, English History, Composition, Drawing: Girls only—Cutting out, Sewing, Knitting, Darning, Marking, &c.

15.—No candidate can compete for more than one of the Special Prizes.

NATURE OF THE PRIZES.

16.—Prizes of books or money will be given to each Candidate who shall obtain such a proportion of the whole number of marks as shall be fixed from year to year by the Committee. Certificates will be given to each Candidate who shall obtain a certain lower proportion of marks, to be similarly fixed.

MACHINERY OF ADMINISTRATION.

17.—Prize Fund to be raised, and kept distinct from the General Fund of the Association.

18.—A Board of Examiners will be appointed yearly by the General Committee of the Association : of these a certain number will be appointed to act as Examiners by the Board, and the questions framed by them will be submitted to and approved of by the whole Board.

19.—Examinations will be conducted entirely on paper.

20.—The first Examination will be held

Suggestions of Plans for retaining the Attendance of Children at School to a more advanced age. By Rev. H. G. ROBINSON, Training School, York.

A *long* preface would agree but indifferently with a *short* argument; I will endeavour therefore to hasten as quickly as possible into the very middle of my subject. I do not pretend to believe that the suggestions which I am about to offer will in anything like an adequate degree meet the requirements of that very important question which this Conference has undertaken to discuss. The difficulties of that question are immense, and all that I, or better men than myself, can hope to accomplish, is to devise some palliatives for the evil complained of; perhaps to illustrate in our schemes the difference between theory and practice; possibly to demonstrate by the very barrenness of our suggestions the necessity for legislative interference whenever—as the saying is—the country may please to consider itself ripe for it. In the meantime the question is, what can be done upon the *voluntary principle?* Parents are not to be *compelled* to retain their children at school up to a later age, but they are to be *persuaded,* as far as possible to do so. Wherewithal then are they to be persuaded? At present they take their children from school at an early age, because in a pecuniary point of view they are *gainers* by doing so. They make a *direct* and *immediate* profit out of the child's labour. Were it possible to offer advantages equally *direct* and *immediate* as the result of keeping the child at school, nothing more would be necessary. But this is not possible. The advantages which the child will derive from a prolonged course of education are indeed *real* and *substantial* enough, but they are less apparent,—they do not take the form of £ *s. d.*, and they are merely *prospective.* Hence, to secure them involves a very considerable sacrifice on the part of the parent; a sacrifice which he will only be induced to make by a very much stronger conviction of the value and importance of education than at present exists. To diffuse such a conviction throughout the country seems therefore the most likely way of accomplishing, on voluntary principles, the reformation we desire. Now, it seems to me that the schoolmaster himself — if he will lay himself out for it — is capable of doing good service in this way. His influence should not be confined to the school-room, but should be exerted in the cottages where the parents of his scholars reside. He should regard himself in some sort as a preacher of education — an educational missionary who must go out into the highways and hedges and compel them to come in. But in order to induce him to make efforts of this kind, he must be paid for making them; he must have a direct and manifest interest in any results which he may be able in this way to achieve.

I. And it is to this that my first suggestion points. I venture to take a hint from the Capitation Grant, and to propose a plan which may be regarded as supplementary to it.

I would suggest that their lordships, the Committee of Council on Education, be solicited to try the experiment of allowing a bonus, say, of 10*s.* on every boy, and 6*s.* on every girl (being the children of labourers and mechanics) who shall have attended school for 176 days in the year, and shall have attained the age of 13 years before the close of the school year for which the Capitation Grant is allowed. This bonus shall be given exclusively to the teacher, and shall be paid at the same time with the augmentation on the certificate and the allowance for instructing the pupil teachers. The efficacy of such a plan lies entirely in the fact that it gives the master a substantial interest in the presence in his school of children of a more advanced age. Now it may be objected that independent of any such premium the master already has a sufficient interest in keeping his pupils at school as long as possible. It is true the more he can do so, the more agreeable will his work be, the more effective its results, and consequently the more satisfactory his position and circumstances. But the *general* feeling that it is a good thing to keep the children in attendance for a longer period is not in itself a motive power strong enough to stimulate him to any direct systematic premeditated efforts to bring about this desirable state of things. But have the courage to call in the aid of the commercial principle — agree to pay the right man for doing the work that you wish to have done — and you may at least feel confident that you have taken the most natural and direct way to the accomplishment of your aim.

But another and more formidable objection is that — with the very best will to the work, the master himself is powerless. Charm he never so wisely (it may be said), he will scarcely by any scholastic incantations persuade parents to forego the profit of their children's labour that *he*, and not *they* or *their children*, may receive a bonus on the children's attendance at school. Now in meeting this objection, I will begin by admitting that no immediate or complete revolution will be effected by the proposed scheme. It will not at once or within a very limited time fill our schools with older children. What then will it do? It will provide an agency by which in due time a public opinion in favour of advanced education may be formed amongst the class most interested. It will make every schoolmaster a kind of crusader and missionary.

He will make it a rule to become acquainted with and to visit the parents of his elder pupils; he will indoctrinate them with arguments in favour of education, and he will in some measure succeed in inspiring them with a sense of its future value to their children. And I must here express my conviction, founded not on plausible conjecture but on positive experience, that a schoolmaster endowed with tact, temper, and patience, and filled with genuine zeal for his calling may acquire very great influence over the parents of his pupils, and induce them to consent to arrangements and submit to sacrifices for which in the first instance they may have appeared quite unprepared. But moreover, *interest quickens invention.* When the schoolmasters of England find the question before us referred so directly to themselves, and associated with such conditions as I advocate, they may be led to consider the best remedies for the evil complained of, and may be enabled out of their homely every-day experience to contribute valuable practical hints towards the solution of this perplexing educational problem.

I do not conceive that any objection need be taken to the scheme on financial grounds. Should the outlay become great, a great work will have been done, and the expenditure will always be in direct ratio to the results.

II. But can any further use be made of this scheme? Can we append to it any arrangements which may act more immediately on parents and children? It seems not impossible to do so. I would propose that the names of those children on account of whom the teacher receives a

bonus be *recorded*. For this purpose a *special register*
should be kept in every school, the master of which
desires to take advantage of the "bonus on prolonged
attendance." In this register the names of those children
on whose behalf the bonus is allowed, together with
the names, residence, and occupation of their parents,
should be entered by the *government inspector himself*
at the time of his visit. The fact of such a register
being kept would not be without considerable effect on
the classes whom it is most necessary to impress. The
register should moreover be open to the inspection of
visitors to the school; employers of labour and others
might by degrees be induced to refer to it and give a
preference to those whose names appeared there. But a
further use might be made of it. The managers of schools
might be allowed to make a return to the Committee of
Council of a certain per centage of the names recorded in
the proposed register. From these returns a *national
list* might be made out, and to this list a certain proportion — it need not be a very large one — of the smaller
government appointments might be assigned, to be awarded
to individuals according to the results of a competitive
examination. Local patrons, civic corporations, and
similar bodies might perhaps be induced to contribute
some of the situations at their disposal to swell the common stock. Thus would some of those incentives to
intellectual culture be provided for the poor man which
have hitherto been overlooked in his case, though we are
all conscious how much they have to do with the spread
of education amongst the middle and upper classes.

III. The present popularity of the examination test
naturally suggests the inquiry whether any use can be
made of the system of public examinations in promoting
the education of the working classes. In other words can
any general movement, similar to that which promises to

be successful among the middle class, be brought to bear upon the lower stratum of society? I venture to think that the scheme is one which deserves to be attempted, and which, if attempted with certain necessary modifications to adapt it to the new field of action, is very likely to be successful — is very likely, at least, to contribute its modicum of help to the end at which we are aiming. No doubt there are difficulties attending the application of such a scheme to the working classes. These difficulties are so obvious that I will not suggest them; so complex that I should need more space and time to dispose of them than are now at my command. I believe however that a system of examination adapted to elementary schools might be brought, at least *partially*, into operation throughout the country. And the first thing to consider will be the organisation by which they should be carried out.

1. I would suggest, then, that the plan must emanate from the Committee of Council. They alone can give *unity* to the scheme — they alone can stamp it with the character of a *national movement.*

2. The immediate agents through whom the Committee of Council must work are the staff of Inspectors of Schools; and it might be found necessary, in course of time, to add to that body one or two officers, whose special business it would be to superintend the arrangements connected with the examinations.

3. But other agencies must be employed, and assistance must be obtained from other quarters, if the scheme is to be brought into extended and effective operation. The services of Diocesan Boards of Education must be secured; the different educational societies must lend their aid; local corresponding committees must be formed; and by the united action of all these, adjusted according to their various spheres of influence, guided by one central and superintending authority, a regular system of national

examinations may be carried on which will quickly produce an effect at least in the more populous districts of the country, and do very much towards supplying that stimulus for the want of which the educational movement is at present languishing.

But in the next place we have to consider what inducements to present themselves for examination can be offered to the class of persons whose education we are anxious to promote. And the only two principles through which we can approach them with any practical advantage are *interest* and *ambition*. Once make them feel that it is their *interest* to acquire a certain amount of information, and to give proof that they have acquired it, and they will not be slow to avail themselves, at some sacrifice of convenience, of the test which the examination will provide. And it lies with the public generally — with the employers of labour more particularly, to make the working class feel that it is their interest to be educated. But a very considerable effect will be produced if we can call forth amongst the people the spirit of an honest ambition. At present this feeling is not very active among them: they are not so susceptible of mere honorary distinctions as the classes above them. Still an *ambition* like a *taste* or a *want* may be created. And the examination scheme would, I think, be available chiefly in this direction.

1. With this view, then, I would propose that all those candidates who passed a satisfactory examination should receive a *certificate of competency*.

2. But besides this, I would suggest that the successful candidates should be arranged in two classes, and that all those whose names appeared in the first class should be presented with a *medal*, bearing the superscription of the Committee of Council on Education, stamped (if possible) with the name of the successful candidate, and designated by some such title as the *National Educational Medal*. I

am inclined to think that the *medal* would produce a much greater effect than the *certificate*. It is, or appears to be, a more *substantial* reward. It is a time-honoured and traditional emblem of honorable distinction.

3. Other rewards and incentives would not be wanting when once the examination scheme was fairly in operation. The advocates of education would not be slow to do their part. Prizes would be offered under various conditions as the recompense for superior diligence and success. Perhaps no reward which private benevolence and generosity could propose would be more valuable than the foundation of exhibitions to some of the middle schools which at present exist, or which the stimulus given to middle-class education will, in due time, call into existence. These exhibitions would open out to the working classes occasional opportunities of attaining a higher and more complete education, and thus of rising to a superior station in life. And it is not necessary that such opportunities should be more than *occasional* or *exceptional*. It is not the *number of chances* in their favour, but the fact that there *are* chances which stimulates to exertion, and disposes to sacrifice. And, indeed, the remark which, in concluding my paper, I wish to make is this, that one great defect of the educational movement so far, has been that it has too easily been taken for granted that the working classes will seek after and love for its own sake that education which those above them acquire under the stimulus of a very great variety of prizes, honours, and emoluments. Let the friends of education take a hint from Horace, and provide a liberal supply of *crustula* in the shape of rewards, honorary and substantial, and there will no doubt be a greater eagerness manifested throughout the country to make acquaintance with the elements of intellectual culture.

On Associations for offering Annual Prizes to groups of Schools (Prize Schemes), with suggestions for their Improvement and Extension.
On Certificates of acquirement, and a Proposal for a Public Examination of all Boys who choose to present themselves for examination on their finally leaving the Day-School. By HUGH SEYMOUR TREMENHEERE, Esq.

WE are invited, in this section of the Conference, to consider the expedients which have been proposed for keeping the children of the " working classes " longer at school.

Interpreting this term "longer at school" by the designation of the Conference, namely, that it is a Conference " *on the early age* at which children are taken from school," and also by the subject proposed for inquiry before Section A., namely, " the fact of the early removal of children from school," it seems to me to leave out of view a part of the problem we have to deal with, nearly as important as that of the early age at which the children leave school, namely, the *irregularity of attendance* of a large proportion of them during their school years.

That the early removal of the children of the working classes from school will be satisfactorily established by communications that will be laid before Section A. there can be little doubt. The facts already published by Her

Majesty's inspectors are very striking in reference to that branch of the subject, and for the purposes of the present paper need not be recapitulated. The substance of the whole is correctly embodied in the following few words by Mr. Stewart, in his Report for 1856-7 : " In that branch of the population to which the public measures apply, all education ceases at the age of 12, and more commonly at 9 years of age " (p. 449).

Equally frequent are the notices in the reports of nearly all the inspectors, of the *irregularity of attendance* of a large proportion of the children during their school years, and many facts are given illustrating that irregularity in reference to individual schools.   Mr. Watkins states (Report for 1854, p. 438), that not half of the children in the Yorkshire schools have been at the same school for one year.   Mr. Marshall shows, from the table of attendance furnished by all the inspectors, that out of the total average attendance of 382,236 children as many as 114,000, or 29·35 per cent., have only been one year at the same school, and only 15,000 have been at the same school as much as four years (Report for 1855, p. 606).   The reports of the inspectors for 1856 reiterate facts of the same import.   Mr. Bellairs shows that in his district 63·19 per cent. of the children had been only one year at the same school.   Mr. Stewart refers again to some striking evidences as to the same point in his present district,—the counties of Cambridge, Huntingdon, Bedford, Hertford, and Buckingham,—having previously commented upon it in his reports upon the counties of Northumberland and Durham, &c.

These tables, however, do not exhibit the whole state of the case in reference to this point of irregularity of attendance ; for although a child may have been only one year at the particular school at the time when the return was made, he may have been previously at others, or at the same school for a certain period some months or years before, and may very probably leave this school and be re-admitted at it, or at others, before he finally leaves the day-school and goes to work.

The causes of this I shall hereafter advert to. I desire at present to draw attention to the fact, which is one that I conceive should not be left out of view, or receive only a passing mention, on such an occasion as the present, when we are met to consider the expedients by which it might be possible to make the elementary education of the working classes more solid and satisfactory. It is one of the most material elements of the subject which we have to consider; and, for my own part, while seeking to satisfy myself as to what expedients might possibly contribute towards the attainment of the object aimed at, namely, the securing for the country the fruits of all its efforts and of its liberal expenditure in the sound elementary education of the working classes, I have kept in mind both the above-named sources of obstruction, the early removal of the children from school and the frequent interruptions in their attendance during their school years; and I have endeavoured to devise measures which might tend to reduce the amount of both.

It may be said that the " Capitation Grant," the offer on the part of Government of from 3s. to 6s. per head for each child who remains at school 176 days in one year, is a sufficient admission of this irregularity of attendance, and that no new facts are needed to remind us of it.

It is desirable to consider for a moment what are the facts brought out by the Capitation Grant as far as it has hitherto been applied. They are these,—that out of the 4800 schools under government inspection in the year ending December 31, 1855, 1096 schools received aid from it. The average attendance at those schools was

102,364; but out of these only 36,929 children, or 36·07 per cent., came within the terms of the Grant by having attended school 176 days during the year. The percentage of the preceding year was 33·94.

We may be allowed to ask, therefore, what is the actual state of attendance among the remaining 66·6 or 63·93 per cent.?

Although it cannot be doubted that the Capitation Grant is operating to encourage masters and managers of schools to do what they can to induce the parents to send their children more regularly to school, and will do so still further under the wider range of operation given to it by the minute of January 1856, nevertheless the fact remains that a large portion of the children of the working classes still attend, and from the effect of existing causes are still likely to attend, school very irregularly, and I believe it may serve a useful purpose or two to present to the Conference a few recent and authentic statistics upon this branch of the subject.

I regret that those I have to offer are so few. I endeavoured to procure a larger number of facts from which to draw my deductions; but the returns I asked for were not easy to furnish with correctness, and having no claim except that of private acquaintance with those from whom I sought them, I have no right to complain of the deficiency. I have only to ask for the favourable consideration of the Conference for what I have to lay before them.

As soon as I was aware, about three months ago, of the intention to hold this conference, I drew up the accompanying form, and sent or caused to be sent a copy of it to fifty schools in different parts of the country. The heads of inquiry are,

The names and ages of all the boys in the first and second classes;

The age at which they first went to school ;

The total number of months' attendance at this and other schools ;

And I added a note requesting that the schoolmasters would obtain the aid of the parents in filling up these re- turns correctly. I confined the inquiry to the boys in the first and second classes, because it may be assumed that the majority of boys arrive at those classes before they finally leave the day-school.

The difference between the time that had elapsed since each boy first went to school and the actual amount of his school attendance would show the amount of interruption that had occurred.

Of the fifty copies of the form, about half were sent out by myself, or through personal friends. I was guided in the selection of the schools or localities to which they were sent, principally by the opinion I entertained that the master or some one of the managers would take pains to have them filled up correctly. The remaining half I sent to three or four of Her Majesty's inspectors of schools, who kindly undertook to forward them to schools where they thought they would be attended to.

Considering the trouble required to fill up these forms correctly, I am not surprised that only thirty-two were re- turned to me. Of these, three were avowedly defective ; leaving twenty-nine to be analysed and considered.

Of these twenty-nine there are *seventeen* schools in which *from one-half to three-fourths of the boys in the first and second classes* have been *absent* on an average *nearly one-third* of their nominal time at school.

These seventeen schools are the following—

Glossop National School, near Manchester.
Rusholme Wesleyan School, Manchester.
St. Thomas, National School, Birmingham.
Boys' National School, Barnsley.
Central National School, Sheffield.

Holy Trinity National School, Sheffield.
National School, Rotherham.
Dowlais Boys' School, Dowlais.
National School, Merthyr Tydvil.
British School, Swansea.
National School, Saham, Watton
„   Foulden, Norfolk.
„   Ashill   „
„   Hockwood   „
„   Oxburgh   „
„   Swaffham   „
„   Carbroke   „

In three other schools, namely,—

St. George's National School, Leeds,
Tortworth   „   Wootton-under-Edge,
All Saints'   „   Wakefield,

one-fourth of the boys in the first and second classes had been absent upwards of *one-half their nominal time at school.*

The returns from the remaining nine show a better attendance.   They are the—

Elsecar (Earl Fitzwilliam's) School, Barnsley.
Earl Fitzwilliam's School, Rotherham.
Charity School, Pontypool.
Mayfield School, Manchester.
National School, Wednesbury.
„   Droitwich.
„   Shirley, Birmingham.
Trinity National School, Nottingham.
„   Watton, Norfolk.

In the above calculations I have left out of view altogether all instances of absence that amounted on the whole to less than than a year.   Had those under a year been taken into account the number of boys who had attended with more or less irregularity would of course have been shown to be much greater; but by noticing only those whose absences exceeded a year, an ample allowance is made for occasional interruptions that were unavoidable.

In the great majority of instances given in these returns there had been occasional interruptions extending from three to twelve months. I gather from the returns themselves that holidays were not deducted in stating the amount of attendance.

In the seventeen schools above-named, there were in the first and second classes, 805 boys. Of these, 331 would, if they had attended regularly from the time they first went to school, have been at school in the aggregate 22,500 months. Their actual attendance amounted to 16,000 months. They were consequently absent more than one third of their nominal time at school.

In the three other schools the attendance of twenty-five (out of ninety-eight in the first and second classes), would have been, if regular, 2309 months. Their actual attendance had been only 1147 months.

I do not institute any formal comparison between the attendance at these twenty schools, and that at the nine other schools named above, for the following reason. Of these nine, two are attended principally by the children of colliers, &c., in the employ, or living on the estate of Earl Fitzwilliam. The master of one of these schools thus expresses himself in a note to the return forwarded to me:—

" This (regularity of attendance) certainly is a favourable view of the district. It must be remembered that the school is well supplied with material, and every inducement for the children to remain is held out. Earl Fitzwilliam's frequent visits, the public examinations, the distribution of prizes, &c. &c., all tend to keep up the interest of parents."

The master of the other school expressed himself verbally to me to the same effect; noticing also the beneficial results of the frequent visits of the ladies of his lordship's family.

From my knowledge of the circumstances connected with four more of those schools, I have no doubt that influences of a similar nature operate upon them to the same end; and while the above extract sufficiently accounts for that regularity of attendance, and describes it as exceptional in the district, it is worthy of particular regard as indicating very justly some of the most effective means that can be taken by persons of influence elsewhere to produce the same result.

I beg to place the original returns, together with this paper, in the hands of this section.*

* There is another point of view from which I venture to think that these returns deserve to be considered.

In the paper following page 134 in the volume of Minutes of the Committee of Council on Education for 1855, entitled " A Summary of a Return for England and Wales, showing the Population between the ages of 5 and 15, &c.," and comparing that population with the total number of scholars returned by the Registrar-General as on the books of both public and private schools, it is stated that the total number of children in England and Wales between those ages was 4,006,174 ; while the total number of scholars returned by the Registrar-General as on the books of public and private schools was 2,108,592.

In public comments upon the above figures it is very often assumed that because only 2,000,000 out of 4,000,000 children were at school at the particular time when these tables were made up, therefore the other 2,000,000 children were growing up without education.

That this is not so in regard to a large portion of the working population must have been observed by most persons conversant with their habits, their practice very commonly being to send their children for two, three, or four years to school, at greater or less intervals during these supposed " school years," according to various exigencies, accidents, or feelings which at the time influence them.

It will probably be admitted that the average attendance at the schools of the working classes, after they have been established for a year or two, does not greatly vary. The common observation, I believe, is that as some boys leave, others take their places, to be replaced again, on their quitting the school finally or only for a time, by some of those who had been there before.

If the limited induction from the twenty schools above named be accepted as confirming this commonly observed fact, then the assumption above referred to, that half the children of the working classes be-

The two great obstacles to the effectual education of a large portion of the children of the working classes who attend school at all having been recalled to our minds, namely, their early removal from school, and the irregularity of their attendance during their school years, it is necessary for the purposes of this paper briefly to advert to the causes of these obstacles.

They are as follows : —

tween five and fifteen are growing up without instruction in schools, must be taken to be erroneous; and if any general inference can be ventured upon from the statistics of the above twenty schools, concurring as the facts there brought out do, as I believe, with common observation, it would rather be that a large proportion of the children of the working classes are absent for one third or one half of their nominal time at school, and that during their absence they are replaced by other children, whose total attendance at school during their school years amounts to about the same.

The general conclusion would therefore be, that to the total average attendance of the children of the working classes in any given year must be added at least one third more who have attended school for some time, and will do so again before they finally leave the day school and go to work, and who consequently will have received, though no doubt very imperfectly, something of the rudiments of education.

Since writing the above I find that the same error has been commented upon by Mr. Kennedy in his Report for this year (p. 394). Mr. Kennedy, to whom I am indebted for procuring for me some of the above returns, has, in his Report, called the attention of the teachers in his district to them, and asked for a full and complete statement calculated still further to illustrate this subject.

The figures quoted in the above-named summary in the Education Minutes are erroneous, as will appear by reference to the Census Report, p. xxviii. (Education), but the argument noticed as having been founded upon them is not affected by the error. The general conclusion which the Registrar-General arrives at, is that, " assuming that all the children of working parents are under education, every child would spend at school but four years out of the twelve (qy. *ten*) which elapse between five and fifteen."

The statistics of the twenty schools given in this paper indicate the fact of irregularity of attendance, and may serve to recall attention to it, and to show that it exists to no inconsiderable extent. The answers as to the age and period of attendance of each boy, prove conclusively that the school-years of a very large proportion of them are between the ages of *five* and *ten* only, and their actual attendance not much more than *three* years.

1. Children are wanted at an early age in a vast number of manufactures, trades, and occupations, at which they can earn wages.

2. They are wanted at home.

3. They are allowed to stay away from school when neither at work nor wanted at home, by, in some and that a large class of cases, the indifference of the parents to the education of their children, arising from their own ignorance; in another large class of cases, by the sensual habits of the parents, who spend in drink and in other ways what would suffice to clothe their children decently and pay for their schooling; and, in many other cases, from the culpable indulgence of parents in permitting them to stay away from frivolous causes.

With regard to these points it is to be observed that, although the children are wanted at an early age in so many occupations, there is no reason, except the indifference and cupidity of parents, why, in a great number of cases, where the father is earning from 12s. to 30s. a week, the child or children of school age should not be kept at school to a later age, and more regularly than they now are. Considering the large proportion of the labouring class earning an amount of wages between the above limits, the low rate of school fees, and the assistance that is rarely difficult to be obtained in case of need towards those payments, there ought, but for that indifference and cupidity, to be a much larger number of children at school, and those at school ought to be kept there more regularly and to a later age.

With the cupidity of such parents it may be difficult altogether to deal; but both to their cupidity and their indifference a powerful counteraction would be applied, if it were possible —

1. To show to the parents some tangible and material advantage to be gained by their children or themselves, to

compensate for the sacrifice of their children's earnings at the earliest age at which they can find employment;

2. To raise the tone of public opinion among the working classes as to the moral value to the individual of a sound education, to excite their emulation, and to bring home to their minds the estimation in which diligence and good conduct at school are held by those above them, and ought to be held among themselves.

With a view to these objects it was proposed by their Lordships the Committee of Privy Council on Education, by their Circular of August 1855, that certificates of good conduct and attainments should be granted to children who are *twelve* years of age, and had been at the same school continuously for *three* years, and had reached a certain standard of attainment; these certificates to be granted by certificated or registered teachers, and by managers of schools, authenticated by Her Majesty's inspectors of schools only as to the signatures of those persons; and it was hoped by Mr. Watkins, who suggested this kind of certificate, that it would be accepted by employers as giving to the holders of it a preference in the competition for employment, and, in certain cases, employment of a higher kind.   Mr. Watkins finds that in his district several employers co-operate with him in giving effect to this certificate; and Mr. Norris has been successful in causing it to be accepted by many persons of influence in Staffordshire and elsewhere.

The objections which I have heard stated to it by many employers are, that there is no security that the masters and managers of schools will not yield to the temptation of granting it on insufficient grounds, and after too lenient an examination; that the disqualifying clause, (clause 4 of the explanatory circular, Minutes of 1855–6, p. 30,) if interpreted strictly, would operate too generally and too severely; and that comparatively few children of the working classes can satisfy its requirements by having attended the same school for 176 days in each of three consecutive years, and until they reach 12 years of age; moreover, that considering the requirements of manufacturing industry in this country, and the importance of an early initiation into work as the great business of life for the "working classes," it is not desirable, as a general rule, to encourage boys to put off until the age of twelve the acquiring the habits and skill necessary to a good handicraftsman.

It appears to me that there is a great deal of force in these objections, and especially in the three last; and I fully concur in the remarks of the Rev. Nash Stephenson, our Honorary Secretary in this section, in his pamphlet on the Educational Condition and Educational Requirements of the town of Birmingham, (Birmingham 1856,) in which he draws attention to the risk the child would incur, and the price he would have to pay, in the endeavour to obtain one of these certificates, from the possible operation of the clause which disqualifies him from obtaining it by "irregularity or unpunctuality of attendance, want of cleanliness in person or neatness in dress, or any single act of gross disobedience or immoral conduct." He may thus have been, in the words of Mr. Stephenson, "detained at school from nine to twelve (three years of his remunerative labour life), and at the expiration of this protracted period of probation" may either fail in obtaining a certificate altogether, or receive one which would be but a small recommendation to him, and in which the employers around him might not be disposed to place much confidence.

It was with a view to the same objects above adverted to, namely, to offer to the parents some tangible advantage to compensate them in some measure for the loss of their children's earnings, if they left them a little longer at school, to encourage them to send them more regularly, to excite emulation among the children themselves, and to raise the tone of public feeling among the " working classes," as to the value of sound education, that in my circular of November 1850, (Report on Mining Districts for 1851, Appendix A,) I proposed to the iron and coal masters of South Staffordshire to form an association for the purpose of offering prizes of some value to be competed for by candidates from groups of elementary schools, and to accompany their prizes with handsomely printed cards certifying the nature of the examination passed, and that the boy's " general conduct and progress in religious knowledge had been first ascertained to be satisfactory."

The facts which led me to the suggestion of these associations were briefly these. It had become evident that, after all the outlay that had been incurred in the mining districts in building new schools and providing good teachers, the children of the working classes, and especially those of the lower grades of the working classes,— the great majority of the whole,—left school at an earlier age than before, having learnt at that earlier age, in consequence of the improved modes of teaching, the little that their parents deemed necessary for them. It was found also that leaving school so young (generally between nine and ten) to go to work, the impressions made upon their minds by what they had learnt at school were so faint that in a few years they had, generally speaking, lost nearly all they had ever acquired.

To induce them to attend more regularly and to stay a little longer at school, until they could show by an examination that they had acquired so much of the rudiments of education as to be able to read fluently, write correctly from dictation, and do the common rules of arithmetic, and that they had been grounded in the elements of religious knowledge, were the main objects of the prize-schemes.

The success that has attended the original association, and the formation of similar ones which soon followed in the adjoining counties, was mainly due to the zeal and ability of the Rev. J. P. Norris, Her Majesty's Inspector of Schools, who was permitted by the Committee of Council on Education to conduct the examinations, and who has given much time and attention to the whole subject. And it must be a matter of gratification to all concerned, to find that Mr. Norris, in his Report of December 1856, (Minutes for 1856–7, p. 829,) is able thus to record his conclusions relative to the effects produced by the four prize-scheme associations under his eye, namely, the South Staffordshire west of Dudley; the South Staffordshire east of Dudley; the North Staffordshire; and the Shropshire : —

"To sum up this Report, I may say, very confidently, that thus far the system of prizes, now at the end of its fifth year of trial, has been a successful experiment.

"It has encouraged the teachers, awakened a more general interest in their work, and induced a large number of parents to care more than heretofore about their children's schooling. For the children it has done much more; it has retained many of them for a longer period under the wholesome discipline of school; it has stimulated their industry ; it has given them a new pleasure, the pleasure of a generous emulation ; and it has taught them that life is a *career* in which honest, self-reliant exertion is sure to bring success, and to win for them the respect of their fellow men."

Joining to the full in the satisfaction suggested by the above extract, I feel bound nevertheless to record my opinion that those prize-schemes are going beyond their original intention, and that the time has arrived for another proposal which may tend to give that original intention a more general effect.

Mr. Nòrris states, in his Report for 1856, that the candidates in these four associations amounted in 1855 to 696, and in 1856, to 799.

This great increase in the number of candidates gives rise to some serious considerations:—

1st. Can the funds of the associations be expected to go on increasing proportionately to the demand made upon them?

2ndly. Can the time of the inspectors be given to the extent required by this increase of candidates?

Mr. Norris answers these questions in the negative, and therefore proposes that the competition for the *money-prize* should be deferred until the candidate has completed *twelve* years of age and *three* years regular attendance at school, and that no one shall be a candidate for the money-prize who has not first gained the Bible-prize, the qualifications for competing for which are two years regular attendance at school subsequently to the age of nine.

Now all the evidence collected by the inspectors and others tends to show that a very small proportion of the children of the lower grades of the labouring classes— and it is to be borne in mind that these are the great majority of the whole—are, or under present circumstances can be expected to be, found at school at the age of twelve at all, still less to have attended school regularly for 176 days in each of the preceding three years.

Consequently it must be expected that the money-prizes under the above arrangement will be gained almost exclusively by the sons of small tradesmen and superior artisans, who stay longest, and in point of fact comprise a large proportion of many schools; and that the only objects within the probable attainment of the children of the lower grades of the labouring class, for whose encouragement to remain at school the money-prizes were primarily intended, will be the Bible-prize and the card that accompanies it.*

As this new arrangement has been adopted, on Mr. Norris's suggestion, by the committees of the four above-mentioned associations, it becomes necessary maturely to consider it, inasmuch as twelve more large associations have recently been formed, and there is a probability of others following.

The twelve alluded to are as follows:

In 1854, one was formed at Kidderminster for a portion of the Archdeaconry of Worcester; and in 1856, another was formed at Worcester for another portion of the same archdeaconry. To these another has been added this year for the district of Stratford; and the whole have been united for the purposes of examination, under the name of the Worcester Archidiaconal Prize Scheme.†

* Out of 3505 children in 31 schools in Mr. Stewart's present district it was found that 1876 were of the middle class, and only 1629 of the labouring class (Report for 1856, p. 463).

† "The examinations all took place on the same day, and the questions were the same for all. The papers being looked over by the same two examiners.

"The prizes were distributed in each district separately, the books, special prizes, and testimonial cards being open to all, and therefore the same in each district, as of course was the standard of merit of each class. The money premiums varied in amount in each district, depending on the local funds raised.

"*Kidderminster District* distributed 122*l*. 5*s*., in sums varying from 4*l*. to 2*s*. 6*d*.

"*Stratford District*, 49*l*. 7*s*. 6*d*., in sums from 1*l*. to 3*s*. 6*d*.

"*Worcester District*, about 83*l*., in sumsfrom 1*l*. 10*s*. to 2*s*. 6*d*.

"In the apportionment of the money premiums regard was had to age of candidate. In the two first classes, boys, as they were above 12, 11, or 10, received in proportion, the whole, $\frac{2}{3}$, $\frac{1}{3}$. This apportionment was not carried below classes i. and ii.

"The numbers from each district that presented themselves and were classed, were—

			Candidates.			Classed.
"Kidderminster	-	-	157	-	-	138
Worcester	-	-	-	156	-	-	135
Stratford	-	-	-	81	-	-	77."

In 1855 the association for Northumberland and Durham was formed by the exertions of the Hon. and Rev. J. Grey and the Rev. D. J. Stewart, shortly after I had brought the subject to the notice of the large employers of labour in that important mining district.

In the course of last year I succeeded in inducing the principal persons in the mining portion of South Wales to form three associations, extending over the whole of that part of the country.

In the spring of this year I was also enabled to cause one association to be formed for the mining parts of the counties of Derby, Nottingham, and Leicester, and two for the mining portions of Yorkshire ; the way for the formation of the two latter having been prepared by the Rev. F. Watkins, Her Majesty's Inspector of Schools, by communications with several of the leading persons in that county.

In 1855, by the exertions of the Rev. Nash Stephenson, the Coventry Archidiaconal Church Extension Association adopted a Prize-scheme, co-extensive with that archdeaconry.

The Birmingham Educational Association also adopted a Prize-scheme in March last.

All these associations have adopted plans similar in all their principal points to the original ones of Staffordshire and Shropshire, and, it seems to me, more in keeping with the primary end in view.

These sixteen associations embrace in their operation nearly the whole of the mining districts of England and Wales, some large districts chiefly agricultural, and the town of Birmingham.

Also, in 1853-4, at the suggestion of Mr. Norris, the London and North-Western Railway Company introduced this mode of encouraging education at their schools at Crewe. About the same time, the same plans were adopted by the Weaver Navigation Company for their schools, but owing, Mr. Norris thinks, to removable causes, with less satisfactory results.*

Two of the above sixteen large associations have not completed their arrangements. The candidates who came forward to compete for prizes in the remaining fourteen amounted in the year 1856-7 to 2,429.†

Should the number of candidates be found to increase in the newly-formed associations as rapidly as in the earlier ones, and experience is tending to show that they will do so, it will clearly be as necessary in their case as Mr. Norris has seen it to be in those he has to deal with, to adopt some means to make the money subscribed go farther than it has hitherto done.

As regards this portion of the question, therefore, I should be inclined to reverse Mr. Norris's proposition, and to suggest to these associations to make the higher prizes more of an honorary character, — such as a handsomely bound book or a medal, — as being likely, with the card, to appeal to the ambition of the better description of parents and their children; and, retaining the money-prizes chiefly for excellence in the more ordinary attainments, to reduce their amount in proportion as the stimulus of the money-prize and the accompanying card are found to

---

* Details relating to all the latest-formed associations are given in my Report to the Secretary of State on portions of the mining districts, recently laid before Parliament (August, 1857), in which Report the suggestions contained in this paper are also embodied.

Associations.				Candidates in 1856-7.
† The Staffordshire and Shropshire	-	(4)	- -	799
The Worcestershire	- -	(3)	- -	394
The Northumberland and Durham	-	(1)	- -	260
The South Wales	- - -	(3)	- -	530
The Derby, Nottingham, and Leicester	(1)		- -	70
The Coventry Archidiaconal	-	(1)	- -	344
The West Yorkshire Northern -	-	(1)	- -	32
		14		2,429

operate upon the children of the lower grades of the working classes.

Mr. Norris further proposes that, as the cards " have been proved by experience to be very highly valued by the parents," cards alone should be distributed " to all deserving children," merely certifying to the fact that they " have attended some school regularly (*i. e.* 176 days, exclusive of Sunday, in each year) for a period of *two* years subsequently to their *ninth* birthday, and that they bear a good character."

I venture to think that such cards would not have the effect of inducing many parents among the working classes to sacrifice for them their children's wages for one or two years, especially as, bearing no testimony as to the amount of a child's acquirements, they would carry very little weight with an employer in an application for work by the possessor of one of them.

On this part of the subject, I beg to offer two suggestions of a larger kind; and I am led to these suggestions by the acknowledged fact of the very considerable effect which these Prize-schemes have had in causing greater regularity of attendance among a certain portion of the children at elementary schools, and in prolonging their school age, and consequently in raising the standard of attainment previously to leaving the day-school.

1. There have been this year, as has been shown, in the associations now at work, near upon 2,500 candidates.

All of these have made increased efforts while at school, and have presented themselves for an examination which implies that they possess the groundwork of education, — namely, that they can read fairly, write correctly from dictation, and do the four first rules of arithmetic, simple and compound, " their general conduct and progress in religious knowledge having been first ascertained to be satisfactory. Many of them can do much more than this.

Of these 2,500, according to the general practice up to this time, about one half will have received prizes of greater or less value, accompanied by the card certifying to the fact, and also as to good conduct and progress in religious knowledge. The remaining half will have received nothing to testify to the efforts they have made, or even to serve as a proof that they were able to join in the competition.

I propose that another card, smaller and less ornamented than the one given with the prize, but still attractive in its style of ornament, should be given to each of the unsuccessful candidates whose examination showed that they had come up to the above-named minimum standard of acquirement.

After communication with the honorary secretaries of the three South Wales, the Derby, Nottingham, and Leicestershire, and the Yorkshire Southern associations, and with their concurrence, I have caused plates to be engraved for these two cards *, the prize-card being larger and more ornamented than the original prize-card, and more worthy of being framed (the mode of preserving it adopted in so many cases by the parents), the "card of merit" being of the same dimensions as the original prize-card.

This card of merit, bearing upon its face the certificate of the inspector as to the examination passed before him by the holder of it, will be a very different thing in the estimation of any employer of labour, and of the children themselves and their parents, from the present government certificate, granted by masters and managers of schools, and authenticated by the inspector as to the fact only of the signatures of those persons.

---

* I have reason to believe that the same cards will be adopted by the four associations of Staffordshire and Shropshire. The West Yorkshire Northern Association have had similar cards engraved for themselves.

2. My next proposition is designed to act upon the vast body of children who are unable to satisfy the conditions of a Prize-scheme by reason of their leaving school to go to work at an earlier age than that which entitles them to join in the competition, or by reason of the irregularity of their attendance while at school.

The fact is established, that the great bulk of the children in elementary schools leave them *before* they are ten years old, and that the attendance of a large proportion while there is very irregular, and that from these two causes combined the little they have learnt has been learnt so imperfectly, that in most cases it is nearly all lost after a few years.

The demands of the labour market, and the present state of public opinion among the parents of that class of children, and, I may add, the state of opinion of the country generally, render it, I believe, impossible to prevent this early removal of children from school by legislation, or by any other means, to any considerable extent.

I am not insensible to the value of those " other means " of various kinds, which have been already acted upon with more or less success, or which have been proposed. The improvements which remain to be introduced in the employment of time at school, by the more common adoption of the practice of learning lessons at home, by which so much time is saved in the Scotch schools,—the giving a more practical bearing to what is taught, as far as is consistent with the sound teaching of what is primary and indispensable,—the judicious use of industrial work out of school hours, which experience has now in so many cases shown to be possible without detriment, and even with benefit, to the school teaching,—all these and other measures of practical improvement in the education given will doubtless operate usefully, each in its particular direction, but I believe much more upon the children of the middle class and of superior artisans than upon the great bulk of the children of the labouring classes.

The Prize-schemes have confessedly hitherto acted far more upon the better class of parents than upon those who are disposed to neglect their children. The opinion of the Rev. William Lea, in a letter to Mr. Bellairs, relative to the effect of the two Prize-schemes for the Archdeaconry of Worcester, is shared by Mr. Norris in regard to those of Staffordshire and Shropshire. Mr. Lea says: " My own idea is, that they have not had much effect upon parents who were indifferent to education " (Minutes for 1856-7, p. 277).

It appears to me to be of the first importance in devising our measures for improving the state of elementary education, to keep more steadily in view than has hitherto been generally the case, the broad fact, that the whole of the children attending these elementary schools are not to be considered as an homogeneous body, requiring the same treatment, and from whom we can look for one great and similar result. They should be looked upon as, what in point of fact they are, belonging to the two great divisions of the labouring class, — one, whose children require only the mere rudiments of education for all the purposes of life, and the other whose children require something more. And as regards the former of these two great divisions, composing the great majority of the whole, I repeat my strong impression, that neither improvements in the mode of teaching or in the things taught, nor any legislation within the bounds of practicable adoption in this country, are likely, in this or even in the next generation, to alter to any considerable extent the existing fact of the withdrawal of the great bulk of the children from the elementary schools before or about the age of 10.

Something more, however, may I think be done by

appealing still further than has hitherto been effected to the principle of emulation among the boys*, and to the natural pride, and to the self-interest of the parents ; and I believe it would thus be possible so to act upon both, that a very considerable proportion of those boys who now leave school so early as to derive very little permanent benefit from it, would be able, before they leave the day-school finally, to show that they can come up to the minimum standard of the Prize-schemes, or even go somewhat beyond it, both in reading, writing from dictation, and arithmetic, as well as in respect to conduct and religious knowledge, although at an earlier age than qualifies them for competition under the Prize-schemes. If they can do this well,—and I believe it quite possible that it should be done well *by the time* a boy is 10 years of age,—they will have had the elements of education so fixed in their minds, that they will be able with the greater ease to go on educating themselves, and will be the less disposed to allow themselves to relapse into ignorance.

As things are at present, the great crowd of boys who pass through the schools rapidly and attend irregularly, not only have no chance of joining in the competition for a Prize-scheme, but must necessarily, generally speaking, end their school-lives without receiving themselves, or being able to show to their parents, or to employers of labour, the least token that their progress, such as it may be, has met with any public recognition. Such boys feel that they have nothing to aim at; and the parents find that the boys have nothing to gain by remaining at school after they have learnt the very little that, in the idea of the parents, comes within the word "schooling."

I propose, therefore, that public examinations should be held every half-year, of all boys, of whatever age, or

* The education of the girls will be considered hereafter.

time of attendance at school, about to leave the day-school finally, or who have left it within the last six months, who may choose to present themselves for examination.

The examination to be, with the exception herein-after mentioned, in writing, in a book, to be provided for every boy by the school managers for the purpose, of the copy-book form, but with a durable and somewhat ornamented cover, for the sake of preservation.

No boy to be sent up by his master for examination unless he can satisfy the minimum requirements of the examination under a Prize-scheme, as above stated.

I propose that groups of schools should be formed, say twenty-five in each group.

If twenty boys left each school every year able to reach the above minimum (a large average), 250 boys would present themselves in each half-year from each group.

In the paper annexed, I have shown how such an examination can be conducted in a few hours, and by whom.

The examination papers, which should contain graduated questions, from the level of the above-named minimum to questions of proportion, fractions, &c., and to grammar and geography, or other subjects that might be thought more desirable, should be set by Her Majesty's inspectors, one of whom should, if possible, be present at the examination. The success of the Prize-schemes is greatly due to the conviction of the complete fairness with which the examinations are conducted and the prizes awarded by the inspectors.

On a day previous to the day fixed for the examination, the clergyman, or the minister of the denomination to which the boy belonged, should examine him as to his religious knowledge in one or more of the following subjects : —

The Catechism,	The Four Gospels,
The Gospel of St. ——,	The Acts of the Apostles,
The Book of Genesis,	Old Testament History,

and certify in the first page of the boy's book (if the fact be so) that his acquaintance with the doctrines of the Christian faith, and his knowledge of Scripture are, for his age, satisfactory.

The master of the school should also, in the same page, certify (if the fact be so) that the boy bears a good character.

No boy to be admitted to the examination without the above certificates in the first page of his book.

On the day of the examination, in the first hour and a half, the boy would first work on his slate, and then copy into his book the most difficult of the sums placed before him that he thinks he can do correctly.

After an interval, to be employed as described in section f of the paper above referred to, the boy would write in his book from dictation; and subsequently, if capable, the answers to some of the questions proposed in grammar and geography, or some other subject.

A short time given to an examination in reading would be sufficient as a test of fluency and accuracy.

One of the committee of masters, or managers, or both, together with the inspector if present, whom I propose as the proper persons to conduct these examinations, would, at their termination, verify the fact by their signatures.

The result would speak for itself. Good writing, correct spelling, correct arithmetic, as far as attempted, and, if the boy was capable of anything further, correct grammar and some little knowledge of geography, or of some other subject, would appear upon the face of a large number of these examination books. If the committee of masters and managers could afford the time to look over all the books attentively, a few words of commendation would give additional value to those especially deserving it.

A new motive for regularity of attendance and diligence at school would be supplied, by holding out to each boy a definite object to work for, namely, that of recording in a book, on a public occasion, his actual attainments previously to leaving the day-school.

It would excite emulation among the boys themselves, and probably lead many to urge their parents to allow them to stay long enough at school to obtain this record of what they could do. It would further tend to counteract the practice of irregularity of attendance during the school years, by making it obvious to any boy, that without regular attendance he could not expect to get on as fast as his neighbours who were more regular, and that consequently he would either be altogether unable to come up to the minimum standard before leaving school, or would be able to exhibit but a poor proof of his progress in comparison with others.

This book would be looked upon with pride and pleasure by the better class of parents, and could scarcely fail to be gratifying to those who are now indifferent to the education of their children. It might be expected, therefore, to lead in both cases to their children receiving better and more durable impressions from their attendance at school.

An employer, to whom this book might be presented by a boy wishing to be engaged, would see at a glance what the boy's attainments and character were when he left school, and might from that form some judgment of the boy's general capacity. I do not think, however, that too much reliance should be placed on the expectation that employers would bind themselves to give a preference in all cases to the holders of school certificates, however creditable to the possessors of them. In most instances,

especially where skilled labour is concerned, an employer
engaging a boy for the first time would, I apprehend, before examining his school certificate, first look at what
nature had endowed him with; and unless he found his
eye bright and intelligent, and his bodily framework apt
for labour, no amount of school-learning would have any
weight with him. Next, the employer would probably
inquire as to the boy's relatives and connexions; and if he
found him to be the son or nephew, or in any way connected with a steady workman already in his employ, he
would give him a preference before another whose school-
certificate might be far more creditable and attractive.
Nevertheless, it may reasonably be anticipated that, in
many cases, such a school certificate may avail a boy
in his application for work even in the employments that
are most sought after, and still oftener in the more ordinary ones, where general intelligence and good conduct,
rather than manual skill, are the things required.

As a proof that trustworthy evidence of general intelligence and good conduct is much sought for and valued by
persons in want of boys' labour in various departments of
employment, it may be mentioned that the application for
boys from the first class at Norwood and other poor-law
district industrial schools is now so great that, whereas
formerly the ages of those boys ranged generally from
13 to 16, and the guardians had great difficulty in getting
them off their hands, now, and since the improved teaching and discipline has taken effect in those schools, they
seldom stay beyond or even until 12 years of age, and it
is difficult to prevent their being engaged before they have
been as long in the first class as is desirable.

The knowledge that these school-certificates had become, in many instances, a recommendation for employment, and perhaps, in some cases, for employment of a
better kind, would soon spread among the parents, and

afford a tangible and intelligible motive to them for giving their children enough "schooling" to enable them to produce a creditable record of it in their examination book.

No boy should be allowed to present himself for this examination more than once. It would, therefore, be his interest to remain at school until he could pass it creditably; and his ambition would be excited to put on record as much as he could beyond the minimum required.

Boys who failed to obtain the "Card of Merit" in the competition for a Prize-scheme might be allowed to present themselves for this general examination; and as it would take place some months after the Prize-scheme examination, they might have made good use of the interval so as to enable them to reach the minimum, and show finally a good examination book if they were obliged to leave the day-school and go to work before the next competition under a Prize-scheme.

By degrees so many boys would be in possession of prizes, cards of merit, and examination books, that it would seem reasonable to anticipate that the combined example and numbers, and the instances of the material advantages flowing from those distinctions, would contribute to form a new kind of public opinion among that class of the population in relation to education, inducing them to fix their mark higher, and leading them by its results, moral and material, to a truer estimate of the value of intellectual resources, and of early moral and religious instruction and training at school.

A boy who had given public proof at one of these examinations of what he could do on leaving the day-school would be greatly encouraged to keep up what he had acquired, and to make further progress.

The "after prize," suggested originally by Mr. Norris in North Staffordshire, and adopted by many of the prize associations since formed, is likely to operate very forcibly in the same direction; being offered to those boys who can produce certificates: (1.) That they have gained one of the preceding prizes. (2.) That they are employed in connexion with the works of some member of the association. (3.) That their character is good. To this I would add, (4.) That, if not the gainers of one of these prizes, they could produce a satisfactory examination book.

This proposition of providing a mode by which a boy can put on record, on a public occasion, the extent of his acquirements, though humble, on leaving the day-school, is but an extension to the elementary schools of the labouring classes of a principle that has been found useful at the universities.

Formerly, at the universities, the class-lists were very restricted. Latterly they have been greatly extended. Every one passing through the university possesses a record of the fact in his degree. Those moderately gifted are content if they can pass the lowest examination, so as to obtain that record. To many, the apprehension of seeing their names among the multitude, or in the lowest class, operates as a stimulant against idleness. The men of greater abilities are urged to increased effort by the higher honours and prizes.

In the elementary schools for the labouring classes there has hitherto been nothing for a boy to aim at beyond the mere steps of his slow and laborious progress,— the more slow and laborious because in so many cases obstructed by irregularity of attendance. He may have been in the habit of frequenting the day-school " off and on" from the age of 4 or 5 until 10, 11, or 12; and he then, in the large majority of cases, leaves it without taking with him the slightest token that any one beyond the precincts of his school has marked or recognised his progress, be it small or great; and it must appear to him to be a matter of perfect indifference to every one beyond that small circle whether he has made any progress or not. It cannot, therefore, be a matter of surprise that he is himself somewhat indifferent, and that his parents are not less so, as to the actual amount of instruction beyond the mere power of reading and writing a little, which he may have acquired, or how soon he loses it.

It would seem reasonable to expect that this indifference both of the child and the parent would be greatly checked, if not converted into some degree of zeal and pride in education, if the stimulus were applied of the public record of a boy's attainments and character at the time of his leaving the day-school, which has been above proposed.

In March last, I laid the first draft of this plan before a meeting of the Birmingham Educational Society, which I was invited to attend to consider with them the details of their Prize-scheme. I then submitted it to the experienced judgment of Canon Moseley, Mr. Cook, Mr. Norris, Mr. Kennedy, Mr. Bellairs, Mr. Bowstead, and Mr. Watkins, Her Majesty's Inspectors of Schools. All, except Mr. Watkins expressed a cordial concurrence in its principle. The details given are indications only of the manner in which it might be carried out, although, I believe, not far from what would be found to work easily.

I was first led to consider this plan in connexion with the Prize-schemes which, as Inspector of Mining Districts, I felt it my duty to suggest and have contributed to form throughout now the whole of the large districts in England and Wales, with the exception of Lancashire and Cheshire. At the same time I believe it to be very extensively, if not generally applicable beyond those districts. Associations of schoolmasters are now very common in all parts of the country. Rural deaneries and archdeaconries have formed associations within themselves for educational purposes. Towns like Manchester and Birmingham have shown that they can form associations for the general purpose of improving and extending elementary education. A committee of schoolmasters could, I believe, always be formed in any given district to promote an object which would give so much encouragement to their own efforts; and a committee of managers would in many places readily second them by giving their aid to the inspectors in conducting the examinations, if the very desirable presence of the inspectors should be granted by the Government, or otherwise doing their best to make the examinations from the inspector's papers fair and impartial.

There are, I believe, at least twenty-five inspectors and assistant-inspectors whose services might be available for the purposes of these examinations. If the Committee of Council would permit them to give up one day every half-year to prepare the questions, and one to conduct the examinations, twenty-five groups of schools might have the benefit of the inspectors' aid and presence, a number which would probably include many of the most important localities in their respective districts, and enough for the satisfactory trial of the above plan.

It may be said, why not unite these general examinations of all boys leaving school or who have left school within the current half-year, irrespective of their age and period of attendance at school, with the Prize-schemes, and abolish in the latter the requirements as to age and regularity of attendance for a certain number of years, for the sake of simplification and of having one examination for all who can come up to a certain standard?

The answer is, that regularity of attendance has a great moral value; that, in so far as it requires effort and self-denial, its effects upon character are good both in the parent and in the child; and that, inasmuch as the exigencies of the labour market are likely to operate continuously in withdrawing children at an early age from school in spite of all efforts to the contrary, the more we can procure regularity of attendance during the few school years, the greater will be the number of children who will have had the opportunity of having the rudiments of education permanently impressed upon their minds, and of benefiting by the moral discipline and the religious instruction of the day-school. Moreover, the higher prizes under the Prize-schemes (whether money or honorary prizes), involving, as is now proposed by Mr. Norris, and adopted in Staffordshire and Shropshire, three years continuous attendance at school, and a much higher standard of acquirement, will operate in a manner which it is not desirable to check in diffusing a higher standard of education among the more highly-paid operatives and the lower grades of the middle-class, from whose improved intelligence and mental power much valuable results may be anticipated in relation to the industry of the country.

In reference to the question of the funds necessary for the purposes of these Prize-schemes, I beg leave to mention that in the autumn of 1855 I took the liberty of addressing a suggestion to the Lord President of the Committee of Council on Education, to the effect that a certain proportion should be added by the Government to the sum raised by the Prize-scheme associations, to be applied as " Queen's prizes" to the most deserving and most advanced of the candidates.

The answer of the Lord President was to the effect " that these Prize-schemes involved a very small outlay ; that they were organised in those parts of the country where there were the richest capitalists ; that they had hitherto succeeded without government aid ; that the sanction of the Committee of Council was sufficiently shown by the presence of Her Majesty's inspector, and by the promoters having at their disposal the advice and

assistance of a public officer of his experience ; and that
much greater liberty of action is possible for all persons
concerned so long as the expenditure of public money is
not to be accounted for, and the degree of encouragement
afforded by the Government stops short of assuming to regulate or answer for the several schemes."

As the outlay required for these schemes increases with
the increase of the number of candidates, and as experience is tending to show which of the several plans is the
best and therefore most deserving of the stamp of government approval, the time may be approaching when this
question may be submitted for re-consideration, especially
if the prizes for the highest acquirements should be made,
as I have ventured here to propose, more and more honorary, in which case, a medal accorded as " the Queen's
prize" would be, in point of money value, of little moment,
but in the estimation of the children who might obtain it
of the very highest, as well as in that of their parents.

One of the advantages of the plan of a general examination of all boys leaving the day-school, above described,
would be (as contrasted with the Prize-schemes) that it
would require next to no outlay ; almost the only expense
attending it that would fall upon the managers of schools
being the little necessary to provide the bound copybooks.
The schoolmasters would, I apprehend, be most ready to
lend their aid to what would give so much encouragement
to their own exertions, and tend to add to the numbers
at their schools.

PROPOSAL FOR A PUBLIC EXAMINATION

Of all Boys, of whatever age or time of attendance at School, about to leave the DAY-SCHOOL finally, or who have left it within the last six months, who may choose to present themselves for examination, provided they can come up to a certain minimum standard of acquirement.

1. Groups to be formed of, say, 25 schools.
2. In each, an average of twenty boys may, every year, leave school, who can come up to the minimum standard required under a Prize-scheme,—namely, who can read tolerably ; write a fair round hand; spell simple words correctly from dictation ; and, in arithmetic, have a fair knowledge of the first four rules, simple and compound ; in all 500 boys, or 250 every half-year ; a high average.
3. It is proposed that every such boy who is about to leave school, or who has left it during the last half-year, should be invited to present himself for examination on some day just previous to the Christmas and Midsummer holidays.
4. This examination to be, with one exception, in writing.

    A book to be provided for every boy for this purpose by the managers of his school.   It should be of the copy-book form, but with a durable and somewhat ornamented cover.
5. The arrangements for the examination to be as follows:—

a. Notice of the time and place to be given.

b. On the day previous to the day fixed, the clergyman or the minister of the denomination to which the boy belongs to examine him as to his religious knowledge in one or two of the following subjects :

The Catechism,	The Four Gospels,
The Gospel of St. ——,	The Acts of the Apostles,
The Book of Genesis,	Old Testament History,

and to certify in the first page of the boy's book, that (if the fact be so) his acquaintance with the doctrines of the Christian faith and his knowledge of Scripture are for his age satisfactory.

The masters of his school shall also, in the same page, certify (if the fact be so) that the boy bears a good character.

No boy to be admitted to the examination without the above certificates in the first page of his book.

c. At the time appointed, a committee of masters, nominated by the masters of twenty-five schools, to meet at the place appointed for the examinations, and to write upon the black boards a series of questions in arithmetic, grammar, and geography, proportioned in difficulty to the ordinary attainments of boys leaving school.   These questions to have been previously prepared by one of Her Majesty's inspectors of schools, and delivered on the morning of the examination. They should be framed from school books in common use.   The subjects might be varied if desired.

d. One of Her Majesty's inspectors of schools to be present, if possible, and also a committee of managers of schools.

e. The boys to be arranged at the desks. and the black boards, with the questions in arithmetic appropriate to each, having been placed opposite to them, they are to be desired to work on their slates. and then to copy into their books, the most difficult of the sums before them which they think they can do correctly.   An hour and a half to be allowed for this portion of the examination.

f. Immediately upon its conclusion the committee of masters, aided probably by the managers present, will look at the answers of the sums, and affix their signatures to each, adding "Right" or "Wrong," as the case may be.

g. The boys to be then separated into convenient subdivisions, and to write, in their book, from dictation.   One of the masters standing before each subdivision, will read out from some reading-book in common use appropriate passages, the first being easy, the latter more difficult.   Twenty minutes to be allowed for this exercise.

h. Questions of grammar to be then placed on the black boards before them ; they will be desired to select the most difficult which they think they can answer ; twenty minutes will be allowed for writing the answers in their books.

i. Questions in geography or other subjects to be then placed before them, and twenty minutes to be allowed for writing the answers.

The name and age of each boy to be written by himself on the last page of his examination.

Fluency and accuracy of reading to be then tested, as far as time allows.

k. The committee of masters or managers, or both, to examine what has been written, and to mark the errors.   The examinations not being competitive, much less time would be occupied in revision. No master to examine the books of a boy belonging to his own school.

l. Her Majesty's inspector, or assistant inspector, if present, and a member of the committee of managers and masters, to sign their names at the end of the examinations in each book, to testify that they took place in his or their presence, and to certify the number of errors. The books to be then delivered to their respective owners.*

March 30, 1857.

The Organisation and the Rules of the "Associations for offering Prizes to be competed for by Groups of Elementary Schools," are, with slight differences, similar to the following Example:—

The subscriptions furnished by the fifteen largest associations amount to between 90*l* and 130*l.* per annum. The contributors are principally either employers of labour, or owners of landed property.

Monmouthshire Association for awarding Annual Prizes among the Elementary Schools of the Working Classes.

President.—Capel Hanbury Leigh, Esq., Pontypool Park.

Vice-Presidents.
The Venerable the Archdeacon of Monmouth.
The Venerable the Archdeacon of Llandaff.

Patron.—The Right Reverend the Lord Bishop of Llandaff.

---

* I have taken a group of 25 schools as a basis of calculation, as presenting less difficulty than a larger area; but that much larger groups might readily be formed is shown by that of the Coventry Archidiaconal Association, which now comprises in its Prize-scheme 51 schools, and sent this year 344 candidates to join in the competition. The total number of inspected schools in England and Wales may now be stated at about 5000. One hundred groups of 50 each would comprise the whole, and would occupy 25 inspectors four days only in each half-year in these examinations, and four in preparing the questions.

Committee.

Thomas Brown, Esq., Ebbw Vale.
F. Levick, Esq., Blaina.
R. P. Davis, Esq., Tredegar.
G. T. Hubbock, Esq., Rhymney.
Sir Thomas Phillips.
Thomas Powell, jun., Esq., The Gaer.

W. Williams, Esq.
J. Firmstone, Esq.
L. Powell, Esq.
Jas. Brown, Esq.
Martin Morrison, Esq.

Subscribers.

	£	s.	d.
C. Hanbury Leigh, Esq., Lord Lieutenant of Monmouthshire, Pontypool Park - - -	5	0	0
Messrs. Darby, Brown, and Co., Abersychan Ironworks - - -	5	0	0
Messrs. Darby, Brown, and Co., Cwm Bran -	5	0	0
Thomas Powell, Esq., The Gaer - - -	5	0	0
Sir Thomas Phillips -	5	0	0
Trustees of the late Thomas Protheroe, Esq.	10	0	0
The Earl of Abergavenny	5	0	0
James Brown, Esq., Brynglas - - - -	5	0	0
Messrs. Banks and Co., Pontymister - -	3	3	0
W. Williams, Esq., for Pontnywynnyd, Varteg, Golynos, and Co. -	10	0	0
Launcelot Powell, Esq., Clydach Co. - -	5	0	0
F. Levick, Esq., for Blaina and Cwm Celyn Co., &c.	10	0	0

	£	s.	d.
Messrs. Darby, Brown, and Co., Ebbw Vale and Victoria - - -	5	0	0
Messrs. Darby, Brown, and Co., Sir Howy -	5	0	0
R. P. Davis, Esq., for Tredegar Ironworks Co. -	10	0	0
Rhymney Ironworks Co.	10	0	0
J. Firmstone, Esq., for Pontypool Ironworks Co. - - - -	5	0	0
Martin Morrison, Esq., Newport - - -	2	2	0
T. P. Price, Esq., Abertillery - - - -	2	2	0
Joseph Latch, Esq., Newport - - - -	2	2	0
W. S. Cartwright, Esq , Newport - - -	1	1	0
W. A. Williams, Esq., Llangibby - -	1	1	0
	£116	11	0

Honorary Secretary and Treasurer.—Sir Thomas Phillips.

The object of this association is to induce parents to keep their children at school longer and more regularly than is at present the custom, and to hold out to the children themselves an additional motive to diligence and good conduct.

Conditions of Competition.

1. Candidates to be boys or girls (not pupil-teachers) who have attended, for a period of at least two years, an elementary school for the working classes, approved of by some member of the association.

2. They must be at least 10 years of age.

3. They will be required to produce a certificate from their teacher, that they have attended the day-school at least 176 days during the twelve months ending the 1st June preceding the examination.

4. Certificates will also be required of good character, and of satisfactory progress in religious knowledge, signed by their teacher, and countersigned by their clergyman or minister.

5. All candidates will be expected to read tolerably ; to write a fair round hand ; to spell simple words correctly from dictation ; and, in arithmetic, to have a fair knowledge of the first four rules, simple and compound.

Those competing for the higher prizes will be examined in decimals and the higher rules of arithmetic, and in grammar and geography.

Girls will be expected to possess skill in needlework, and should bring with them the requisite amount of material for cutting out and making some article of clothing.

§ A. The above rules have been drawn up with a special view to the first year's examination. In subsequent years it may be judged expedient to modify them.

§ B. Managers of schools, who wish to send candidates to take part in the above competition, must forward, on or before the 1st day of June next, a list of such candidates, specifying the age of each, together with a certificate that the school is approved of by some member of the association, to the Rev. H. W. Bellairs, or J. Bowstead, Esq., Her Majesty's Inspector of Schools, Privy Council Office, London.

§ C. The examinations for the year 1857 will be held at Newport, in the month of July next.

The day and hour of the examination will be duly announced by public advertisement.

§ D. Prizes, not exceeding on the whole 100*l.*, of 3*l.*, 2*l.*, and 1*l.* each, will be given to the successful candidates according to their proficiency, as shown by the examinations.

Smaller prizes in addition to the above may also be given on the recommendation of the inspectors.

The name of each successful candidate will be registered in a book, to be provided by the association, to which reference may always be made.

A handsomely printed card will be given to each successful candidate, certifying that he has gained a prize. The prizes and the cards will be delivered to the successful candidates at a public meeting, which will be held after each annual examination.

A " Card of Merit " will be given to such of the unsuccessful candidates as appear to deserve that encouragement.

The expenses of the successful candidates, in attending the examination and the meeting, will be defrayed by the association.

The printed cards will form a lasting certificate of good conduct at school; and will be not only a just object of satisfaction to the possessors of them, and to their friends, but a valuable testimonial to any employer.

In some parts of the country, the employers of juvenile labour have signified their intention of giving a preference to those children who are possessed of certificates of good conduct signed by Her Majesty's inspectors.

§ E. In order to encourage boys to keep up and extend their knowledge after leaving school, to show them the value of good character, and to teach them habits of economy, it is further proposed to offer, in subsequent years, prizes of 5*l*. each, to candidates who pass a satisfactory examination in some one or two books, which may be selected from a list of works to be hereafter advertised, and who can produce certificates, signed by their minister, and also by some member of the association,—

a. That they have gained one of the preceding prizes;

b. That they are employed in connection with the works of some member of the association;

c. That their character is good.

This prize will only be awarded once to the same individual.

The sum will be invested in the savings bank in the name of the successful candidate; and, at the expiration of two years from its being awarded, the savings bank book, containing the statement of the original sum and the interest, will be given over to him.

If any boy who has become entitled to this sum dies before two years are completed, the money will at once be given over to the parents.

A printed card will also be given with this prize.

I endeavoured to obtain some public documents from the United States that might throw light upon the state of attendance at the elementary schools of the principal towns and cities in that country.

The only documents which have reached me are the annual reports of the school committee of the City of Lowell, for the municipal years 1853, 54, 55, and 56; and the annual reports of the "controllers of the public schools of the City and County of Philadelphia," for the years 1852, 53, 54, 55, and 56.

The Report of the Lowell School Committee for 1853 speaks of "a changing population, and a pupilage generally younger than is found in schools of the same rank in other cities." The Report for 1854 refers to "the extent of the manufacturing establishments, the number of young persons employed in them, and the very many poor familes whose chief dependence for subsistence is upon the earnings of their children." The conditions therefore of the problem, in the Manchester of the United States, are analogous to those in the manufacturing towns of this country.

Accordingly, it appears from the Reports for 1853, 1854, and 1855, (the analysis being omitted in that of 1856), that out of an aggregate of 8190 pupils belonging to the primary schools during those three years, only 181 had attended constantly one year; 473 had attended constantly two terms, and 1600 had attended constantly one term. (The terms are, 1, from January 7th to April; 2, from 14th April to 1st July; 3, from September to 25th December.)

The causes of this are stated (at p. 12 in the Report for 1856) to be "the too great haste on the part of parents and teachers in pushing the children forward to higher schools." "From the time the scholars enter the primary schools till the time they leave the high school, there is a constant hurry and rush." "Our children must be promoted as rapidly as possible," say the parents. The consequence is "a want of thoroughness in the instruction, which the committee lament as one great defect" in their schools. And at p. 19 of the same Report, "the cause of frequent absences is thus adverted to:—

"Some allowance must be made for the fluctuating character of our population, and the fact, that many children, under the age of 14 years, are in the schools but three months in the year.* But these facts do not furnish the whole cause. May it not be frequently observed in the ready indulgence of parents — the permission of absence on trivial excuses? We are not in a position, nor would we assume such, to dictate to parents in a matter of personal duty, as this is. But we would suggest to them, that a too ready compliance with their

---

* By the "Factory Act" of the State of Massachussetts, no child under the age 15 years shall be employed in any manufacturing establishment unless such child shall have attended some public or private day-school, where instruction is given by a teacher qualified according to law to teach orthography, reading, writing, English grammar, geography, arithmetic, and good behaviour, at least one term of eleven weeks of the twelve months next preceding the time of such employment, and for the same period during any and every twelve months in which such child shall be so employed.

children's wishes in a matter like this, or some transient whim of opposition to the teacher's mode of discipline, or some caprice of disin-
clination, is not altogether for the children's benefit.   *   *   *
Parents, who are mindful of their children's interest, and of the
character and progress of our schools, will not be negligent in respect
to such a subject as this. We commend it to their respectful attention.
If our school advantages are worth anything at all to us, they are
worth improving. Our schools are supported at a large expense; the
services of competent and faithful teachers are secured. It certainly is no mark of respect or appreciation to allow such frequent
absences as now occur."

The exertions of the "Truant Commissioner"—an officer appointed by law to send "truants and absentees" to school—are
highly commended in the Reports of the Lowell School Committee for
1854 and 1856.

In the first of those years the Commissioner had disposed of 788
truants and absentees; of whom 166 were of American and 620 of
foreign parentage. Two of these were sent to the House of Employment and Reformation for Juvenile Offenders for two years, three for
one year, and four for six months. The rest were sent to school, except four for whom employment was found.

According to the Commissioner's Report for 1856, he had disposed
of 876 truants and absentees; of whom 236 were of American and 640
of foreign parentage.

And the Committee justify the employment of this kind of agency
by stating (p. 20 of Report for 1856) that they have in Lowell "the
class of vagrant children,—almost as proportionately numerous here
as in larger and older communities,— exposed to the same perils, and
growing up to be the same dangerous classes with those that are to
be found in other cities in the land. If there are ten or fifteen thousand of such children in New York, there is a proportionate number
in Boston and Lowell."

In the Reports of the "Controllors of the Public Schools of the City
and County of Philadelphia" for the years 1852 to 1856, the notice of
the "Night Schools" presents several points of interest. The following is the account given of them in the Report for 1852 (p. 14):

"The night schools, into which are admitted adults as well as
minors over 14 years of age, who cannot attend the day schools in
consequence of being compelled, by force of circumstances, to engage
in some employment, having been in operation for the past three years,
may now be regarded as a part of the system of education in this
district. The desire manifested by those entitled to their benefits, to
avail themselves of the privilege, indicates that much good is effected
to individuals, and a happy influence produced upon the community
through the instrumentality of these schools.

" These schools were opened about the 20th October, 1851, and
closed the early part of March, 1852.

" The number of teachers employed were 43 males and 150 females.

" The number of pupils in attendance 7161.

"The average age of the pupils was, males 17 years 11 months, females 16 years 11 months.

"Of the whole number admitted 4063 were of foreign birth, and 3898 were born in different parts of the United States.

"The cost of supporting these schools during the past year was as follows:—

Salaries of Teachers - - -	$13,106 90
Superintendence and Cleaning -	2,660 63
Books and Stationery - - -	1,774 80
Making a total of -	$17,542 33

or $2 20 for each pupil for the term."

The Report for 1853 gives the following account of these schools for the past year.

"The night schools may be regarded as a highly important part of the system in this school district, affording as they do, to those to whom circumstances may have denied the advantages of education in early life, to supply that deficiency to a useful extent, as also to those whose necessities will not permit them the privilege of attending the day schools, to share the benefits of that mental training so necessary to fit them to become useful citizens, while society also shares the advantages which are sure to follow.

"While there is abundant reason for congratulating the community upon the beneficial results which have attended the establishment of these schools, there is nevertheless cause to regret that the attendance of the pupils is as a general rule too irregular to be productive of the same advantages that would follow from a more regular attendance; it is therefore earnestly urged upon the sectional directors to use their efforts to correct, so far as they can, this evil, and upon parents, guardians, and masters, to aid by their counsel and influence, and if need be, by the exercise of their authority, to secure a more general and punctual attendance upon these schools.

"The number in attendance upon the night schools during the winter of 1852—53, was, males 5776, females 1996, total 7772.

Average age, males 17 years 4 mos., females 16 years 9 mos.

Born in Philadelphia,	males 2404,	females 831,	total 3235 ⎫			
Other parts U. States,	„ 1083,	„ 369,	„ 1452 ⎬		4687	
Of foreign birth,	„ 2286,	„ 796,	„			3085

Total,   7772

"Of this number when admitted there were

638 males and 315 females	who could not read, ⎫							
769 „ „ 112 „	who could not write, ⎬ - -							1127
1164 „ „ 779 „	who were entirely ignorant of the							
use of figures	- - - - - -							1397

2524

While the remaining number of those admitted had a very limited knowledge of either of the studies named.

" Of the whole number at the close of the schools there remained but 151 males and 79 females who could not read,

478 „   97 „   who could not write,
153 „   112 „   who were unacquainted with the rudiments of arithmetic.

" The want of success on the part of these may be attributed to their irregular attendance.

" The cost of supporting the night schools, as appears by the foregoing statements, was $16,907 02 for 7772 pupils, or $2 17½ for each pupil for the term."

In the Report for 1854 very few particulars are given of the night schools. The numbers attending are stated to be 5385, and the average cost per head $3 25.

In the Report of 1855 it is stated that " It is a matter of deep regret that most of the night schools, while in the full tide of success, had been closed for the want of adequate appropriation. * * * The number of adult persons applying for the advantages of the night schools has never been so large as during the last year."

It appears, by the Report of 1853 (p. 14), that in that year a law was passed requiring " a tax to be levied and paid to the county treasurer," for the support of these night schools. No sufficient appropriation was made, and it would seem that the persons above referred to as " applying for the advantages of night schools" had not been disposed to incur the expense themselves.

The report of 1856 mentions that the night schools had been continued " to the extent allowed by the appropriations."

In the years when these night schools were most successful, namely, 1851-2, and 1852-3, the attendance at them was, as shown above, 7961 and 7772 respectively.

During the same years the attendance at the whole of the day schools (Primary, Secondary, Unclassified, Grammar, Normal, and High Schools) was 49,635, and 50,085 respectively.

The population of Philadelphia in 1850 (the latest enumeration) was 408,762. (American Almanac for 1857.)

In the Report of 1853 it is stated that " the cost of supporting the Primary, Secondary, Unclassified, and Grammar Schools, with an attendance of 49,052 pupils, is $6 84 for each pupil."

On the Working of the Staffordshire Certificate and Registration Scheme, and on the best Method of its Extension to all Schools. — By Rev. J. P. Norris, Her Majesty's Inspector of Schools.

I HAVE been asked to furnish the Conference with an account of a scheme which has been in operation for rather more than a year in Staffordshire, having for its purpose the promotion of a more regular and prolonged attendance of children at school.

The scheme may be described in very few words; indeed, its most characteristic feature is its simplicity.

Twice a year the managers of *all* elementary schools in the county are invited to send by post, to two registrars, the names of such children as they can certify to have attended school regularly for at least two complete years subsequently to their ninth birthday. The registrars enter these names in books kept for the purpose, and return by post to each school certificate cards to be given to the children so registered. At the same time, efforts are being made all over the county to induce employers of labour to recognise these certificates, and to give a preference to children who are able to produce them.

More than 1500 children have thus been registered already, and many of the leading employers of labour have promised their cooperation.

Such, in brief outline, is our scheme. I hope, before I have done, to show how it might very easily, with scarcely any cost, and without any legislative interference, be extended to the whole country. But, first, I must describe rather more fully its origin, purpose, and mode of operation.

The scheme grew out of several conversations which I had, in the early part of the year 1855, with the schoolmasters and schoolmistresses of Staffordshire. The subject of these conversations was the early removal of children from school, and the strong desire on the part of the teachers that the Legislature should interfere to check the evil. They pointed to the efforts which had already been made, and especially to the Prize-schemes and to the scholars' certificate scheme, and complained that, beneficial as these schemes had been, and highly as they valued them, yet they had failed to reach the mass of their children, and could in no way be said to have placed the uneducated child under any disadvantage as compared with the educated child in the labour market; concluding that the only remaining resource was an extended application of the principle of the Factory Acts to all sorts of juvenile industry.

In reply, I endeavoured to explain how insuperable would be the difficulty of enforcing such a law, and how futile the law unless enforced; and added, that so far from the resources of voluntary effort having been exhausted, it seemed to me that the first and most obviously necessary step towards obtaining the cooperation of employers had never yet been taken. This step was simply to provide all children who had received a decent amount of schooling with a certificate, which they might produce when they went to seek employment. Until this were done, it seemed to me in vain to expect the cooperation of employers; for any promise on their part to favour educated children would involve themselves, or their agents, in a course of most troublesome inquiries into the previous history of each child who presented himself for employment. If this trouble were reduced to simply asking the child whether he had a certificate of schooling, it was my belief that many employers, who now shrugged their shoulders, and excused themselves on the ground that the thing was impossible, would no longer decline to cooperate with us.

The notion was approved by the teachers, and they expressed their conviction that the plan would be popular, — adding, that even if we only partially succeeded with the employers, yet the mere registration of the children would do good: parents liked to have something to show for their childrens' schooling; and many a mother, who was hesitating whether she would not take her boy away from school, would be determined to leave him a while longer, that he might have his certificate like the rest.

Some of my friends, to whom I explained my views, seemed to see other advantages in the plan. They said the statistics so gained would be very interesting; that public attention was being more and more concentrated on the evil of the early removal of children from school; that *something* was sure to be done ere long; and that, whatever that *something* was, whether in the nature of voluntary effort, or of legislation, such a registration of school children could not fail to be useful, and indeed must almost necessarily form the basis of any further operations.

When they suggested that I should put my proposals into the shape of a pamphlet, I told them that the world was tired of pamphlets, and had ceased to read them; and that a far better plan would be to get the thing tried first over some given area—say Staffordshire; and then, if it were found practicable and likely to answer, we should be in a position to go before the public and say,

" This scheme is not a mere theory; it has been tried and found feasible; if you wish to see it at work, go down into Staffordshire."

This, then, is what we have done. The scheme has been at work for more than a year in Staffordshire, and this Conference affords me my first opportunity of bringing it into more general notice.

I thought I should best explain its purpose by thus giving a brief narrative of its origin. I must now make a more formal statement of the nature of the scheme as developed in Staffordshire; and then I hope to show how easily it might be extended to the whole of the country.

The principles of the scheme may be set forth under the following heads:—

1. The scheme professes to have but one immediate object, viz. to set a mark upon children who are reported to have had a certain amount of schooling. It does not propose any standard of education; it does not profess to define what a child ought to know before he goes to work; it does not aim at raising the standard of instruction. All this it leaves to other agencies already at work. Whatever amount of good the existing schools give to a child within the prescribed period of schooling, with that the Registration Scheme is content. Hence it proposes no examination test, but simply requires that children, in order to be registered, shall have attended school regularly for a certain period.

2. These registration tickets are given to children in the hope that they may prove an advantage to them when they come to seek employment. Now it is clearly in vain to expect employers of labour to give a preference to certificated children over non-certificated children, unless the supply of the former be in some degree commensurate with the demand for children's labour. Consequently, in

determining the period of schooling, regard was had, not
to the wishes of the educationist, but rather to the demands
of the labour market; and therefore the standard of requirement was pushed down to the lowest amount of
schooling that could be considered to have any real value
—two years of regular attendance subsequent to the
ninth birthday.

3. The scheme addresses itself to *all* employers of
children's labour—whether they be churchmen or dissenters, whether they happen to live in districts where
the schools are good, or in districts where they are not
good. It follows necessarily from this, that the scheme
must offer to register children from elementary schools of
all sorts, denominations, and degrees of efficiency.

4. Although it is the intention of the scheme that none
but deserving children should be registered, its administrators disclaim the responsibility of determining who are
deserving children, and who are not. They throw upon
the teachers and managers of the schools the responsibility,
not only of ascertaining the period of schooling in each case,
but also of determining whether the children are deserving
of registration or not. Accordingly, in the circular which
is sent round to the schools, it is stated that—"managers
of schools have a discretionary power of withholding such
certificates in any case in which they are dissatisfied with
the scholar's conduct or progress."

To each of these four principles objections may be
raised, which I wish briefly to anticipate, and, so far as I
can, to answer.

1. In the first place I can imagine that what I hold to
be the chief merit of the scheme, viz. the absence of any
examination, may appear to some to be its great defect.
It may be asked—"why forsake a simple and obvious
means of ascertaining whether the child's time at school
has been well spent or ill spent? If your certificates

guaranteed not only attendance at school, but satisfactory progress while there, you would double their value.

Now in answer to this I ask, do examinations really ascertain the amount of good gained at school in the case of young children ? I wish to repeat here what I have said in almost every Report that I have addressed to the Committee of Council on Education—that the chief good resulting to a young child from attendance at an efficient school, is of a sort that cannot be ascertained by examination. I hold most strongly that, in the case of young children, and especially of girls, the main value of schooling lies, not in the amount of learning acquired, but in the effect which cannot but be produced on a child's character, by living for some years of its life in daily converse with the mind of a wise and good teacher, in a well-ordered society, under wholesome laws, firmly but kindly enforced, where good behaviour is the rule, and misbehaviour a marked exception.

This sort of discipline, or training, or moral culture—call it what you will—is what we wish to secure for all our children before they go to work; and, what is no less important in this matter, it is precisely that side of education which farmers, manufacturers, and employers generally, most value. The question then is, could we ascertain this by examinations ?

Now I quite grant, that in nine cases out of ten, the fact that a school-boy has qualified himself to pass an honest and careful examination in the higher subjects of school work, implies that he has undergone this kind of moral training. Excellence of this sort can hardly be attained without integrity and patient industry ; and in the administration of the Prize-schemes, in which I have been so much engaged, I have always rejoiced to believe that our examination did virtually, to a very great extent, test the moral as well as the intellectual character of the children examined. But in order that this may be so, it is necessary that the examination should be extremely careful, and the standard sufficiently high.

Could either of these conditions be fulfilled in the case of this registration scheme? I think not. The number to be examined would be immense, and the standard must necessarily be very low. The facilities for passing the examination by fraud, or by a few weeks' cramming (if I may use a vulgar word for a most vulgar thing), would be so great and obvious, that the result of attempting it would simply be to discredit, and so break down our whole scheme.

This answer to the question — " Why do we propose no examination?" seems to me so sufficient, that I need hardly pause to point out other reasons for having no examination; as, for example, the great cost of providing a board of competent examiners, and of holding collective examinations up and down the country; and again, the almost insuperable difficulty of finding a standard of proficiency that should suit a mass of children drawn from widely different schools and localities. For these reasons we declined to made intellectual proficiency a qualification for registration. And those who have taken part with me in the administration of the scheme, agree with me in thinking that we owe to this, in a great measure, its success thus far.

2. I now come to the second feature of the scheme, the very limited period of schooling with which we propose to be content. I know it will be objected, that in making this concession to the existing state of things, that in offering our certificates to children of 11 years old, we seem to recognise this as a suitable age for leaving school; that though in many schools they leave before this age, yet that in some they stay beyond it; and that in our en-

deavour to raise the standard of the former, we run the risk of lowering the standard of the latter.

‚ In answer I have only to refer to our prospectus, by which it will be seen that the danger has been anticipated, and provision has been made against it. It is there said that "the scholars should be urged to continue their regular attendance from half-year to half-year; that for each additional half-year's attendance a fresh registration ticket will be issued, marking the increased length of schooling, and that in this way the tickets will go on accumulating value as a school testimonial."

3. Against the third principle of the scheme, which admits to registration children from all sorts of elementary schools, whatever be their denomination, and whatever be their degree of merit, it might be objected, that by putting bad schools on a par with good schools, so far as the purposes of this scheme go, a valuable opportunity is lost of giving a premium to good schools, which would tend to raise the standard of our schools throughout the country.

My only answer is that I would gladly so arrange it, were it possible; but, for the reason stated under this third head, it is impossible. If the scheme aims at embracing the whole field of juvenile labour, it must also cover the whole field whence that labour is drawn. And even if it were possible to confine its operation to any select class of schools, this selection would commit the scheme to more than it professes. It was judged best, therefore, in this as in other matters, to confine ourselves to our one simple purpose, and for the rest trust to the other agencies which are yearly and almost monthly improving the quantity and quality of the means of education offered to the people.

4. After what has been already said about the absolute singleness of purpose which characterises the scheme throughout, I need hardly anticipate any objection to the

fourth principle, in which the administrators of the scheme disclaim all responsibility with respect to the returns made to them.   All responsibility for the correctness of these returns is thrown upon the school authorities.   In these matters responsibility cannot be divided.   The responsibility of deciding who are deserving of registration, and who are not, must rest either with the registrars or with the school authorities.   If the school authorities come to me and ask "What am I to understand by the words 'deserving registration?'"   I answer, it is our especial wish that you should interpret the words with just so much strictness as you may think wholesome and good for your own school.   Different schools will doubtless adopt different standards, according to their state of discipline; and so it may be that as this comes to be known, certificates, borne by scholars from one school, will acquire a higher value than certificates from another school.   This I should regard as fair and right, and in no way impairing the integrity or usefulness of the scheme.

I have now explained the four main principles of the scheme.   I will very briefly recapitulate them.

1st. We do not profess to test the proficiency of children.

2nd. We are purposely content with a small amount of schooling.

3rd. We admit *all* elementary schools to the benefits of the scheme.

4th. The responsibility of the certificate rests entirely with the school authorities.

The first three principles answer the question —

" What are the qualifications of those who are to receive the certificates ?"

The fourth answers the question —

" What authority is to grant them ?"

It will be seen at once that the registrars have in fact no responsibility in the matter.

My first idea was to have the children registered by the registrars of births, deaths, and marriages : but I soon found that this would not do, and that the scheme would be unpopular if they were connected with it. It was suggested that one or two registrars would be better than many, and that they ought, if possible, to be persons whose signatures would give weight to the scheme. It ended in our determining to have two registrars, a *clerical* registrar and a *lay* registrar — giving to each school the option of sending its names to the one or to the other.

Canon Hutchinson, Honorary Secretary to the Diocesan Board of Education, most kindly undertook to be the Clerical Registrar ; and Mr. Hand, the Deputy Clerk of the Peace for the County, most kindly undertook to be the Lay Registrar. To the kind co-operation of these two gentlemen is due, in a very great measure, the success which has thus far attended the operation of the scheme.

I need not enter into the several reasons which led to this arrangement. It is sufficient to say that the two-fold registration helped materially to render the scheme acceptable to all parties, and that the month which I spent in corresponding, first with the registrars of births, deaths, and marriages, and then with the clergy and supporters of schools, before any definite agreement could be come to, helped to show me how impossible it is for a man to foretell in his study what plan is likely to work, and what not; and how essential it is to bring a thing to the test of practice before one can propose it with any degree of confidence for general acceptance.

As I said at the beginning of the paper, the scheme thus far has worked well. The number already registered

(1500) shows that. It is popular in the county; no hostility to it of any sort or kind has been shown (which in England may be counted a rare success). I hear on all sides that the parents set store by these certificates; and indeed this is proved by the very gratifying fact that of the 1500 children registered, 540 have received their second half-yearly certificates, and 157 have applied for their third.

My five months' absence from England has prevented me from sending a circular (as I had intended) to the principal employers of labour in the county, asking for their co-operation. But nearly all with whom I was able to speak on the subject in the course of last year expressed their approval of the plan: and I have by me letters from several of the most influential among them promising to recognise our certificates.

I feel justified, therefore, in bringing the subject under the notice of this meeting; and I am emboldened to hope that if its principles be approved, measures may be initiated by this Conference for its extension over the country.

I will in conclusion indicate the machinery by which, as it seems to me, such a result might be accomplished.

I should propose that a Central Association should be formed in London, representing as many as possible of the counties of England: that this central body should draw up a prospectus of a model County Registration Scheme: that each member of the Association should undertake to communicate with two or three friends of education in the county or counties with which he happened to be connected; and through them bring about the formation of local committees: and that these local committees should organise County Registration Schemes after the proposed model. The scheme might thus by degrees be propagated over the country, very much in the same way that the Reformatory School movement has been.

I have thus traced the origin of the Staffordshire scheme, explained its purpose and leading principles, and indicated a way in which it might perhaps with advantage be extended to other counties.

I have carefully abstained, according to the instructions of our Committee, from proposing anything which would require legislative interference. It seems to me a decided commendation of any scheme connected with popular education that it seeks no support from Government. At the same time, should any gentleman wish to see the scheme so modified as to serve as a basis for a legislative enactment, I have by me a copy of some suggestions which I wrote out in June, 1855, at the request of a member of the Legislature, who did me the honour to consult me, as well as others of my colleagues, on the subject of an extended application of the principle of the Factory Acts.

PART IV.

PAPERS ON HALF-TIME SCHEMES AND EVENING AND
FACTORY SCHOOLS.

——◆——

On the Operation of the Half-Time Scheme in Factories.
By ALEXANDER REDGRAVE, Esq., Inspector of Factories.

THE object of the Conference is to induce employers of
juvenile labour to assist in procuring a postponement of
the period at which children are withdrawn from school,
for the purpose of becoming agents in the productive
power of the country. It is not proposed to invite the
Legislature to establish conditions under which children
shall be employed, or to impose obligations upon parents
or employers which shall compel children to attend school,
but to excite the attention, and to rouse the sympathy of
the employers of juvenile labour to the amount of ignorance now existing, and to commend to their consideration
the adoption of some means or other of ameliorating the
sad state of things which, by universal consent, demands
the most profound solicitude from all who seek to lay the
foundations of a sound national education.

If we had been desired to prepare for general acceptance a scheme which should provide, under the authority

of the Legislature, means for the acquirement of instruction by the children of the labouring classes, it would
have been our duty to propose that all of us should be
required to submit in some degree or other to restrictions,
to which individually we might have some objection, but
in which, for the sake of the great public good to be obtained, we cheerfully acquiesced.   If, for instance, it were
proposed as an abstract principle to be decided upon by
the Legislature, that any child between the ages of 5 and
15 should attend school regularly, or that every child, when
employed in any labour, should attend school daily during
the continuance of such labour, or if the employment of a
child were illegal unless it had previously attended school
for a fixed period, or possessed certain attainments, we
should propose a very considerable interference with the
rights of labour, with the right of earning wages; and it
would require not only very powerful reasoning to convince many persons of the necessity of such an interference
by the Legislature, but a very powerful party in the state
to carry such a proposition.

If I understand the object of this Conference, it is rather
to consider in what manner such an interference of the
Legislature may be rendered unnecessary to awaken the
public interest to this subject, as a question which may be
treated as a private arrangement, but at the same time to
show that this great question of the education of the
children of the labouring classes cannot be left to itself,
that it will not advance without extraneous help, and that
that help must be immediate and effective.

The persons by whom that help can be given are the
employers of juvenile labour.   It would be futile to elaborate a scheme upon paper, which shall apparently provide for the difficulties of securing the education of the
young and of not interfering with their obtaining wages,
without first obtaining the concurrence of employers to the

scheme. The half-time system of education possesses, in the abstract, all the elements of success; but in practice it has entirely failed. It has not been the means of extending the duration of school attendance, and it has driven from labour a vast number of children who have been deprived both of labour and of education. The half-time system supposed that children would remain at school from the age of 8 years to the age of 13; and if that anticipation had been realised, the half-time system would have been a great success; but in fact the *average* length of time during which half-time children attend school is less than the general average of schools under inspection. This will show the extreme difficulty of interfering between the employer and the employed in any manner which imposes restrictions obnoxious to the one or to the other. There is a feature in the half-time system which can only be known by those who have had experience in the working of it. It is not looked upon as a system of education, but as an adjunct to employment. I do not speak of those manufacturers distinguished in their own districts for their benevolent and painstaking efforts for advancing the welfare of their poorer neighbours, nor of the more enlightened and intelligent of the operatives, but I do speak of the great mass of parents who send their children to earn wages in a factory, when I say that they regard the half-time as an incumbrance to their right in the wages of their child. And it is to improve the moral sentiment of this very class that the efforts of this Conference appear to me to be directed. If such be the prejudice of a very large class, it is certainly unwise to seek to extend the influence of such a prejudice. Education ought to stand upon its own merits—if they be not sufficiently attractive to induce parents to appreciate it, or to appreciate it only as an appendage to the obtaining of wages, some other principle should guide us in promoting the education of the labouring classes. The labouring classes do not value education, because they are ignorant of its value; they do not perceive in what manner it can bring happiness to their homes; they do not see that it can add to the weekly earnings of a family. It does not appear to be sufficient simply to announce to the poor man that his children would be happier and better members of society if they were educated; it is necessary to prove the truth of this assertion, to make him feel its truth before the truth becomes apparent to him.

How often is it enforced that the moral condition of the lower classes cannot be ameliorated until their social habits are changed, until decency is introduced into their dwellings, until cleanliness is a system and no longer an exception! It is not expected that the abstract beauty of morality can be admired until the observers have been educated to discern wherein its beauty consists. In like manner perhaps we cannot hope to appeal to the better feelings of parents, and to induce them to retain their children at school until they have been prepared to consider and to find that they themselves will reap advantages by their children's school attendance, over those who have been careless of the education of their children.

As I have before mentioned, it is to the employers of juvenile labour to whom we must look as the chief agents in promoting *voluntary* education. Their influence combined would be all-powerful. To that, however, it would be vain to aspire; a gradual and increasing appreciation of instructed labourers is the most that can as yet be hoped for.

The most prominent of the schemes which have hitherto attracted public attention, are the half-time schemes and the certificate system. To these a serious objection would at once be found in their disarrangement of labour. An employer may be willing to adopt the half-time system, but he will find many difficulties arise which are not easily surmounted. In the first place he will require twice as many children as he formerly employed; in the next place, he has to satisfy the parents with half the weekly wages for their children's labour; the school fee has to be provided for; if left to the parents, they will too often neglect and refuse to pay it; if the employer does not exercise some control over the school attendance it will be irregular, and the absences very frequent. But judging from the effect of the half-time system in factories, employers will cease to employ young children whenever the supply of children of a riper age is sufficient, and thus the half-time system would be valueless to the children. But the chief objection to a voluntary half-time or certificate system, would be the partiality of its adoption. If parents presented a memorial to employers, urging them to adopt the half-time or certificate system, or to postpone the age at which children would be admitted to work, then we might reasonably expect employers, as a body, to concur in such a memorial; but can employers of juvenile labour in the present day, when competition in price is most severe, a competition frequently depending upon the cheapness of manual labour, can they be expected voluntarily to restrict the class from which the cheapest labour is to be obtained? The scrupulous employer refuses the labour of children, and his profits suffer; his competitor accepts the cheapest labour accessible to him, and carries all before him in the market. After all, parents are greater obstacles to the extension of education than the demands of labour; and the great difficulty in the way of a voluntary educational arrangement would be the readiness of parents to consent to the employment of their children without any condition touching their instruction.

The principle of a certificate system is that which I would support as thoroughly sound in principle, as really effective for the children themselves, and as capable of adaptation, with the authority of the Legislature, to all classes of labour in this country. I look to the eventual establishment of the principle that education is not mere attendance at school for one or two years, but that it is sound instruction gained in school or at home ; that the possession of instruction should place the possessor at an advantage compared with him who is ignorant. But a thorough recognition of such a system, which I endeavoured to illustrate in a paper read before the Society of Arts in February last, must be enforced by the Legislature.

Considering the great sacrifice which a voluntary adherence to a certificate system would demand from an employer surrounded by employers of labour, many of whom might refuse to join in the scheme, and whose choice of labour would therefore be unfettered ; considering the objections of parents and their strenuous efforts to obtain, under any circumstances, remunerative employment for their children ; I fear an attempt among a section of employers to adhere to a certificate system would be an unproductive one, unless the certificate were compulsory by law.

In proposing for the acceptance of employers generally any arrangement which may possibly interfere with the economical details of their establishments, or which may possibly require some concession at their hands, it will be evident that such arrangement should be as simple and require as little trouble as possible ; anything approaching to detail should be avoided, for no system of detail can be relied upon, unless the details are satisfactorily cared for. A broad general rule may be followed by general concurrence ; that which requires investigation, invites discussion, creates doubts, and is followed by modified and varied approval.

For these reasons I venture to think that an urgent

appeal to employers of juvenile labour to give the preference to children who have been at school, and to those
who have been for the longest time at school, would at
the present moment have more effect than an attempt to
induce them to adopt the details of a half-time or of a
certificate system.   Such an arrangement would not bind
them to employ none but those children who had been to
school.   It would not demand of them to forego economical
labour, and to resort to a more expensive class of hands; but
it would pave the way for a more comprehensive arrangement hereafter, by accustoming parents to the principle
that education is a necessary antecedent to employment.
It is simply an attempt to prolong school attendance by
inducing parents to send their children to school at an
earlier age than at present.   I cannot satisfy myself that
a postponement of the age at which children should be
employed could be realised with any prospect of success,
except by the authority of the Legislature; but if when
the labour of children were required, it were sought for
at the schools in the first place, I feel confident that the
effect would be to increase the number of scholars very
considerably.   The trouble or responsibility upon the
employer would be very small; when he required fresh
hands (children) a message to the school or schools which
he supported would bring him the supply: to applicants
the answer would be, "We seek our hands from the
school."   If parents found that the usual avenues for their
children's advancement were rendered difficult of access
unless they attended school, the necessity of qualifying
them to earn wages would quicken their appreciation of
school attendance.   A general concurrence among employers to adopt such an arrangement would not lessen
their supply of labour; it would not have the effect of
altering the rate of wages; it would not be a prohibition
of employment of children, because by attending school

they would qualify themselves for it. It is, moreover, an arrangement which has been tried and is now practised by several factory owners, who refuse to employ any children except those who have attended their own schools. These gentlemen experience no peculiar difficulty in obtaining, subject to that condition, a sufficient number of children, although their factories are surrounded by others in which no such restriction exists; and I have heard from Mr. Wilson, the excellent director of Price's Patent Candle Company, that after the rule was laid down by him that the children required for the works should be obtained from the school, " the parents sent plenty of pupils." The experience, moreover, of the progress made by the children employed by the factory owners to whom I have referred, warrants the assertion that the previous school attendance has been of essential service compared with the ordinary schools attended by factory children; the attainments of the children in these particular schools are far in advance of the children attending the ordinary schools.

If the voluntary postponement of the age at which children are withdrawn from school be of somewhat difficult attainment, it is still an object of scarcely inferior importance to promote at any age the prolongation of school attendance. Perhaps I may be permitted to urge that the establishment of a feeling in the minds of the lower classes that education will lead to employment, that without some attempt to obtain it children will not readily find employment, will prepare the way for an extended use of certificates; that it will tend to eradicate many of the objections which now exist, from the value of education or school attendance being considered by parents as a matter rather of sentimental than of material benefit to children.

An appeal to the employers of children, many of whom

are enlightened and earnest advocates of education, showing how they may be able to advance the cause of national
education with little interference in the economical arrangements of labour, coming from a body of gentlemen
constituting this Conference, would be received with respect, and be considered with an earnest purpose; and
I humbly conceive that the fundamental principle of your
recommendation should be the greatest amount of good
that can be obtained with the least possible interference
in the relations between the employer and the employed.

On the Principles to be observed in Schemes for promoting School Attendance. By the Rev. W. J. KENNEDY, Her Majesty's Inspector of Schools.

SIR,—I propose to offer to you the results and deductions of my experience, generally, respecting the working of any voluntary machinery for the promotion of education, and in particular, respecting the value of schemes for awarding prizes and certificates to children with a view to create among their parents an appreciation of education, or of schemes for inducing employers to give a preference to the holders of such certificates.

My object is three-fold. First, To caution against too sanguine expectations from the schemes now being agitated. Secondly, To suggest the principles requisite to be observed in any efficient plan for promoting school attendance. Thirdly, To suggest a feasible and efficient plan for promoting this important object.

I entertain no doubt whatever that during the last quarter of a century the attendance at elementary schools has gone on slowly but steadily improving,—improving in respect of the numbers in schools, in respect of regularity of attendance, and in respect of the age at which children leave school.

I also entertain no doubt but that many of our poor children never go to school, and that far greater numbers go so irregularly, at such wide intervals, that their schooling is worthless.

Non-attendance and irregular attendance — here are two serious evils.

What are the causes?

What are the remedies?

The causes are patent. But, omitting certain minor causes, they are now mainly three.

1st. The indifference of parents arising from their not being themselves educated, and therefore having no conviction, no inward sense, of the value of education. This moral deficiency, and not want of love for their offspring, renders them careless and negligent about their children's schooling.

2nd. The poverty of parents, and consequent inability to pay school fees; which poverty also induces them to fall in with what I will call the

3rd cause of the evil, viz., the demand on the part of employers for juvenile labour, which checks and stops the attendance at school, even where the parents are not indifferent nor too poor to pay the fees.

These are the main *causes* of the evil.

What are the *remedies?*

One thing is clear, that the remedies (if any direct remedies can wisely be applied) must be brought to bear upon two parties; upon parents, to remedy indifference, or poverty, or greed; and upon employers, to remedy the demand for juvenile labour.

Here, then, we have two parties to deal with, parents and employers.

This brings me to the declared objects of this conference, and of this section in particular.

I. One of the proposals is to carry into extensive operation the scheme devised by that truly excellent man, Mr. Sey-

mour Tremenheere, viz, for the educated classes to form
voluntary associations, and by means of public examinations, of prizes and certificates, and a show of zeal for education, to act upon the minds of the parents among the
poorer classes, in order to dissipate their indifference, and
inspire them with such an appreciation of education as
shall induce them to send their children to school, and that
with regularity.

Such associations, effectively worked, must do some
good, both in respect of the end in view, the promotion of
school attendance, and in other ways. I have been connected for some years with such an association, and I believe it has been to some extent useful.

Pardon me, however, while I express my fears, while I
endeavour to show, that such associations are not likely to
extend far or to last long. It is with diffidence that I differ
at all from such a person as Mr. S. Tremenheere; and to
point out difficulties is a disagreeable and invidious task,
but perhaps not altogether a useless one.

First, then, my experience convinces me that in the
working of any voluntary association, it is important that
the machinery should be very simple, and should not involve much correspondence, and many details. But in
the carrying out of these prize schemes year after year,
there is requisite the active co-operation of very many
persons, the arrangement of numerous details, and the
careful discharge of much laborious work. And all this
has to be done, not in one single case at a head office,
but in the case of each one of all the hundreds of associations which would be necessary to be formed.

Secondly, all this work, all this machinery, involve much
annual expenditure; for, to say nothing of the expense of
the annual prizes, it never has been found that such work
can be kept up, even if it be started, without duly paid
officers, &c.

But what hope is there of raising the necessary annual incomes for all or even for many such associations?

The voluntary principle is often found efficient for a single grand effort, to raise one large fund by a great spurt (so to speak); it is *not* found adequate for sustained energy and annual drains of money. The few cases in which it is found at all adequate for annual money calls, are those in which there is some building and institution to be kept up, or in which the object is strictly religious, especially if the religious object bear a party character. But it is now pretty generally felt and thought that the voluntary system is overtaxed and overstrained even in these cases. Educational associations, even under the best auspices and circumstances, have never flourished. Look to Diocesan Boards; are they flourishing? Look even to the training colleges; have they a superabundance of voluntary annual support? Nay, look even to the Mother Society in Church Education; has the National Society, in spite of its prestige, in spite of all its machinery of clerks and collectors for raising funds throughout the country, has it a large income? I regret to say that these bodies are all, more or less, allowed to languish for want of funds.

It may be that certain jealousies and rivalries impede the efficiency and curtail the incomes of Diocesan Boards and training schools, and the National Society; but all these same jealousies and rivalries will exist in Prize Scheme Associations, with the superadded heartburnings of clergyman against clergyman, manager against manager, and teacher against teacher, causing the love of many to wax cold.

Add to this, these Prize Schemes assume that the great body of the educated classes are in very great earnest in behalf of national education. It is, however (to say the least), doubtful whether such be the case. I am one of those who think such earnest feeling is confined to the few, and that a general zeal for education has yet to be created. I could bring forward various evidences of various kinds in support of what I say. I will mention one fact only. In 1853 the government brought forward a bill giving corporations the power to levy a rate for the support of all the schools in their towns. Adequate annual support for schools was then the first great want— a want which has since led government to give the capitation fees. Nevertheless, I am told that not one corporate town petitioned in favour of the bill; and that, in fact, not one was disposed to support it.

Such are some of my grounds for fearing for the success of Prize Schemes. What I would advise then is not to abandon the effort to carry them on wherever there is a special opening for them, but not to attempt to get up a cry and to excite a *furore* in their favour, and so set them on foot on any grand scale. Let the beginnings be small and humble, advisedly so; then, if there is any principle of life in them they will GROW.

The greatest help to the success of Mr. Tremenheere's Prize Schemes would be, if they could be hooked on to and worked by some stable, permanent institution. Thus, a great hit has lately been made in middle-class education. An enlightened and benevolent man, Mr. Acland, had been for some time planning and fostering public examinations and prizes in connection with middle schools; but the good he had brought about would have died with him, if not before, had it not been for the judicious and successful advice of Mr. Temple, who has got these middle-school examinations attached on to those deep-rooted and stable bodies, the Universities, thus securing for them a permanent character and position. But I see little opening of this kind for elementary school examinations and certificates: and it is a truth of universal application that deep-rooted social evils, like the one we are now considering, cannot soon or easily be eradicated. The amelioration of a long standing social evil is not to be effected by spasmodic efforts, fitful zeal, or *dilettante* associations, and still less by the mock zeal of ambitious aspirants; it must be the work of long years, effected—if effected—by some agency which operates with the regularity and persistency of a law of nature.

The best and only hope of much good from such schemes is, if, at some future time they should form one item in a legally established national system of education.

II. This section of the Conference does not propose to touch the second cause of the evil, viz., the poverty of parents and consequent inability to pay school fees. I therefore pass on to the other scheme treated of in this section, which proposes to act upon the difficulty thrown in the way of national education by the employers of labour.

The employers are to be asked to combine, and to engage to give a preference to those young people who hold educational certificates, even though the employment be one of physical strength or manual skill.

The deficiencies of this scheme seem to be,—

First, that it assumes that it is feasible to grant universally educational certificates; certificates, too, which are worthy of reliance, as being true and fair: all which appears to me to be more than doubtful.

Further, I would observe that it has been found that employers, especially the small capitalists (who are very numerous), will not fetter themselves in the labour market. Their grand object in the eager competition, the life struggle, with home and foreign rivals-in-trade is, not *educated* labour, but *cheap* and *skilled* labour, and skilled manual labo uris constantly found among the uneducated.

Moreover, it looks like a hardship upon an honest industrious lad, perhaps the support of infirm parents, to shut the door of labour in his face, for want of a school certificate.

But even if local associations could be organised by which employers of labour should all agree to give a preference to those who could produce certain school certificates, and if the certificates could be universally and fairly awarded, I fear the scheme would prove futile. Such associations could never be anything but local, scattered here and there. But our population—especially our town population—is very migratory in its habits. And both those who held certificates, and more particularly those who did not, would be ever shifting to places where there would be no question of certificate or no certificate, but all would be on an equal footing.

The late lamented Lord Ellesmere, wishing to improve the education of his colliery children, laid down the benevolent and well-intentioned rule, that no child should be employed in his collieries under the age of 11 years, though the law prescribes 10 years only. But this local rule proved nugatory, because the parents either moved away, or sent their children between 10 and 11 years old to neighbouring pits. Thus all Lord Ellesmere effected was to do himself a pecuniary injury, by not employing boys under 11 years; and the rule proving useless as well as injurious, was of course abandoned.

But such voluntary local associations to impose certificates, or other tests, as a condition of employment, are not merely futile; their operation is always unfair: because it is found that employers ever evade their own rules of this sort, unless the evasion is punishable by law; indeed, they evade them even then, as I well know. The reason why the half-time system of cotton and silk mills has worked well, on the whole, is, because its operation was enacted by law, and universal throughout Great Britain, and because it has been closely watched and diligently superintended and worked by paid officers, like Mr. Leonard Horner and others.

Consider, moreover, that while school fees remain high (as they unfortunately do in some places) the want of education and non-possession of the certificate may result from poverty. This is no fanciful case, but one of far greater prevalence than is usually supposed. In 1851 it was ascertained by a very intelligent person, the chief constable of Salford, in a personal house-to-house visitation, and from diligent inquiries about each case, that there were 1111 children between the ages of 2 and 14 in that borough who were wholly uneducated, from undoubted inability on the part of the parents to pay the school fees; besides those who were absent from school owing to other causes. I ask you whether these poor children ought to be excluded from employment because they cannot produce school certificates?

We must not forget, too, that such a scheme, if it were universally acted upon, might seriously narrow and otherwise affect the labour market. I don't see how it could fail to do so; but any experiment on the labour-market in a country like ours is not to be made lightly.

For these reasons, because the scheme has failed where it has been tried,—because its operation (when attempted on a voluntary and partial system) must be futile and unfair,—because it would often be a punishment on meritorious poverty,—and because it would tend to interfere with the labour market; for all these reasons I should say that no attempt ought to be made to effect local combinations of employers for the object of giving preference to those candidates for employments who produced certain so-called certificates of education. And my conclusion is, that as regards influencing the employer, we ought not to attempt any direct influence at all by means of voluntary associations.

III. Not that I am in favour of compulsory attendance; far from it: because it is opposed to the genius and temper of our people, particularly perhaps in the case of the population of our northern counties.

Asiatic races bow to authority, the Celtic races readily combine into organised political communities and lose their individuality in the state of which they form atoms. The Anglo-Saxon people retain their independence and their individualism (if I may so speak) in a high degree. They neither readily bow to masters, nor lose their individual completeness in the life of the state. Transplant a Lancashire man to-morrow to the backwoods of Canada, America, or Australia, he feels no want of the highly organised political and social life he left behind. He feels as complete in his state of squatter and backwoodsman as he did in England. But hence, for one reason, the extraordinary repugnance which such a race would feel to compulsory state education.

Another chief reason for deprecating state compulsion I have already alluded to; I mean, the danger there is in interfering with the labour-market. Those who are not conversant with commercial subjects can hardly imagine what an enormous difference may be created in the commercial world by what might seem a trifling matter. To take one instance: — Grievous mischief, in a merely educational point of view, arises from the children going into coal mines at 10 years of age. But if any legislative interference should cut off the labour of these children, who shall say what rise there would be in the cost of coal per ton? Then, if the price of coal rose, it would affect not only the comfort of the poor at their firesides, but would very seriously affect our manufacturing interests in every branch, whether of iron, of cotton, of wool, of silk, of glass, or of pottery-ware,— in short, of almost every important article. I dare not therefore wish for State compulsion as a remedy, unless it be in the mild shape of some very cautiously framed half-time system.

The half-time system of the Factory Acts has worked beneficially on the whole in consequence of its enforcing great regularity of school attendance, while the Print Works Act works injuriously from its not enforcing regularity. But even a half-time system must be extended cautiously so as not to injure the labour market or trench upon personal rights. I see much danger on the side of over-legislation.

IV. Bear with me if at this point I cannot refrain from suggesting to you, on this topic of school attendance, a view of the question which may not have occurred to some now present—a view which is not hopeful and encouraging to us educationists, but which may possibly have something in it.

Have we then in England any reason or any right to expect that the labouring classes shall be generally well educated. Is it consistent with our manufacturing pre-- eminence, our commercial greatness ?

There is a reverse side to every picture ; and in all affairs of this world, none of us, I think, can have failed to note that all advantages and excellences seem to have their reverse side, seem to carry with them what may be called a corresponding, or, so to speak, a correlative defect—for the excellence seems almost to imply the defect. Among men, the robust athlete is generally an intellectual dullard ; the amiable disposition is generally infirm of purpose. Among lower animals, the dray-horse lacks speed, the race-horse is not adapted to draught ; the nightingale has dull plumage ; the peacock has a harsh voice. In short, we cannot, we are not allowed to, combine opposite advantages.

In like manner, is not cheap labour, that is juvenile labour, the opposite of an educated people? Can we English cover the backs of half the globe with our cottons, feed half the globe out of our pottery ware, arm half the globe with our muskets, and so on,—in short, outstrip all nations of the earth in manufacturing and commercial enterprise and success, and yet debar ourselves from the cheapness of juvenile labour? Can we undersell all other nations, and yet educate duly our youthful labourers?

I incline to believe that, *to some extent at least,* we must make up our minds to sacrifice the one object to the other. And I don't think that we are prepared to part with any portion of our manufacturing and commercial greatness.

If there be any thing in this view of the case, then we may continue indeed to promote and improve school attendance, and we ought to do so; but we must ever do this *within the limits compatible with our commercial pre-eminence.* Our natural productions, our position on the globe, our sea-bord, our personal qualities seem to destine the English to be the greatest manufacturing and commercial people of the world. We must follow up our destiny.

This may seem strange advice from one, like myself, devoted in every way and on all accounts to promoting the education of the working-classes; but I have an illustrious example in the advice given by the great artistic poet and peaceful shepherd Virgil to his countrymen, whom he bade to neglect both peace and the arts, and to follow the manifest bent of their genius, viz., war and empire,

> " Excudent alii spirantia mollius æra,
>   Credo equidem : vivos ducent de marmore vultus ;
>   *   *   *   *

Tu regere imperio populos, Romane, memento :
Hæ tibi erunt artes ; pacisque imponere morem,
Parcere subjectis, et debellare superbos."*

V. To sum up : If what I say holds good, then the principles which should be observed in any scheme to remedy the evils of non-attendance at school seem to be the following :—

I. The scheme, especially if a voluntary one, should be simple in machinery and operation. But

II. It must *not* depend upon precarious voluntary annual subscriptions.

III. On the contrary, it should be connected with some moneyed body, for it must have paid officers, as well as many other expenses.

IV. It must be connected with, and worked by, some permanent body, for social evils are not remedied save in long years.

V. It must not trench upon personal rights or commercial interests.

VI. It should not be brought to bear directly upon, or interfere with, employers of labour : unless it be by some very cautiously framed legislative measure for securing a regular attendance.

VII. It should be brought to bear upon parents, with a two-fold operation, viz., operating with a view to dissipate their *indifference*, and operating where necessary to remove the *plea of poverty* by supplying the school fees.

All the seven foregoing principles would be observed by the following plan :—

Let the country be marked out into educational districts, either Poor-law Union Districts or others. Let

---

* The foregoing remarks point to the immense importance of Night Schools. They do not take people from work, and they keep them from mischief while they improve and interest the mind.

there be legally established an officer in every district, whose sole duty shall be to attend at two fixed hours every day at his office, to receive applications from parents who profess inability to pay school fees, and who should be bound to spend the rest of his time every day in visiting the dwellings of the poor, in recording the children not at school, and the reasons for it, in communicating with school managers, and in bringing to bear upon the parents of neglected children every possible agency and moral inducement to send their children to school.

Where necessary, let him be empowered to pay the whole or part of the school fees.

This plan, if any, would surely sweep all our children to school, and would keep them to it with regularity.

1. It would be simple in machinery and operation.
2. It would not depend on precarious annual support.
3. It would have paid officers, and a moneyed body to rely upon.
4. It would be worked by a stable permanent body.
5. It would trench upon no personal rights or commercial interests.
6. It would not coerce or otherwise interfere with employers of labour.
7. It would operate upon parents, rousing them from indifference, and where necessary aiding their poverty.

I might add, that it would carry with it many incidental advantages.

It would provide the most complete statistical facts about the attendance and non-attendance of all children at school which can possibly be devised.

It would add enormously to the funds of schools by filling them with children paying the school fees.

Finally, I will only add that this scheme is being tried,

in all its essential features, by a voluntary body, and with the most complete and triumphant success.

In Manchester an association has been quietly at work for the last three or four years, making no noise, but employing paid agents, to visit parents and sweep the neglected children into school. Three thousand such children are at this moment thus sent to school, who would not otherwise be there. The parents are left free to choose the school. In many cases the parents are now paying all, in others they pay half the school fees. The regularity of the children's attendance is secured by simple machinery. And 1200 a year is added to the schools at which these 3000 children attend.

I know of no other voluntary association, of no other scheme, of equal value for the promotion of school attendance.*

But knowing the precariousness of any mere voluntary association dependent on annual subscriptions, I am anxious to see the same work done, but done by some permanent institution of the country.

W. J. Kennedy.

* Persons who might desire further information about this scheme, would do well to apply to E. R. Le Mare, Esq., Manchester.

On Factory Schools. By J. FAWKENER WINFIELD, Esq.,
one of the Hon. Secretaries of the Birmingham Educational Association.

I SHOULD not have presumed to address so large and influential an assembly as the present had I not for many years past given much practical attention to the great and vital subject of juvenile education; and being intimately connected with a large number of the industrial classes in the town of Birmingham, and having had last year the honour of assisting to found in that town an association for the removal of obstacles to education,—an association which has done, and is doing a great work, whose influences will extend far beyond a county or borough boundary,—I venture to ask your attention for a short time to the subject of the importance of Evening Factory Schools.

Thankful indeed I am to see the great and good of the land assembled here together to discuss the question of questions of the present day. It is a bright sign of the times in which we live to find in this metropolis,—while statesmen cannot agree upon any great national plan of education,—to find men of all opinions meeting in conference together as the friends of the working classes to devise means for the improved education of the working classes.

Good it is to try to reform juvenile criminals. It is better rightly to educate juvenile vagrants, to place the power, naturally given to the parent, in other hands when that parent does not use it aright, and thus brings up his children as a nuisance, and eventually a vast expense to the country; but it is better still to frame measures by which the children of our honest hard working artisans can be usefully educated, and led in right paths—to devise plans by which we can hope that when we are gone, our places will be supplied, and our workshops filled, by an educated and a Christian people. I venture to urge upon you the importance of evening factory schools. I speak from my experience in the town of Birmingham, but hope that the experience of others in large manufacturing towns will agree with my own. To quote the words of Mr. Horace Mann, which have been so well referred to by the Rector of St. Martin's, Birmingham, in his letter urging the establishment of evening schools in connection with the noble institution founded in that town by King Edward the Sixth:—

" There can be no doubt but that evening schools form a very important part of educational provision. When it is considered that the principal obstacle to the continued education of the working classes is the great demand for early labour causing constant occupation through the day time, it would seem that evening schools presented just the remedy required. It is indeed objected that the previous toil is likely to unfit the child for study; but a well conducted evening school might easily make study so attractive as to be in truth a recreation."

On reference to the statistical tables recently issued by the Birmingham Association, to which I have referred, I find that in one district of one-fourth of the poorer classes of scholars, their day school life ceases at 9; that of nearly two-fourths their school life ceases at 11, and that after this age barely one-fourth of the number, who would come from the families of the more respectable artisans, have prolonged their education to between the ages of 12 and 13. Children are brought to work at the average of 9½ years. For the 32 per cent. of children who are vagrant through the poverty, the indifference, or the vice of their parents, we trust legislative enactment will soon find useful and effective provision.

I feel most strongly that the early age at which children are brought to work in Birmingham is a great evil. I see many difficulties in the way of remedying it. I know the objections raised to a factory act in the hardware districts, but I do hope that employers generally will unite to see if something cannot be done.

The limited means of parents compel them to send their young children to work at an early age. The 2s. 6d. or 3s. a week they earn is of great importance in aiding the family fund. It is hard for a parent, earning from 16s. to 25s. a week, with a large family crying for daily food, to allow his feeling for their mental improvement to predominate over his desire to feed and clothe them, which, without their united help, he could not do. Again, manufacturers who employ juvenile labour *could* set apart portions of each day in the week for the education of the children in their works, but deduction could not be made from the wages of the children as an equivalent for such time devoted to education and thus lost from work; and in these days of great competition, when each man is trying to increase demand by underselling his neighbour, I fear there are few who would be inclined to give not only the time in the day and provide the instruction, but also suffer the more serious loss which would result from change of hands. Generally speaking, in hardware manufactures, children wait on the workpeople and "feed" the machinery. From the result of inquiry that I have made among manufacturers in Birmingham in the button, steel toy, hook and eye, pen, and jewellery trades, I find that change of hands would be attended with inconvenience and loss.

In the branch of trade with which I am connected, generally termed brass and iron founding, we could easily dispense with early juvenile labour; but I am convinced that in Birmingham trades as a whole, as their organisation now exists, remembering they have a foreign as well as a home competition with which to contend, the employment of children is necessary. I give the fullest force to all these and other objections, and I long for the day when the hardware districts will adopt some general measures by which a longer education can be given to the children. Looking then at our statistical tables, and at the present employment of children at an early age, I think I have a good case on which to prove to you the importance of evening schools, and evening factory schools in particular. If evening schools do not exist from a very early age, the education of these little " workers " is neglected. As a rule, work ceases in Birmingham at seven in the evening. I wish the manufacturers there would all combine and say, as regards our children, it shall cease at six; for then our evening schools would be more effective than they are. If there are no schools, where do our children released from work go? I ask all who know large towns to remember the temptations which exist for the young in them.

Look at the saloons, the gin palaces, the penny theatres. Look at the number of children who frequent these places. Is it not better to provide more wholesome attractions? Is not a school better than the street? Look at the children workers in the day who swarm the streets by night. If evening schools were more general, would not this evil in a measure be obviated? From the evidence of our zealous and devoted clergy and ministers of religion in Birmingham, we find that, with few exceptions, evening schools connected with places of worship are inefficient.

They fail when conducted on the voluntary system. Teachers and masters must be paid; and at the commencement of such schools the attendance of scholars should be compulsory. Ministers of religion have not the power to compel attendance; masters of manufactories have. I therefore conclude that, as evening schools are desirable, evening factory schools are the best to remedy the evils which arise from the too early employment of children. For excessive hours of juvenile labour I think there is no excuse, and I do not envy the masters who desire to get rich from the destruction of mind and body of children toiling from an early till a late hour, with no change.

In conclusion, I venture to bring before you a case which will prove the truth of my remarks. I am one of the owners of one of the largest works in the kingdom for the manufacture of varied kinds of hardwares. About fourteen years since, being deeply interested in the condition of the youths we employed,—seeing from their conduct in the shops and their rude behaviour on leaving work, their deficiency in education, we established, with a view to their improvement, an evening school on the voluntary principle, with voluntary teachers—voluntary, not compulsory, attendance. This did not answer: teachers and boys were most irregular: little good resulted. We found, as many others have done, our plan a failure. The lads paid a penny each week for their instruction, and they too often brought the penny and said to the master, that will do, I shall go home. In about a year after our first commencement, we again started on a new plan. We built large, well ventilated, and comfortable school-rooms; engaged a well trained, certificated, and highly competent master and teachers, the sole duty of the former being to attend to the evening school, and to visit the homes of the boys during the day. We have a good organ and full instrumental band, and every quarter give concerts. We make it a rule that every lad in the works under the age of 18 shall attend school,—indeed, when they are engaged it is a part of the agreement; they can only leave the works in an evening by an order from the school-master.

We endeavour to give them a useful practical education,—a sound religious and moral training,—an education adapted to the meanest capacity, all based upon the Bible,—a religious, not a sectarian education. Our lads, in number between 200 and 300, as a rule come to work at eight in the morning. They have ten minutes at eleven o'clock, one hour and a quarter for dinner, half an hour for tea. At seven in the evening the bell rings, they all go to the washing rooms for half an hour; at half-past seven school commences by singing, accompanied by the organ. We teach them reading, writing, arithmetic, drawing, grammar, and, composition, making them write letters and themes, and, from dictation, geography and history. We have occasionally lectures upon practical philosophical subjects. We have half-yearly examinations, and give three prizes in each class. We close school at a quarter to nine with singing and prayer. We have regular school on Monday, Wednesday, and Friday; drawing taught by a master from the Government School of Design on Thursday; vocal music on Tuesday; instrumental on Saturday afternoon, when all our people have holiday. Drawing and music we teach as a reward for good conduct, and the attendance is not compulsory. We give the whole education free. Each month I meet the teachers, and carefully examine the state of their classes. In the summer we frequently take the lads into the country in the evening, and have six weeks holiday in the year. Our school-rooms cost about 180*l.*, and the whole expense of the school averages annually from 200*l.* to 300*l.*

The head-master has a register of all the boys admitted

into the works, and, if any are absent, looks them up and reports to the principals. We make it a point to personally attend the school regularly.

Now what are the results?

Taking, as an average number for the past twelve months, 230 boys as in regular attendance, I find that, on admission, taking their ages from 10 to 18,—and by far the larger number of our boys are on admission from 12 to 16,—that

> 19 could read well,
> 58 could read fairly,
> 98 could read a little,
> 55 could not read at all,
> 187 attended Sunday schools;

showing that 15 in every 23 cannot read when admitted.

We began by compelling attendance. This is not now necessary, though we continue it as a rule.

Sometimes when, through shortness of work, the youths are not in the works during the day, we find them come voluntarily to school at night. They are anxious to come, and generally grieved to stay away.

Corporal punishment is rarely needed. Their behaviour in school is good; their conduct in the works is changed; we have rarely a case of dishonesty, of bad language, or disobedience to masters. All our foremen notice the marked change. Many are the cases each week which I could bring forward of parents making a personal application for the admission of their children into our works, because they say we are so anxious for them to come to your school, to be kept from evil and to be taught what is good.

I am not drawing too bright a picture; I am giving facts; and we are, from the results, thankful that we have established our evening school.

I am convinced that, looking at such work in the lowest

point of view, money spent in factory schools is well spent. Your people become attached to you. They serve you from a love to you, because they feel you care for their best interests. They are not eye-servants. We have no strikes, no disorder. I have our lads at my house under perfect control; we can trust them, and look upon them all as members of our own family. Workmen and children prove by their conduct their gratitude; and though from knowing our own schools best, I could speak more fully of them did time permit, yet I could go away from them and refer to others, in proof of the success which has attended factory schools.

The noble efforts of our friends the Bagnalls, and the Chances, and others in our district, in furthering the education of their children, the glorious results which have attended these efforts, the self-denying labours of Messrs. Wilson at Price's Candle Company,—men worthy of the highest honour—these and many, many other such instances might be brought forward to prove the vast importance of factory schools, and especially of evening factory schools, as a great remedy for the evils existing. I at once answer the common objection to evening schools, by saying that in our own case we find children not fatigued, but rather amused, by the change of occupation: their country excursions with their teachers they look forward to ; and if in regular school lads get weary, I find it to be the fault of teachers rather than the confinement of the lads. During the hot summer months I make a point of frequently sending them out a country walk. I allow that our school would be better if we commenced at an earlier hour; but if any works are closed at six for children all must be, or it is a loss to those who do close early. I also allow that if we could insure children taking healthful exercise and having good training at home, I had rather release them from school at eight than at nine ; but I only ask any one to walk through the streets of our large towns at night, and to tell me how many children he sees, and how they are employed, and then to tell me if it is not better to provide amusement and instruction in a comfortable room, and exercise under supervision of teachers, rather than turn them loose into the streets.

One great question arises. Admitting the importance of factory schools, how are they to be supported? First of all, if teachers are paid, the Privy Council will give to such schools the benefit of their examinations, inspection, and payment. Every manufacturer, however small, may find some little room for his lads in an evening, and he can give an evening or two each week to teach them himself. He will receive an ample reward: his people will love him and will serve him; and if he has no room himself, there are many ministers who would gladly arrange with him for his children to occupy their school-rooms, which in an evening are too often empty. The working-classes have hearts to feel and hearts to appreciate kindness. If their masters treat them as friends they in return will devote their energies to such masters, energies stimulated by loving and grateful hearts.

I appeal, then, to the great manufacturers of our country, to men who are gaining thousands from the labour of young persons. Capital and influence have their duties; and whatever may be the distance between employer and employed, no elevation of the one can separate their common interests; and those who neglect the interests of others will themselves eventually suffer. If employers will educate their people, their labour and expense will return tenfold into their own bosom; they will give joy and happiness and prosperity to many a dark and desolate home; they will, as faithful stewards, discharge their duties; and they will be blessed and rewarded by Him who loves children, who wills not

that one should perish, and who says, " inasmuch as ye
have done it unto one of the least of these, ye have done
it unto me."

I earnestly and respectfully urge the importance of
factory schools, and especially factory evening schools, as
a remedy for the evil existing in the too early employment of children in manufactories; and I would venture one remark which surely belongs directly to the
subject I have advocated. When I think that, in
our evening school, out of every 23 admitted, on an
average only 15 have been able to read, — and be it
observed that our children are those of the more respectable working classes, — I cannot, in justice, shrink
from the conclusion that some effective measures should
be taken to secure for these children, who must be the
strength or weakness of future generations, some fair
and adequate instruction before they *can* be admissible
into the workshops. Then, indeed, our evening schools,
with a due period of daily labour, may prove, blessed by
God, of incalculable benefit.

On Voluntary Half-time Schemes. By the Rev. C. H. BROMBY, M. A., F. S. S. of Cheltenham Training College.

IN entering upon the questions whether the half-time measure now applied to our factories can be extended to other departments of labour, whether without legislative interference, and within what limits success may be anticipated, we, I fear, must exclude every element of philanthropy, and simply reduce the question to one of profit and loss. We must, in other words, limit our investigation to the inquiry,—How far can we persuade the employers of labour that the half-time measure will not diminish their material profits? In looking for an answer we must keep distinct the different departments of labour. It may be sufficient to recognise three.

(1.) *Factory Labour.* (2.) *Agricultural Labour.* (3.) *Desultory Labour.*

In applying the question first to the department of *factory* labour, there can be no doubt of the true answer. The system of half-time has been tried and found to work well; both as it regards the child and the employer. There is but a single opinion, among those who are entitled to give one, that the experiment, so far successful, should be extended to at least kindred spheres of labour. Wherever a given number of children are employed by the same capitalist, and there exists the facility for marching them from work to school, and from school to work, not only the interests of the children but the interests of the truly-enlightened employer in his relation to a rival employer should be protected by direct legislative enactments. It is an anomalous state of things which many an industrial town presents, where one factory stands by the side of another externally alike, each containing the same inner juvenile life, the one at a given signal sending forth its children to a school where the rights of childhood are respected, the other extorting an unnatural amount of service, and then consigning them to the temptation of the street, or the worse temptation of a neglected home. What has been already done was tentative, and has been unquestionably successful. Extend the experiment so modified as to suit the conditions and meet the wants of other departments of wholesale labour. Collieries, and foundries, and potteries, and glass works, may require an adaptation different from cotton and silk works. In some the half-day, in others the half-week system will interfere least with the interest of the labour-market, and in others, as a *dernier ressort*, the system of the night-schools. The object of this Conference I apprehend to be to step between the legislature on the one hand, and the employer and labourer on the other. It seeks to encourage experiment. If the result shall show that voluntary association is fully successful, the work is done. If it fail, as it will fail to a considerable extent, it will point out where legislation must begin its efforts, and complete by its authority what voluntary association fails to effect by its influence. On one point we are all agreed, that something must be done, if the people's education is to be real and not a sham. All agree that the increasing votes of state money on behalf of National Education afford a deceitful index of progress—that they are devoted to the expensive work of covering the land with a large net-work of schools, which are becoming annually more and more emphatically the receptacles of mere infants, as the demand for juvenile labour is allowed to progress unchecked by any condition which the interests of childhood should impose, and that our Normal Colleges are rearing, at a large cost, effective infant schoolmasters (for they are becoming little else), who shall relieve the mothers of the locality from the duties and cares of their maternity. All agree school-work at present possesses no real or lasting hold, produces no real or lasting effect. All agree that the evil is to be traced to the tender age at which children are removed from school, and that the evil is increasing with the increasing development of British industry, and the consequent demand for cheap, *i.e.*, for juvenile labour. Among all the remedies proposed, there is no doubt that the *half-time scheme*, if practicable, will meet the evil most effectually. At present so frequent is the interruption of school-attendance through the demand for labour, that the teacher looks upon it as vain to inquire into the cause of absence ; and the upshot of it all is that from *short* attendance little is learned, from *irregular* attendance that little is learned imperfectly ; while, in respect of the moral virtues of punctuality, attention, order, discipline (to omit training more distinctly *religious*), the real school-work of England's peasants and artisans is feeble and ineffective, and, in many localities, absolutely valueless. The great and pressing want is not *schools* but *scholars*, not *hives* but *bees*. It cannot be too frequently repeated that the object of this Conference should be to take such *practical* measures as shall supply data to the Government for determining how far *Government aid can* be extended, and where *Government interference must* begin. It is no purpose of this Conference, I apprehend, to condemn the compulsory acts already in operation, or to deny the position that the principles of those acts, if sound and successful, should be extended, as soon as tentative efforts should fail, to kindred fields of juvenile labour. Surely if the principles of those acts are sound, and their working is proved to be beneficial, we should recommend their *extension;* if otherwise, pronounce them at once legislative mistakes, and recommend their immediate *repeal.* Where the parent and the manufacturer take limited views of their own interests, and combine to sacrifice the interests of children to a narrow-sighted *greed,* it is just there where the State should step in. As a question of political economy, none can deny that England's future prosperity requires *skilled and educated workmanship.* Since steam-power has made the accidental possession of mineral wealth — the source of our present greatness —less valuable, in consequence of the easier transport whether of our raw material or manufactured goods, the nation which multiplies the most abundantly her skilled artisans will be the foremost in the future mercantile race. The after duty, then, of the State to herself will be clear when voluntary effort has been tried.

By collecting the opinions of large manufacturers I find that, though they differ, they differ not so much upon the absolute unfeasibleness of the half-time scheme, as upon the degree of the practical inconvenience which will attend its application, and as to the varied modifications required. I take one town of South Wales in illustration. The letter which I read is from a large employer of juvenile labour in Llanelly. [The opinions of large manufacturers were here read from letters, and quotations from a petition signed by almost all the South Yorkshire proprietors of coal mines in favour of the Factory Act.] The Forest of Dean, in my own neighbourhood, would afford an excellent opportunity for making an experiment. The works, extending over a large area, are in the hands of a few capitalists, who, as I am able to state from personal knowledge, take large views, and are deeply interested in the welfare of their workmen. The most extensive proprietor, Mr. H. Crawshay, informs me that "he does not think that an extension of Lord Ashley's Factory Bill is necessary in collieries or mines, simply because children are not allowed to work in them under 12 years of age, and both men and boys work but 8 hours out of the 24, which leaves ample opportunity for self-cultivation or instruction out of school." He adds that night-schools would meet the case most effectually, and that a night-school is to be opened in the centre of his works (Cinder-ford) at the close of the autumn.

The half-time system in the cotton, woollen, and silk districts works excellently. Whatever were the feelings of jealousy with which it was first received, it is now universally popular. The time has now arrived for its extension to other fields of labour, and the only question is, what shall be the *modification* which will secure the favourable co-operation of our manufacturers? Where there is no concurrence among employers in any locality, an evil at all times incidental to voluntary associations, or where employers in one district are favourably disposed towards the half-time, and those in a neighbouring district are opposed, a diversion of juvenile labour would ensue; and the same would be true (till there was time for the evil to correct itself) of those localities where the demand for boys' labour fell short of the supply. On the other hand, in some towns, as in Birmingham, the number of children is such as that the voluntary half-time system would produce a double benefit; it would secure to boys who are now overworked the blessings of instruction, and, by the introduction of relays, it would double the number of those who would be transferred from the alleys and streets into some of the departments of remunerative labour. Most places would fall under one or other of these classes, and they clearly demand different modifica-tions of the rule as at present applied by law to cotton and other manufactures. To prevent the diversion into other fields of industry, where the demand for labour is greater than the supply, a very considerable modification must be attempted; but in the other case, where the supply is greater than the demand, the Factory Act might be applied in its full stringency. No disturbing element, as shown in the time or cost of producing manufactured goods, would be introduced into the labour market; the growth of pauperism would be arrested, and the moral and material interests of society immensely promoted.

Mining Districts.—The provisions of the Factory Act must be very considerably modified to meet the necessities of children grouped in large masses *during eight continuous hours* of the day. I find opinions tending in the same direction among those who have examined the difficulties connected with the working of our mines, viz., an enactment (for such general concurrence would admit of legislative enactment in this case) compelling all boys between the ages of 10 and 14, who work underground, to attend school a certain number of hours every six months, after the precedent of the Print Works Act. My own opinion is that the number of hours should bear an inverse ratio to age. At least I recommend that 150 hours each half-year should be insisted on between the ages of 10 and 12; and 100 hours be substituted between 12 and 14. And here I could lay stress upon the fact that a smaller number of school-hours at a later age is worth much more than a larger number at an earlier age. It is of the first importance that young persons, as the Act calls them, should be kept after 14 a few hours a week. These 100 hours at 14 each half-year, as they tell upon the future man, are worth 200 at 12. The habits of attention and reflection then formed will remain more fixedly through life; the opportunities of good advice and wholesome sympathy will leave a more lasting effect; the means of self-education and the power of retaining what is already learnt in the primary school will be less likely to pass away, and all the benefits of moral and mental education will be more real and abiding. The experience which I have of the working of Sunday schools, and of their tendency, though sadly inefficient to keep alive the power of reading, convinces me that four or five hours a week at 13 or 14, and much more at 15 years of age, by the fixedness which they would give to the habits of discipline and self-control, by the direction they would give of the mind to questions concerning social, religious, and material welfare, would tell immensely upon the interests of real education.

To bring my personal reflections and experience to a practical result, I lay down the following propositions in regard to Factory Labour :—

(1.) The diversified character of manufactures must be considered.

(2.) The *half-time scheme* will be applicable to the more extensive manufacturers.

(3.) The *night-school* must be resorted to in departments of labour (as in collieries and mines) where children are detained during *continuous but less protracted hours of the day*.

(4.) The night-school will also apply best to those localities where employers of boys' labour are smaller and more numerous.

(5.) To make either the half-time school or the night-school effective, all employers should require boys before their engagement, to produce the school certificates that their earlier education has not been neglected.

Rural Labour.—When we pass to the department of rural labour, the difficulty of forming an opinion how far the half-time system will succeed is increased, and we have no actual experience to appeal to, as in those factories to which Lord Ashley's Act applies. Parents attach no value to the education of their children, and employers entertain a positive objection to it. The conversion must clearly begin with the employer. In the case of large landed proprietors, who, like Lord Hatherton, are resolved to employ and to instruct upon the system of relays, all difficulty vanishes. But until farmers can be persuaded that the labourer is not unfitted for his work by education, nor until the practical hindrances can be removed, there is no hope of associating this class in giving effect to any half-time scheme. Our inquiries, then, should be twofold:—

1.—What are the farmers' objections to education?

2.—What are the difficulties that stand in the way of a half-time scheme in the country districts?

In answer to the *first* question, it may be safely said that some of the farmers' objections are futile, and some have a show of reality. Mere unreasoning prejudices are natural to any class of men who, destitute of educational advantages themselves, are jealous of their extension to those classes below them in their own employment. These prejudices will give way as middle class education advances; and it is a hopeful sign that at this moment the farmers are looking with considerable distrust upon their hereditary boarding school. To this want of education in themselves must also be attributed their blindness to the fact that the educated labourer must prove the most valuable, in both a moral and economical point of view, to themselves. All the farmers' objections, however, are not prejudices. Some carry with them a show of reason. The boy who has never been inured to labour before 12 or 14, will, for a season at least, be less capable of enduring the labourer's toil; he will sigh for the ease and luxury of the school-room. This loss the farmer can appreciate, but he cannot appreciate the advantages of geography and history, of which he is himself at the same time profoundly unconscious. This, perhaps, is the farmer's strong ground against the School Managers, the Inspector, and the Council Office. We all believe that the labouring boy may be benefited by the mental training and the taste for self-improvement which geography and history are capable of giving him. But would not other subjects more kindred to agricultural life have served the same end? Would not the embryo labourer feel a deeper personal interest in the rotation of crops, the chemistry of manure, the geology of the neighbourhood, and, above all, land measurement, and the farmer cry, " There is some sense in that education"? And the parent, whose valuation of education must be borrowed from his own and his boy's employer, would more probably make an investment in the shape of a present sacrifice which he could foresee must be hereafter fruitful in a material point of view. If we are not prepared for legislative action, we must adopt the principles of expediency, and expediency suggests whether it would not be wise to propitiate the farmers by cutting down the subjects of instruction to reading, writing, and arithmetic in the rural primary school, superadding in the highest class, especially if it included boys who work upon the half-time system, those subjects of instruction only which will bear upon their after-life. The farmers would abandon many of their more reasonable prejudices if, in the half-time school class, the children were learning daily lessons in practical life one part of the day, and were positively engaged in manual labour during the other, the two dovetailing together — prejudices to which the boy himself, growing up to manhood a more intelligent, a more economical, and a more skilled labourer, would become a living contradiction.

Our *second* question was—What are the difficulties in the way of the half-time scheme in rural districts? We specify three.

(1.) *Distance from school.* (2.) *The fact that the farm-house dinner often constitutes a large portion of the boy's pay.* (3.) *The parent's poverty.*

Distance of the school from the home of the boy, and the distance of both from the scene of labour, present a main obstacle to the half-time scheme in numerous districts.

The proprietorship over the family of the labourer presents another grand difficulty. In innumerable cases the labourer's family lives in the cottage of his employer, and the boys who are engaged upon his acres have their chief meal at the farm, which constitutes a principal part of their wages. The relay system would knock on the head this arrangement, and deal a fatal blow against the feudal right which the farmer possesses to the entire services of his cottage tenants.

These are two principal difficulties,—the evil of distance may be obviated by the system of alternate weeks or days, and in many instances such a system would meet the case. It would succeed in those cases where the employer kept his superintendent of the gang of boys. It would fail where the superintendent was the school officer. Where the difficulties are insurmountable, the only resource is the night school; not, however, the modern night school, which carries with it the elements of self-destruction, but one in which the evil must be avoided of introducing all subjects of instruction except those which have to do with every-day life ; they must *not* be kept by amateurs, nor yet by masters already exhausted with the previous day's school work.

The aim in such cases must be to make the school education *remunerative* in the eyes of the parent and employer. It must be borne in mind that the parent does not object to the schooling of his child, but he does object to sacrifice his claim upon his services; neither will oppose the half-time scheme, if the parent on his side finds it to contribute to the support of the family, and if the farmer on his part is persuaded that it prepares for him labourers who have acquired habits of skilled and disciplined industry. It is, however, impossible to determine the relative advantages of the *half-day* or the *alternate week* plan. The character of the locality, and the feelings of the people, will have much to do with it. If the whole of agricultural England were divided into estates as extensive as Teddesley, and all proprietors were Lord Hathertons, then the half-day system would be universally applicable to the immense moral and material advantage of the whole community. But where the employers are many, and no single overseer can undertake the charge of the relays, the farmer's acres must form part of the school. Pupil teachers, with the master of the school, by a more liberal arrangement of the Committee of Council, might become the subordinate taskmasters of the field, responsible to the farmers, on the one hand, for the execution of their allotted work, and to the parents, on the other, for the earnings of the child. Time would soon convince the reluctant employer that half-day labour is as remunerative as a whole day, for not only would the boy in his moral and physical being delight in the alternation of head and hand labour, longing for the activity of the field when tired of his books, so that his labour would be more hearty and more real, but it would be also the labour of skilled and disciplined hands. In this opinion, I am borne out by all the masters who have tried the allotment system. I have quotations from the letters of masters of agricultural schools, and from the reports of Inspectors of mines and schools. One, writing to Mr. Norris, Her Majesty's Inspector of Schools, to whom not only I, but every advocate of popular education, is much indebted, observes: " The greater number of my

elder boys are now employed out of doors half their time,
and I do not find that they lose any of their book knowledge by being thus employed ; on the contrary, they are
so much more diligent in their studies at school, than if
they were at their books all day, that most of them are in
advance of those few boys who do not work on the half-
time system.   All agree that the boys are active, intelligent, useful, and willing, and that they require no captain,
except the farmer himself, or one of his workmen."   Mr.
Tremenhere, in one of his reports upon mines, and Mr.
Kennedy, before the Committee of the House of Commons,
confirm the position in regard to other departments of
labour,—that the half-time school entails no loss upon the
school-life of the child in consequence of the valuable
regularity that it secures.

In summing up my views, I am compelled to acknowledge that I am unable to furnish definite replies to the
questions proposed in the circular published by the Committee, unless it be the last of the four.   To the first
question,—*Whether certain hours of the day on certain
days of the week for school attendance are to be preferred?*
my general reply is, that where circumstances allow of it,
where distance from school forms no difficulty, and where
the supply of boys' labour is in excess of the demand so
as to allow of relays, the simple division of the day into
school and work is the best.   This rule will apply to large
factories and large farms; but where distance from school
is great, although labour may be redundant, *alternate days
of school and labour are preferable.* Where again, however,
a different state of things exists, as in many rural districts,
and where there are many and petty employers, as well
as in places which admit of the easy diversion of juvenile
employment into other channels of labour where like restrictions do not exist, then, however imperfect be the
regulations, I would follow the more latitudinarian prece-

dent of the Print Works' Act, and be content to bind
employers to so many hours in the half-year, or, what is
better, to so many hours in the week.

In reply to the second question— *Whether the time at
school ought to be greater or less than the time at work?* I
would reply, that before the age of 10 the school-time
should be largely in excess of work-time; that from 10 to
13, school-life and work-life should be, if possible, equal;
and that from 13 to 17, attempts should be made to keep
up attendance at school, if only for some hours a week.

In reply to the third question— *Whether a portion of
the school-time may be taken in the evening?* I have to say,
Yes; in mineral districts and in all unfavourably circumstanced agricultural ones.

To the fourth question— *Whether the appeal in favour of
the half-time scheme should be addressed to the parents or to
employers of children?* I state my opinion most unhesitatingly;—the appeal should be made to the employers.
By their opinions, distinctly expressed in their practical
preference of educated boys to neglected ones, not only
will they directly influence the opinions of the labouring
classes, but they alone will be able to stamp the children's
education with a commercial value.

There are two substantial reasons for this opinion.
First, because parents, themselves uneducated, are little
likely to value the education of their children. The exigencies of poverty, on the one hand, in rural districts,
and the over-abundance of wages in other localities, secured without education, on the other, are not likely to
beget any high value of school in the minds of the parents.
The second reason for beginning with the employer is
this—that the employer knows that, with uneducated
work-people, the increase of wages in prosperous times
leads to an increase of profligacy, and the shirking of the
usual amount of work at the beginning of the week, the

result of which is, that capital is crippled in the hands of the employer, and the cost of production increased to the public. The employer must know that skill and industry advance with the advance of a sounder education, and that subordination, resistance to agitation, and whatever else is calculated to ward off a social crisis at home, and to enable him to keep his own amongst the growing competition abroad, are thereby secured.

In every case, in factories, in mines, or in farmhouses, the first step is to require *an educational test*, or a certificate of two years past attendance at school *before employment; i. e.* before 10 years of age. The Factory Act has overlooked this requirement in factories, though from that age up to 13, it has made provision. In *similar occupations* my opinion is that the same enactment should be at once extended. The foremost and most benevolent capitalists positively desire the law to protect them against the results of unprincipled competition. In *mines* and *collieries* let the Print Works' Act, in a modified shape, be applied, requiring six hours a week to 14 years, and three hours till 18. In agricultural districts, where there happen to be large farms and landed proprietors, the factory system of relays will be the most practicable, while in others less favourably circumstanced, the precedent of the present Print Works' Act should be followed, but with still greater latitude; while in rural districts, thinly populated, outlandish, and impracticable, I am not sure whether I am not prepared even to recommend a system of itinerant schoolmasters, who shall visit different farmhouses on different nights of the week.

There is another feature in the half-time system which I would not overlook — its tendency to promote *moral training*. The highest object of national education, restricting the term to the labouring classes, is not intellectual development so much as the formation of moral habits. Instruction, mental or religious, has no tendency in itself to restrain crime. The daily and hourly practice of self-control, right behaviour one to another, victory over selfishness, are the qualities of real education. Such an education is rarely possible within the walls of a covered school-room, where natural animal restlessness is only kept in check by the fear of animal punishment. The boy, to be really educated, must be educated amid the circumstances of *real* life; and it is in the workshop, and more especially the field, that natural activities will manifest themselves, and afford to the educator the opportunity of their correction and direction. The habit early formed of uniting industrial occupation with mental improvement will be likely to assert its claim when school-life is closed; and the youth formed upon the model of the half-time system will be more likely to look to the Mechanics' Institute or the local night school for the employment of his leisure hours, than the boy who left school at an earlier age, taking away with him no one association of school-life which suggested to him either profit or pleasure.

In conclusion, I cannot withhold the sentiment, that enthusiastic as I am in the advocacy of popular education, my enthusiasm only belongs to it as to one of many instruments of improvement which the present social condition of our people requires. The social evil is too gigantic to be assailed by any single weapon. It has taken its growth in the rapid progress of civilization, the increased luxury of the opulent, the widening chasm and diminished sympathy between class and class, the struggle between wealth and poverty, and the wide destitution of one portion of the poor, which has robbed them of all heart, and mind, and power; and in the habits of intemperance and sensuality of another portion, in imitation of the luxurious living of their social betters. We need new organizations to raise the educational condition of the people, but co-ordinately, and *pari passu*, we need more efficacious instruments for improving their physical condition. The extension of bath-houses and dwelling-houses, the legislative control of Savings' Banks and of Insurance Societies, the restriction of the sale of moral poisons, as well in publications as in beer and spirits, the suppression of places devoted to low debauchery, the parallel encouragement of popular games, concerts, and public parks, and whatever else encourages the hoarding instead of the dissipation of the wages of industry, and so elevates the mind by elevating first the physical condition of the poor, will, at least, in another generation, do more to secure the co-operation of parents on behalf of their children than all the theories and tentative remedies *put together*, and brought to bear upon a mass too sunken and degenerated to value life, except as it ministers to sensual, animal, and transient pleasures. *

* In many instances the children's wages are essential to the parent. This is the case in agricultural districts. On the other hand, the children's earnings induce unthankfulness and improvidence in the parent. Make the parent more provident and grave ; take from him the temptation of trusting to his children's labour. A Paisley weaver out of employment is supported by the earnings of his family, and a correspondent of mine urges the fact against the extension of the half-time system : but teach that weaver to spare something of his abundant wages when in full work, and the necessity would cease for reversing the apostolic maxim — " The children must not lay up for the parent, but the parent for the children."

On the Plan of Juvenile and Adult Education adopted in the Writer's Manufactory. By EDWARD AKROYD, M. P. for Huddersfield.

MR. AKROYD, M. P., wished, as a large employer of juvenile labour, and as one who took great interest in the extension of national education, to state in what way he endeavoured to carry out and extend the educational clauses in the Factory Act. He employed about 1,100 juveniles in his works between the ages of 8 and 13; all of whom, in accordance with the Factory Act, were compelled to attend school half the day, the other half of the day being devoted to work. Now, although their attendance at school could not but be under any circumstances beneficial, he had discovered, that owing to the entire ignorance of the children when they first became short-timers, and to the too early cessation of the period when they are by law compelled to attend school, the results were not so satisfactory as could be desired. He had endeavoured to remedy these evils by establishing an infant school, as a preliminary to factory education, and for children from 3 to 8 years of age, a charge of twopence per week was made; and since the school numbered 380 infants, it was almost self-supporting. The energy and special talent of the trained mistress attracted the confidence of the parents; and as children under 8 cannot be employed in factories, there was no countervailing motive on the part of the parent to take them from the infant school. The charge was paid most cheerfully, and the children themselves attended most willingly. He might further observe, that he had always recognised the importance of not oppressing the infant mind, either with a complication of subjects taught, or too intense and continuous application in teaching; and he had always endeavoured to pay due regard to moral culture and physical development. Supplementary to the factory schools, he had instituted a Working Man's College, for the education, by evening classes, of youths and adults above 13—the period when factory education ceased. The college comprised junior and senior divisions: the former for youths from 13 to 18 years of age; the latter for adults above 18; an arrangement which removed from the minds of the elder students the objection which they naturally felt at being classed with younger and perhaps brighter pupils. The college was under the superintendence of trained and certificated masters, whose abilities and earnestness in their work had secured the respect and esteem of the students, and stimulated in them a thirst for knowledge. There were now about 150 students. As an inducement for healthy out-door exercise, he had encouraged the students to join a Recreation Society, for whose advantage he had opened a play-ground, a cricket-ground, and a bowling-green. He had also opened allotment-gardens, as a tempting and profitable inducement to out-door labour and industrial training. To the more deserving of the students, he annually distributed certificates and prizes — also silver and bronze medals for good conduct. Besides a Working Man's College, he had instituted, with even greater success, evening classes for young women, reserving one day in each week for industrial training, and for the cultivation of useful domestic arts, which were too often neglected in the manufacturing districts.

About 160 young women diligently attended these classes, which were conducted by a well-trained and zealous schoolmistress, whose heart was in her work. Alluding to the certificate system, he remarked, that for two years he had given to the half-timers, when they attained the age of 13, a certificate of their attainments in reading, writing, and arithmetic, stating whether their progress had been " pretty good " or " very good," and also what had been their conduct at school, " good " or " bad." The certificates added a recommendation to the parents to continue children at the evening school or college for at least three years longer. In employing " full-timers," he always gave a preference to those who had satisfactory certificates, placing good conduct as a primary quali-fication. He attached the more importance to this cer-tificate plan, because it was one capable of very general application. If some such certificate were made impera-tive upon all employers, that they should not employ for " full time " any child above 13 without such a pass, under a penalty upon both the employer and parent, a great advance might be accomplished, and a stop put to the evasion of factory education, which the employment of " full-timers," who had never attended school, now permitted. The total number of day scholars and students for whose education he had made provision, was as follows : —

Factory children, from 8 to 13, at Halifax and Copley Mills, about - - - - -	1,000
Non-Factory children, of the same age - -	110
Infants under 8, about - - - -	380
Working Men's College - - - -	150
Young Women's Evening Classes - - -	160
Total - - - - -	1,800

At these day schools were educated the children of parents of all sects and denominations. Whilst, there-

fore, he had been desirous to implant those broad principles of Christian faith and charity which are common to
all Christians, and which lie at the root of Christian
morality, he had guarded against any doctrinal leaning or
attempts to convert the children of Dissenters towards the
Church of England, to which he himself was attached.
For this reason, the catechism was not taught in his
day schools. Doctrinal and special religious teaching
was given on Sunday to about 800 Sunday scholars,
whom he accommodated in his schools.

Rudimental instruction in reading and writing having
been previously disposed of during the week, the whole attention of the teachers of the Sunday-school was devoted to
religious culture. For this purpose he preferred teachers of
decided piety and earnestness, in whose conduct and character appeared satisfactory proof of the sincerity of their
profession. The usefulness of these schools depended much
upon the energy of the incumbent of Haley Hill district, the
Rev. C. R. Holmes, and the Rev. J. Hope, who had Copley
under his charge—both of these gentlemen being ably
supported by the self-devotion of the teachers and others
who assisted. He had every reason to be satisfied with
the result of his plans, and he begged to remind the section
that all his schemes were based on the Factory Act. He
asked, why not extend the provisions of that act, modified
according to circumstances, to all sections of the community? If the act was fair applied to millowners, it was
equally fair when applied to other employers of labour.
Why should one class of men alone be singled out for
legislation? He contended that if the provisions of the
act had answered their object—and he fully believed they
had—then there could be no reason against extending
them. If, on the other hand, they were unjust, then
abolish them altogether. Diverging from the results of
his own experience, Mr. Akroyd took a wider view of the

objects of the Conference, which invited "the friends of the education of the working classes to consider the early age at which children were taken from school." Of this fact of early removal there could be no question. In Mr. Marshall's report of 1855, containing the results arrived at in sixteen districts, it appeared that out of 382,000 children at schools under inspection, nearly one half, or 156,000, were under eight years of age. Then, as regarded the duration of attendance, nearly one-third, or about 114,000 of the 380,000, had only been one year at school. The term of factory education, from 8 to 13, contrasted most favourably with this wider view. Altogether there were about 44,000 factory children at school; and although no large proportion might attend school for the whole period from 8 to 13 years of age, yet, where the labour of factory children was in request, a more prolonged attendance at school was secured than could be obtained by any other means, or was practised elsewhere. The Factory Act required the attendance of half-timers for five days in the week, and for three hours in each day. One-twelfth of the children's wages, to the extent of 2*d.* per week, might be appropriated to the cost of schooling; so that, in fact, the child paid for its own education. The principles of factory education might be thus briefly stated: — 1st. The responsibility of the child's education rested conjointly upon the parent and employer, who were both equally benefited by the child's labour. 2ndly. Compulsory attendance was combined with voluntary provision for education; thereby the religious difficulty was avoided which had wrecked all other educational schemes.

The parent had the choice of the school, and could therefore select one where the master might accord with his own religious tenets. But, practically, the occasion for the exercise of such scruples seldom arose. He had never heard of an objection to the system pursued, although he had children whose parents belonged to different denominations. So far from checking voluntary exertions, this compulsory attendance had a directly contrary effect — *it filled the schools.* At present, in many districts, voluntary provision for school accommodation is at a stand still. Employers bade high for children's labour; and this bribe outweighed the natural desire of the parent to educate his child. Should not then the law step in to protect the child from this cruel usage, as it did already against bodily maltreatment? Was the mind of less consequence than the body? And whilst prevented from starving and ill-using the one, should the parents be allowed with impunity to stint and degrade to hopeless decrepitude the other, the noblest faculties which God has given to man? But where is the machinery to carry out the general education of the people of this country? If the short-time provisions of the Factory Act have worked well for factories, then there exists no intelligible reason why similar provision should not be applied to all other trades. Nay, in many trades, they were more necessary, from the fact that they were less under the public eye, less amenable to the influence of public opinion—and, therefore, the persons of tender years employed in them were more liable to abuse and neglect. That it was not possible for the voluntary efforts of benevolent men to effect these objects, he was convinced; and to prove that this conviction did not rest upon slight grounds, and that the experience of the voluntary system tended in the same direction, he would read a paragraph from a morning paper of the 21st of May of this year. It was as follows:—

"At the annual meeting of the subscribers to the Voluntary School Association, held at the Milton Club, Ludgate-hill, Mr. Samuel Morley in the chair, the secretary read the report, which stated that nine years had elapsed since the Voluntary School Association was first established, and it had been enabled to render much valuable aid to the cause of popular education. At the last annual meeting, the committee obtained the sanction of the subscribers to close the normal schools of the society, in order to devote its entire resources to the support of necessitous schools throughout the kingdom conducted on the voluntary principle. In accordance with this resolution, they had been engaged in this course ; and grants of money and school materials, from 5*l.* to 15*l.* each, had been made to 37 schools. In the schools thus aided by the society during the past year, there were upwards of 3100 children receiving a sound and scriptural education, and being trained up in a manner calculated to render them virtuous and useful members of society. The amount of school fees received from these children during the past year was 866*l.* 9*s.* ; while the further sum of 377*l.* 8*s.* 4*d.* had been contributed in the form of subscriptions and donations to the schools, assisted by the friends of education in the several localities. The society was the only one in existence that devoted its resources exclusively to the furtherance of the voluntary principle. The committee having expressed their serious disapprobation of the Educational Bill introduced into the House of Commons last session by Sir J. Pakington, stated, that it was proposed to make a vigorous and systematic effort, during the year on which the association was now entering, to render its principles and operations more widely known, and to endeavour to secure for it a much larger amount of public support. The work in which the association was engaged was one which should command the sympathies and pecuniary aid of all who were interested in the promotion of scriptural and unsectarian education ; and the committee could not doubt that, as the importance of its operations was better understood, its funds would be more commensurate with the requirements of the case. At the present moment the income of the association was altogether inadequate.

"The balance-sheet showed the receipts for the year to have been 979*l.* 9*s.* 2*d.*, and the expenditure less than that amount by 272*l.* 13*s.*"

Now, unless it had appeared in their own authorised report, it would have been difficult to have credited the fact that during the past year, so important an institution as the Voluntary School Association should, while objecting to government action, announce the closing of their normal school, and actually take credit for granting to the necessitous schools throughout the kingdom, the paltry sums of 5*l*. to 15*l*. each to thirty-seven schools; while the whole receipts of the year by this National Voluntary Institution had been under 980*l*., and it had distributed less than 708*l*. for educational purposes! It was impossible for him to adduce stronger evidence of the utter inadequacy of pure unsupported voluntary efforts to cope with the defects in our present means of instruction, and to uphold any broad general system which deserved the name of national education.

Mr. Morley explained that the gentlemen with whom he was connected, had another and a very good normal school, besides that which had been shut up; although he admitted the correctness of the report which had been read.

The chairman, after putting several questions to Mr. Akroyd as to the practical details of his educational plans, which he highly eulogised, proceeded to call upon Mr. Winfield to read his paper.

APPENDIX.

—◆—

Mr. Redgrave, Inspector of Factories, in his last Report, page 76, says—

"The half-time system may be concisely described as follows : —

"Daily attendance at school, combined with daily employment for half-time.

"Daily pecuniary responsibility of the employer, and of the parent, for the regularity of the school attendance of each child."

He adds : — "The system is carried into effect in practice, by means of the following regulations : —

"Every child between *eight* and *thirteen* years of age must pass three hours in school on each of five days in every week during which it is employed.   Such three hours to be between 8 A.M. and 6 P.M.

"The mill-owner must every week procure certificates, proving that the proper number of hours have been passed in school by each child during the previous week, and no child can be legally employed during the succeeding week who has been absent from school without cause even for one day.

"The labour of the children cannot exceed seven hours per day ; it must be taken between 6 A.M. and 6 P.M., and the whole of the daily labour must be commenced and completed either before 1 P.M. or after 12 at noon.

"If the hours of work in a factory are reduced to ten hours per day, the attendance at school may be on alternate days ; the children are then employed for the *whole* of one day, going to school for at least five hours on the succeeding day ; their employment at all in any factory on their school days being illegal."

HALEY HILL SCHOOLS.

Certificate.

No.

I certify that _____ has attended

the Schools for _____ months ;

that he can read $\left\{\begin{array}{l}\text{pretty}\\\text{very}\end{array}\right\}$ well ;

that he can write $\left\{\begin{array}{l}\text{pretty}\\\text{very}\end{array}\right\}$ well ;

that he is a $\left\{\begin{array}{l}\text{pretty}\\\text{very}\end{array}\right\}$ good accountant ;

that h   conduct at school has been $\left\{\begin{array}{l}\text{very good}\\\text{fair}\end{array}\right\}$;

Signed _____ School-$\left\{\begin{array}{l}\textit{Master.}\\\textit{Mistress.}\end{array}\right.$

Date _____

N.B. It is earnestly recommended to h   parents that they continue h   regular attendance at the Evening School for at least three years longer, in order that the child may retain and extend the little knowledge which a short attendance at a Factory School affords.

No. _____

Name, _____

Residence, _____

Employer, _____

Reading, _____

Writing, _____

Arithmetic, _____

Conduct, _____

Date, _____

WORKING MAN'S COLLEGE, HALEY HILL, HALIFAX.

Certificate.

WE HEREBY CERTIFY that_____
has attended Classes at the College regularly during the past
Year, that his Conduct has been steady and persevering, and
that he has passed the Annual Examination with_____
Credit._____

_____

_____*President.*
_____*Senior Tutor.*
_____18_____

ALSO that he has attended regularly during the past Year,
that his Conduct has been steady and persevering, and that he
has passed the Annual Examination with_____Credit.

_____

_____*President.*
_____*Senior Tutor.*
_____18_____

ALSO that he has attended regularly during the past Year,
that his Conduct has been steady and persevering, and that he
has passed the Annual Examination with_____Credit.

_____

_____*President.*
_____*Senior Tutor.*
_____18_____

On Feeding Schools and Evening Schools, the former as a means of prolonging and the latter as the means of resuming Education. By JOHN THACKRAY BUNCE, Esq., Honorary Secretary of the Birmingham Educational Association.

I HAVE united in this paper the classes of schools called "Feeding Schools," and "Evening Schools," because I regard both as supplementary means of instruction, forced upon us by a false and artificial system of labour. There can be no doubt that in a state of society undisfigured by the social evils that unhappily we encounter on every hand, there would be no need to attract children to a day school by giving them food, or to keep them so closely at work as to force them to attend school in the evening, if they desire to increase their scanty store of knowledge. We have, however, to deal with two great evils — the poverty of a large class of people, and the absolute necessity which has been created for the employment of children at too early an age, and for too long a time. These difficulties must be met fairly and promptly. We cannot hope to destroy their causes, and so to cure them; the only mode of dealing with them consists in adopting expedients approved by successful practice, or suggested by a common-sense view of the actual state of the case. I do not undervalue prize schemes, certificate schemes, or half-time schemes (I wish most heartily it were possible to obtain the last named); but I am strongly inclined to believe that there is a large class of children who can only be *enticed* to school, and for whom, therefore, the " feeding " school will be found invaluable ; and that there is a still larger class, anxious to extend their knowledge, but who, from the requirements of labour, cannot attend a day school, and to whom evening schools are the only means available for obtaining instruction. In the town where I live the numbers of these classes of children are very large, and probably nine-tenths of them are beyond the reach of half-time, whether voluntary or enforced. The immense number of trades carried on in Birmingham and its immediate district; their peculiar nature; the conditions under which they are conducted ; and the fearful pitch to which competition has risen, all combine to forbid the adoption of a half-time scheme, and combine also to forbid any hope that the demand for children's labour will materially decrease. In many trades it would be impossible to introduce a new set of work-people during part of the day, or part of the week; and in other cases so many trades are carried on in private houses or small shops, that it would be impossible satisfactorily to enforce a half-time scheme, even if backed by severe legal penalties. A *voluntary* half-time scheme is, I fear, entirely out of the question, because many of the smaller manufacturers are themselves so ill-instructed that they are utterly careless about ensuring school training for the children they employ. A few, but only a few, of the leading and more liberal manufacturers have already established schools for the children in their works, but the exigencies of trade prevent them from extending school instruction to any portion of the time usually allotted to work in the factory.

Although there is in Birmingham a large demand for the labour of children, there is also unfortunately a class of children—not inconsiderable in number—who are neither at school nor at work, though certainly of full age for the former, at least; if not for the latter also. From a valuable report presented by the Statistical Committee of the Birmingham Educational Association[*], I find that, of 1373 children between 7 and 13 years old (whose ages and occupations were ascertained by house to house visitation, in districts selected to represent the whole town), 42 per cent. were at a day school; 33 per cent. were at work; and 25 per cent. were neither at school nor at work. It is then with the 33 per cent. of workers, and the 25 per cent. of idlers that we have to deal; and I propose to show, from experience had in Birmingham itself, expedients by which these classes of children can be brought under the influence of instruction. I may remark before going further, that the educational position of Birmingham is certainly not lower, and is probably higher, than many other large towns, and that the remedial measures I am about to lay before the section, are therefore applicable, not only to Birmingham, but also to the other large towns of the kingdom.

First as to "FEEDING SCHOOLS." — In 1849, the Honourable and Reverend Grantham Yorke, rector of St. Philip's, Birmingham,—finding that in his parish there was a large number of persons not only too poor to send their children to an ordinary school, but even too poor to provide them with proper food whilst in attendance at school, — opened a school for the children of parents not absolutely paupers, but who were still too poor to pay even twopence a week. This school was

---

[*] Birmingham Educational Association: Statistics of Education. A Report of an Inquiry into the State of Education of the Children of the Working Classes in Birmingham, as affected by the Demand for Labour, and by other Causes. London: Simpkin and Marshall. Birmingham: Hall. 1857. Pp. 19.

entirely free. It soon became popular; and, by the aid
of benevolent persons, Mr. Yorke was enabled to erect a
suitable building, which has from time to time been
considerably enlarged, and in which the school is now
carried on, its plan having been so far modified as to
admit a considerable number of inmates, many of whom
are orphans of soldiers killed during the late war. There
are now 106 inmates, who are fed, lodged, and clothed, a
stipulated payment being annually made by their friends,
or by persons who take an interest in them. There are
also 130 day scholars, of whom 50, on five days weekly,
receive two meals in the school — dinner and supper;
in return for which they are expected to work for a
given time, the boys in the tailor's or shoemaker's shop,
and the girls at sewing. Whenever vacancies occur in
the "feeding," or, as it is called in the school, the "working" class, children are draughted from the other day
scholars into that class—preference being given to the
very poor, and especially to those who have remained
longest in the school. The working time is arranged in
the proportion of two and three quarter hours at work to
four and a half hours at school. The working or feeding
class children are expected to be at school at eight o'clock
in the morning. At one o'clock they have dinner in company with the inmates, and at seven o'clock supper is
given them, and they are dismissed for the night. Such
is the eagerness amongst this class to attend school, that
the superintendent, Mr. Thomas, tells me he has frequently found the children waiting at the school doors as
early as seven o'clock in the morning. Such is the *necessity* for schools of this class, that I learn from the same
authority that children are frequently sent without having
broken their fast, and some poor creatures have even
fainted in the school-room for want of the food which
their parents are too poor to provide for them. The

kindness manifested towards these poor children produces results in which the sustaining principle of heroism is conspicuously apparent. I recollect hearing of the case of a girl, about eleven years old, who was in the "feeding" class. When the time came for her to attend school, her mother—a widow—cried bitterly because she was obliged to send the child away without food. "Never mind, mother," said the courageous girl, "I am not *very* hungry. I can keep up till one o'clock; and I shall get some dinner then!"

The benefits resulting from the "feeding" class are clearly apparent if we compare them with the other day scholars in point of regularity and duration of attendance. From a return supplied to me by Mr. Bellamy, the schoolmaster, I learn that the average age of the children in the "feeding" or "working" class is 10 years; and of the other day scholars only 7 years and 11 months. The average length of attendance in the "feeding" class is 2 years and 1 month; of the other day scholars, only 8 months. The regularity of attendance on the part of the "feeding" class is as 91 per cent. compared with 65 per cent. on the part of the other day scholars. When I add that the cost per week for feeding each child only averages $11\frac{1}{2}d.$, and that part of this cost is returned in the value of the work, I shall have said quite enough to show the important advantages resulting from the establishment of "feeding" schools.* I should also mention that great care is taken to impress on the children the habit of cleanliness, that washing materials are provided for them in the school buildings, that they bathe once a week, and that they are taught to mend their own clothes. It is impossible not to believe that these habits, taken together with careful moral and religious training, must produce a good effect

---

* For Time Table and Dietary, see Appendix.

on the parents as well as the children, and that many a drunken father and careless idle mother are enabled to trace their reformation to the influence of a child trained in the Free Industrial School. I am aware that some other schools of this class are in existence, especially in Scotland; but I have chosen to enforce my argument by a reference to the school with which I am best acquainted; and the result of my inquiries tends to this — that for a large proportion of the poor, probably 25 per cent. on their class in our large towns — " feeding " schools are the best means of bringing children under instruction. I earnestly trust that the example set in Birmingham will be followed in other large towns. The cost is comparatively very trifling — old shopping may readily be fitted up for school purposes; the cost of maintaining twenty children will not amount to more than twenty shillings per week, and if they are judiciously trained to industrial employments, a portion of this cost may be recovered. I will not trouble the section with further details (which I shall be glad to supply in discussion); and from the necessity of further argument I hold myself absolved by the self-evident nature of the case I have stated. I proceed, therefore, at once to offer a few suggestions for the establishment and improvement of—

"EVENING SCHOOLS." — This agency for prolonging, or rather resuming, instruction, seems to me to have been very partially adopted and imperfectly carried out. It is undoubtedly true that evening schools are frequently established, and for a short time conducted with some degree of spirit; but when the attendance begins to flag, the teachers lose interest in the work, and the schools die out almost before their existence becomes fully known to the class for whose benefit they are designed. In order to render them thoroughly efficient, evening schools require to be founded on a principle different to that hitherto adopted.

In the first place they should be planted as nearly as possible in the midst of the districts in which the persons live who are sought to be influenced by them. A boy or a young man who has been closely engaged at work for ten hours during the day feels disinclined to undergo further physical fatigue, especially when the object is to attend a school which can be rendered attractive only by the exercise of a high degree of skill on the part of the master. If schools are brought close to the doors of the working classes, they are far more likely to be well attended than if the pupils can reach them only at the cost of a long walk to the rooms, and a long walk home again. It may be urged as a difficulty, that suitable buildings cannot always easily be procured near the dwellings of the working class; and in such an objection there is this force — that school buildings attached to churches or chapels would doubtless be best adapted for use as evening schools. But such buildings are not indispensable; as, in the case of "feeding" schools, old shopping may easily be converted into a decent school house at a very limited cost, and there are very few streets in manufacturing towns where disused shopping may not readily be obtained.

Evening schools should be placed under the direction of trained masters, if not of a master superior even to the class of teachers employed in day schools. My own experience in evening schools convinces me that amateur teaching, unless directed by a skilful master, is almost, if not entirely, useless. Volunteer teachers are generally incapable of imparting the knowledge they possess (and in many cases they possess very little); they are quickly disgusted by the uncouth manners and sometimes insubordinate behaviour of the pupils; and they are apt to assume a manner so dictatorial as completely to repel the confidence of the youths placed under their care. Too frequently they regard their attendance to teach as an act of condescension rather than of duty; and entering on the work with this lamentable feeling, they are keenly sensitive to any want of deference on the part of the boys. I am borne out in the statement that highly trained masters are necessary for evening schools by the opinions formerly expressed by many of the clergy of Birmingham in answer to questions addressed to them by the Rev. Dr. Miller, Rector of St. Martin's, who has recently published a very interesting pamphlet on the subject of evening schools.* The clergy to whom I refer, many of whom have great parochial experience, concur in expressing their belief, founded on their own knowledge, that evening schools can never prove successful unless certificated masters are appointed to conduct them.

Such masters cannot be provided without Government grants, and hitherto Government has extended very little aid to the persons who desire to establish evening schools. This subject requires to be pressed on the attention of the Committee of Council. They may multiply day schools by hundreds, and furnish them with the most costly educational appliances; but there will, in all manufacturing districts, always be an enormous number of children who will never be able to enter them, or if they enter, to remain longer than about twelve or sixteen months at the outside. Wherever the demand for labour is overwhelmingly great,—and it is increasing day by day,—children will be sent to work as soon as they are physically able to contribute to the family earnings. The only mode of meeting this evil is the establishment of

---

* A Letter to the Rev. E. H. Gifford on Evening Schools for the Working Classes. By the Rev. John C. Miller, D.D. Birmingham : B. Hall. Price Sixpence.

evening schools; and it must be regarded as short-sighted policy on the part of the Committee of Council that they do not, by every possible means, and by liberal agents, encourage the foundation of such schools. Even if the plan were to fail, it would be worth trying; but it would not fail. There is a sufficient desire for knowledge amongst the working boys and girls to induce them to attend an evening school, provided the quality of the instruction is sufficiently high, and the mode of imparting it sufficiently interesting. If the Committee of Council do not choose to expend a large sum on evening schools, let them contribute a moderate proportion of the masters' and mistresses' salaries, and extend the system of capitation fees, similar to that existing in the day schools, but with the difference of an increased amount, and a shorter term of attendance. From what I know of the feeling of the working class in Birmingham, I am sure that at least twenty evening schools, on a comparatively large scale, might be put into successful operation, if some such plan as the one I suggest were adopted.

It is objected by some persons that the hours of labour are too long to permit young persons to attend evening schools. I should be glad to see the hours of labour shortened, but I confess I do not clearly see the way to effect so desirable an object. I would, however, in the meantime endeavour to meet this difficulty by rendering the evening schools places of recreation as well as education; and also by adapting the instruction to the wants of the district, and in some measure to the class of trades most generally followed. I would set aside at regular, but not too frequent intervals, evenings for actual amusement, to which an educational tone should be given. For instance, the magic lantern might be put in requisition to illustrate the natural sciences, and the illustrations might be accompanied by short lectures, or explanations couched in familiar language. Concerts might be given, in which the pupils themselves might be trained to take part; harmless sports might occasionally vary the graver recreations: I name these amusements simply by way of illustration; others would readily occur to an experienced teacher. In this way the help of amateur teachers might be rendered available. Care should be taken that the "amusement evenings" do not occur so often as to interfere with the regular course of instruction; but they should be sufficiently frequent to serve as a relief. They should be used as means for ensuring regular attendance; no pupil should be admitted to them without a card, and no card should be issued to any pupil who had not attended school a given number of evenings, and had not made satisfactory progress in school tasks.

The instruction given in such schools should, as far as possible, have a practical bearing on the trades in which the majority of the children are engaged. Reading, writing, and arithmetic are insufficient to satisfy the wants or engage the attention of a boy who has been at work all day. But it is more than probable that a worker in metals would take an interest in having explained to him the nature, properties, and simpler combinations of the metals in which he works; in being enabled to trace the sources from whence they are obtained, and the various uses to which they are put. A lad from a cotton, silk, or worsted factory would be equally interested in being familiarised with the materials used in *his* trade. Such teaching would exert a reflex influence upon employers, who would find their boys growing up into steadier and more intelligent workmen than if their knowledge had been confined to the horn book or the multiplication table. Indeed it would not be too much to hope that the certain effects of such a class of schools would eventually influence employers to shorten the hours of

labour in order to afford their younger workpeople larger
facilities for acquiring instruction ; for I believe there
never yet was a master, who, when he looked the question
fairly in the face, did not find that the better his people
were educated — in the best sense of the word — the better
and more valuable workmen they became.   Numerous
other practical suggestions have occurred to me for rendering evening schools more efficient; but this paper has
already extended beyond the assigned limit, and I will
therefore only add that it might be desirable to offer
prizes of some value to the best pupils in these schools ;
that the value of personal cleanliness should be strongly
impressed upon them, that lavatories should be attached
to every school ; that the pupils should be taught to consider themselves as members of a family rather than
merely as scholars ; and above all that nothing should be
done to check, but rather everything to foster that spirit
of independence, self-respect, and self-reliance, by which
our best artisans are so favourably distinguished, and without which schoolmasters, clergymen, and teachers, may
labour in vain to advance the real *education* of the working
classes.

APPENDIX.

———

BIRMINGHAM INDUSTRIAL SCHOOL DIETARY.

BREAKFAST, AT EIGHT O'CLOCK.

MONDAY, Bread and Milk.
TUESDAY, Bread and Coffee.
WEDNESDAY, Bread and Milk.
THURSDAY, Bread and Coffee.

FRIDAY, Bread and Milk.
SATURDAY, Bread and Milk.
SUNDAY, Bread and Coffee.

DINNER, AT ONE O'CLOCK.

MONDAY, Boiled Rice and Sugar.
TUESDAY, Roast Meat and Vegetables.
WEDNESDAY, Suet Pudding.
THURSDAY, Boiled Beef and Potatoes.

FRIDAY, Soup and Bread.
SATURDAY, Bread and Cheese.
SUNDAY, Roast Meat and Vegetables.

SUPPER, AT SEVEN O'CLOCK.

MONDAY, Bread and Dripping.
TUESDAY, Bread and Milk.
WEDNESDAY, Seed Cake.
THURSDAY, Bread and Milk.

FRIDAY, Bread and Treacle.
SATURDAY, Bread and Treacle.
SUNDAY, Seed Cake.

———

TIME TABLE.

MORNING.

9 to 9¼ Prayers and Singing.
9¼ „ 9¾ Religious Instruction.
9¾ „ 10½ Copy Book Writing and Dictation, alternately.
10½ „ 11¼ Reading and Spelling.
11¼ „ 11¾ Catechism and Tables, alternately.
11¾ „ 12 Wash and prepare for Dinner.
12 „ 1 Dinner, Play, &c.

AFTERNOON.

1 to 3¾ Industrial Classes.
3¾ „ 4 Play, Wash, and prepare for Tea.
4 „ 4¼ Tea.
4¼ „ 5 Exercise in Play Ground.
5 „ 6 Slate and Mental Arithmetic, alternately.
6 „ 6½ Reading and Spelling.
6½ „ 7 Singing, Prayers, and Dismissal, in Dining Hall.

The Children take their Baths every week.

Every Child's hair to be cut short; and the state of the Child's education to be examined by the Committee previously to being admitted into the School.

———

HOLIDAYS.

CHRISTMAS, Two Weeks. EASTER, One Week. MIDSUMMER, Two Weeks.

PART V.

PAPERS NOT FALLING UNDER THE ABOVE HEADS.

———◆———

*On Endowments created for the Apprenticeship of Chil-
dren, and on the Application of such Funds by way of
Premiums or Rewards, as an Encouragement in the
Education of the Poor, and for promoting their longer
Continuance at School; and on the Employment of other
Charities founded for undefined Purposes in aid of the
same Objects.* By THOMAS HARE, Esq., Inspector of
Charities.

IT is well known that, amongst the public charities of
this country founded in past times, there is a large
number dedicated to the purpose of apprenticing the children of the poor. It is not easy to ascertain the amount
of the funds applicable to that purpose; but I have caused
the printed Digest of the Reports of the Commissioners of
Inquiry to be examined, and the sums which thereby appear to be exclusively applicable to the purpose of apprenticeship to be extracted; and I find that, as they are
stated in those reports, they amount to an aggregate sum
of 31,670*l.* a year. In addition to this, there are charities

producing about 69,200*l.* a year, which are applicable partly to apprenticeship, and partly to other purposes. If no more than one-seventh of these funds are to be employed in the purpose of apprenticeship, which I do not think would be an unreasonable supposition, the annual income to be disposed of in this manner would exceed 40,000*l.* This estimate, it is to be remembered, has been formed upon statements prepared more than twenty, and some of them nearly forty years ago; during which period many of these endowments have greatly increased in value; and I think it is probable that the income of the apprenticeship charities will be found to amount to little, if anything, short of 50,000*l.* a year.

These funds arise from endowments, of which but a very small part is of recent creation. They are mostly governed by wills made in the seventeenth and eighteenth centuries, and are generally limited to the children of parents living in particular towns or parishes. The sums which are provided as premiums vary greatly—5*l.* is perhaps the minimum sum, and few afford more than 25*l.* Some of these charities are administered by existing corporate companies, some by the municipal trustees of corporate towns, who have succeeded the old corporations,—some by the minister and churchwardens, and other parochial authorities, and a large number by trustees appointed from time to time, and not having necessarily any other public capacity. In the mode of administration there is of course great variety. In the best examples of such administration, they are applied in the apprenticeship of the children of old servants or labourers of the trustees, or their friends, of small tradesmen who are in some way connected with the municipal or corporate bodies, or the children of persons in more or less straitened circumstances, who happen to be known to the trustees. In many cases the apprenticeship fee is believed to be, by an underhand arrangement, divided between the parent and the master to whom the boy is apprenticed. It cannot be said that a certain amount of temporary benefit is not conferred; a certain relief or assistance is given to persons to whom it is no doubt valuable, although they are, perhaps, rarely those who stand most in need of it; but the condition of the poor is left as it was. A few pounds are placed at the disposal, in the great majority of cases, of persons who would, without such aid, have probably done as well for their children as with it; for there is no system of administration which in general cases affords any certainty of reaching those who, without such relief, would be destitute, except those stern yet necessary tests, which the administrators of the produce of a compulsory rate are bound to apply. The charitable, in the spontaneous dispensation of their own private funds, are not unfrequently deceived in the choice of their objects; and I am satisfied that, as a general rule, it will be found that the dispensers of endowed charities are content with much less evidence of the necessity of the recipient than they are in the habit of requiring before they give their own money. To say that these funds are to a large extent distributed as a matter of personal favour, and under the influence of motives wholly independent of the relative merits of those whom they assist, is only to say that trustees are led by appeals to which men are ordinarily most accessible. These powers of disposition give to trustees some influence and patronage, until many of them come to think that this possession of influence and patronage is as much a part of the essence of the trust as is the benefit which it is intended to confer on the poor. There are, however, many trustees who are not satisfied with the manner in which their apprenticeship charities are administered,— who would be glad to be furnished with a rule that would protect them from solicitation, and assist them in the choice of the objects,—and to whom it would be a great additional satisfaction if they could be so applied as to promote education.

In truth, the most conscientious and enlightened trustees feel the peculiar difficulties which exist at this day in the administration of these particular charities. Those who are desirous only of procuring the premium for some friend or neighbour, are readily satisfied; but when an anxiety is felt that the best should be done for the youth who is to be apprenticed, the want of an organised system is immediately felt. In the agricultural parishes especially, there is an extremely narrow range of trades. A very large proportion of boys are apprenticed to the trades of tailors and shoemakers. These trades are nearest at hand, and the masters in them are amongst the most necessitous, and to whom, therefore, a premium of 5*l.* or 10*l.* is an object to be sought after. Little security exists that the boy shall be taught his trade. In great numbers of cases the business is given up ; the master and apprentice separate, or the boy runs away, and no efforts are made to compel him to serve out his term of apprenticeship, and for any useful purpose to the child the premium is lost. Many sets of trustees, in order to guard against this consequence, adopt the rule of paying half the premium at first, and the other half at the middle of the term ; but this is a very insufficient remedy, whilst it strongly exhibits the small degree of confidence the trustees have in the person with whom the youth is placed. It is obvious that any system, by which something like what is contemplated in Clause B. of the heads of consideration, as to the certificate schemes in this section of the Conference,—such as a corresponding committee, opening to the rural and town districts a wider range of employment, a more extensive circle of trades, and a more respectable and responsible class of masters,—would be a great encouragement to those trustees who have a fund for setting forward a youth in life, but do not know how to employ it with safety and advantage.*

Another circumstance which has altered the position of these endowments within the last half-century arises from the changes which have taken place in the state of society, and in the manner of life of the trading classes. The apprentice in most trades was formerly taken into his master's house, and became a member of his family. This custom has almost ceased to exist, and ceasing, it has contributed still further to narrow the range of choice of employment, for the boy is almost necessarily placed in such a situation as will enable him to live with his parents or relations. It moreover increases the danger of his position, he being under the control of the master only during the hours of employment, and too often partially liberated from that of his parents; and at times, the apprentice is too apt to abuse the freedom, and misemploy the leisure which he has not learnt how to use. This again suggests the great value of a system, such as that pointed to under the same head, by which youths on embarking in life might have the advantage of some discreet persons watching over their interests, and to whom they may look for sympathy and guidance.† Multitudes of trustees would,

---

* A system of this sort—an interchange of powers and means—becomes necessary as we advance in an artificial state of society. In times when a community or a family were capable of subsisting as it were within themselves,—the makers of their own rude implements, and the manufacturers of their own apparel,—the range of industrial life was necessarily narrow. Whether this primitive state of things were more or less happy than that we have substituted for it, it is useless to consider. We cannot return to it. Labour is now infinitely divided in its forms, and without comprehensive organisation the social economy must be imperfect. The means by which this can be supplied,—the labourer led to the fitting work,—and the whole connected with instruction in youth,—is that which is to be sought.

† By this watching, I mean regard for those interests which require to be cared for, whatever the employment may be; aid may be

I am persuaded, avail themselves of it with great satisfaction.

Another fact to be adverted to is, that in a great number of trades in which it was formerly the custom to take apprentices, that is no longer the course pursued. I find in many trades, and with the most respectable masters, that a tolerably instructed boy will be taken and immediately employed at wages, when no premium will be accepted, and that a boy who has had less elementary teaching will not be taken on any terms. Extensive communication with the employers of labour will be extremely valuable in furnishing information upon this subject.

If this could be brought about by organising a system of communication between the trustees of charities in different parts of the kingdom,—the trustees of rural parishes with those in the seats of manufacturing and commercial industry,—it might not only promote the immediate object, but also tend to enlarge the sympathy of local authorities and bodies, who at present commonly struggle, with a narrow jealousy, chiefly to secure or extend some special or petty privilege or advantage in favour of their own town or parish.

The rules for disposing of the apprenticeship gifts, so far as relates to the choice of the objects, might be to the following effect:—

1. That no child shall be eligible for the benefit of the funds of charitable endowments created for apprentice-

---

given to obtain for a youth, when he leaves his home, an abode as far as possible free from exposure to physical or moral evil, and an opening to such modes of employment for his leisure as may carry on that teaching which he has before received. Any interference between the employer and the employed, when the connection is once constituted, however prompted by a view to the interests of the latter, would, I apprehend, be fatal to any hope of obtaining the cooperation of masters.

ship (except under special circumstances), unless he or she shall have attained the age of . . . . years, and have attended some school for . . . . . . days in each of the two years preceding that in which he or she attained such age.

2. In the selection of the children to receive the benefit of the apprenticeship endowments, amongst those who are eligible according to the preceding rule, regard shall be had to the conduct and character of the candidates, and to their proficiency in the subjects of instruction in such school; and no child will be considered eligible who does not read and write freely, and show an acquaintance with the common rules of arithmetic.

3. The trustees of apprenticeship endowments shall be empowered to apply them towards the expenses of prolonging the education of any child who shall be elected to participate therein, or otherwise to apply the same for his or her advancement in life, in any case in which it may appear to them that such mode of application will be more beneficial than applying it in the form of apprenticeship.

On the first two rules, I defer entirely to those who are conversant with the existing schools, and know better than I do what may be expected or required. On the third rule, I would only add that I hope means may at no distant period be found to combine the operation of some of our great educational institutions, whereby good conduct and successful competition at one school may be the means of advancement to another; so that whilst every child may receive suitable instruction, the poor may yet know and feel that an avenue is open from the lowest to the highest, through which diligence and talent may pass. Mr. Temple, in his paper in the Oxford Essays (1856), has referred to a possible adaptation of the wealthier institutions to these purposes; and as the benefits of such an enlarged scheme become apparent, it may be hoped that any opposition founded on a mere love of patronage or influence, or on any other narrow or selfish motive, would in this, as it has in other things, gradually disappear.

This is not a place to express any views of the right of the state to modify the uses of its charitable endowments, on which I entertain personally strong opinions; but in making it compulsory on trustees so to employ apprenticeship charities (subject to any exceptions in particular cases which the charity commissioners may for sufficient reasons approve), I do not, I think, propose to depart from the substantial intentions of founders. The foundations mostly took place under a different social state; but the apprenticeship system, provided for the poor child another, and generally a better home, and formed the industrial school of that day. It is fair to believe that they, who so wisely connected their bounty with the advancement in life of its objects, would at this day have availed themselves of every improved means of accomplishing the same end; and that he who provided a method of benefiting one or two children, would have been rejoiced if he could have extended the benefit to twenty.

I will not delay you longer by adverting to other endowments, but will rather refer you to a printed paper, in which I, early in the last year, proposed to apply the charities of a considerable city in such a manner as to benefit in the largest way I was able to contrive, the youth of both sexes. The suggestions in this paper the members of the Conference will better peruse at their leisure.

On Industrial Training as an Adjunct to School Teaching.
By JELINGER C. SYMONS, Esq., H. M. Inspector of
Schools.

To judge how far it is requisite that schools for the
working classes should be more practically industrial, in
order that the working classes should avail themselves
more of schools, I must state very briefly the evidence,
first, how little they avail themselves of them now : and,
secondly, that working people fail to make sacrifices for
education, because it fails to supply what they think will
repay its cost.

And here, on the threshold, I would venture to remark
that it seems to me a hasty and harsh conclusion, that the
poor do not value education, because they do not value
the schooling to which we give that name.

First, I beg leave to show how much larger is the non-
attendance at schools than we were told yesterday; and
consequently how great the ignorance of the working class
children in this country. There are, according to the
census of 1851, no less than 4,908,696 children, between
the ages of three and fifteen, a period which, as regards
the working classes, comprises the whole span of the
school age. Mr. Mann, in his elaborate report on the
Education Census, makes several natural deductions from
this gross total, in order to arrive at the number who ought
to be at school. Without, however, taking advantage of

this large deduction, and assuming that the whole number of children at a school age may at some time and for some period attend school, and giving the census the benefit of the whole 4,908,696, it is yet demonstrable that it largely overstates the number who can possibly be at school at any given time, in returning them as 2,046,848.

Mr. Mann says that he deduces "from the experience of able writers and instructors," that "whilst among the middle and upper classes the average time expended on their children's school education is about *six* years, *the average amongst the labouring classes cannot much exceed four* years," meaning, doubtless, to include the stay at dame and infant schools.* He also supposes, with probable accuracy, " that the children of the middle and upper classes form a fourth part of the whole number of children between three and fifteen ;" and the working classes, consequently, three-fourths. Applying this division of classes to the whole of the 4,908,696 children between those ages, there would thus be 1,227,174 upper class, and 3,681,522 working class children. The whole span of the school age being twelve years, it follows that as the upper class children stay but six years, one-half of their number alone (or 613,587) can, on the average, be at school at once ; and similarly, as the working class children stay only four years out of the twelve, only a third of their number (or 1,227,174) can be at school at once. But these two figures give us only 1,840,761, as the largest number which, according to Mr. Mann's statements, can by any possibility be at school at the same time.

But is it true that every working class child does stay on an average four years at school? Mr. Mann appends to the same page of his report some strong testimony from the Rev. Mr. Burgess and from the Rev. Mr. Watkins,

* P. xxiv and v. of the 8vo. edition.

Her Majesty's Inspector of Schools, to the effect that the average stay is considerably less than four years; and I believe that no single school teacher in populous districts could be found who would state the average as high as three years. If so, the number at school is still less. For the shorter the duration of stay, the smaller the number of children at any given time at school. For example, suppose there were 30 children, each of whom went to school on an average two days in the month of June, there would be an average attendance of two children: reduce the stay of each child to one day, and there would be an average attendance only of one child at once. It may indeed be said, "Increase the total number of children, and then the actual attendance need not be thus lessened." True, but the population presents a limit: and I have given it its utmost tether, and in fact have gone beyond it: for there are, as Mr. Mann observes, at least 50,000 children who never go to school, as being educated at home; and to these must be added the much larger number who are wholly uneducated, and never go to any school. Assuming these at only 50,000 more, we have thus a total of 1,740,000 children, in round numbers, who alone can, on the most liberal assumption, be present at the same time; instead of 2,046,000, as the census incorrectly states, being an excess of 306,000, or 17·5 per cent.

And now what shall be said of the kind of instruction given? Can it be held that a child not taught to write at all, is being educated for any of the ordinary purposes of education? But the teachers of the schools themselves return only 56 per cent. as even "learning to write," and 46 per cent. only as learning arithmetic: so that it may, on the showing of the census itself, be said, that not only are nearly two-thirds always absent at once from school, but that only one half of those that are there—namely, one-sixth of the whole—are receiving at any one time even the rudiments of the most meagre scale of education !

But ought education, even for the poor, to be limited to the mere instruments of mental faculty ? Is not the mind itself to be informed, intelligence enlarged, and the application of these abstract powers taught ? And above all, are not the moral principles and feelings to be evoked, nurtured, chastened, and Christianised ? Putting aside for the nonce all mention of the development of industrial aptitude, how dare we call that an EDUCATION of beings endowed with soul and mind, which falls short in one of these essential requirements ? And how many of our schools fulfil them ? The evidence abounds of their defects and short-comings.

There were in 1855 only 506,009 children in all the schools inspected by the Committee of Council; of which number it would be a most liberal estimate to say that one-seventh, or in round numbers 72,300, were being well educated. I fear the non-inspected common schools would give a less number, for they include all the dame schools, which swell the census returns.

I cannot enlarge upon this great subject, and must therefore state tersely the results only which I gather, first, from the widely spread evidence of them ; and, secondly, from personal examinations of every kind of school for the working classes during twelve years, both at home and abroad.

I believe that the *first* classes in the best of the common schools are now receiving sound and useful instruction in all elementary school attainments. I believe it to be in many instances superior to that which a large number of our own children in the higher classes are obtaining in the same subjects ; for such subjects are, in our rank of life, often sacrificed to the early study of the classics, mathematics, languages, and accomplishments.

In the next generation it may chance to come to pass that the more favoured of our bourgeoisie will far excel the gentry in those branches of instruction which are the sinews of success in life : and the tendency of this change, in a country where wealth and cleverness always obtain ascendancy, may be to further plebeian aggrandisement, and narrow the dynasty of old families.

This elevation of the lower classes is fragmentary and exclusive. It is an uplifting of thousands at the expense of millions, with little regard to moral merit, but chiefly on the strength of scholastic attainments. The lower classes in our common schools are still, with few exceptions, obtaining a very inferior instruction : little, in short, but a smattering of the same instruction given to the forward children, of which the lower classes receive a meagre modicum, and of which (regarding the short period of their average attendance) they will retain next to nothing. I refer for proof of this statement to the experience of every one who has thoroughly examined such classes, and to the statements, though worded with due caution, in several of the reports of Government and Diocesan Inspectors. Their instruction is not defective in amount, but it is of a wrong kind. It usually partakes, however ignorant the children are, of the same advanced range which alone befits the forward scholar, and it is administered, not by the intelligent master, but mostly by monitors or pupil teachers, in whose hands its fruitfulness is not likely to be enhanced. It is not uncommon to find such children wading through formidable columns of long division, or entangled in the rule of three, who cannot tell you the price of a pound of butter at three farthings an ounce, or what change they must have after spending $17\frac{1}{2}d.$ out of half a crown. In fact, mental arithmetic, as it requires mental exertion in the teacher, is very often neglected. It is much easier to point to a sum in the

Irish Arithmetic Book, and say, "Work that on the slate."
In Scripture I find nothing commoner than a knowledge
of such facts as the weight of Goliath's spear, the length
of Noah's ark, the dimensions of Solomon's temple, what
Gad said to David, or what Samuel did to Agag, by children who can neither explain the atonement, the sacra-
ments, or the parables, with moderate intelligence, or tell
you the practical teaching of Christ's life.   Their spelling
and English are often equally bad.

Such instruction of the lower classes is pretentious,
superficial, and abortive.   It dabbles in high things, and
leaves common things untaught.   It aspires to rear a
showy capital without base or shaft.   Unhappily, however, the classes thus dealt with, added to the number
who are avowedly learning nothing, form the bulk of the
future generation of our laborers and servants.   They
are the broad substratum of society.   And such (subject
of course to some cheering exceptions) is the sterile character of the instruction we mainly give to them, even in
the routine and prescriptive studies of the school-room.
Is it probable that the parents of such children will value
an instruction thus intrinsically worthless, and of which
the pretentiousness entails on it the ready sarcasm of the
class just above them, who most of all influence their
judgments and inspire their prejudices?

Diverging from these studies, let the examiner next
inquire how much instruction directly bearing on the
future labor life of these children, supplements and com-
pensates for the sterility of their school attainments?   In
nearly ninety-nine cases out of a hundred the inquirer
will find that not a vestige of it is even attempted.   Ask
the child who has been gabbling over a lesson on the
geography of the globe, or in one of the rival systems
which perplex grammar, to give you a truce of zones and
predicates, and describe the chief agricultural or mineral

features of his own county —to explain what determines
rates of wages—how to plant potatoes, feed pigs, or to
make a pudding—or to describe the special duties of each
kind of domestic service, and the character required for
each when hired—and I will undertake to say that not
one out of fifty school children will give you a good
answer.   And yet these and ten thousand more things
of the same practical use to the after life of the child, are
the things it requires to know ; and are moreover the
things which its parents (who are themselves hard pressed
by the stern practical question how to live) require that
it should be taught : and if they be not taught, and you
are not advancing the child one step, either by instruction
in the school or by actual labor done out of it, towards
that aptitude for industry on which his future livelihood
depends, —how can you expect that the parents will sacrifice both their means and the child's time, for the sake of
that barren and contorted culture you prescribe for him
as a fine thing, under the prostituted name of education ?

I am well aware of the practical difficulty we encounter
in establishing washhouses, kitchens, or dairies, as an adjunct
to the girls' school-room.   I am conscious how many are
the impediments, even to the best of all boy employments
—spade husbandry : and though in most cases these difficulties vanish before perseverance and decision, there are
cases in which these glorious helpmates of our work are
impracticable.   But I deny that a single case exists in
which it is not perfectly easy to teach, as a primary school
study, such industrial knowledge as is admirably given in
books like Longman's "Domestic Economy," Groombridge's
" Village Lesson Book," the Irish Society's " Agricultural
Class Book," Baker's "Circle of Knowledge," and many
of the Finchley Manuals of Industry.   I am quite aware
that this does not harmonise with the aspirations of highly
educated school teachers.   But it is by no means on that

account the less needful for the poor children who are to
be taught. It ought to be insisted upon by every manager
of every common school; whether the teacher likes it or
not. I am also, after ten years' experience in the constant
inspection of Union Schools—most of which annex active
industrial training in household work for girls, or spade
husbandry for boys—able to attest, in the most unqualified
terms, the increasing success of real industrial schools. I
can point to the district school at Quatt as an eminent
and enduring instance of this success. At that school
farm 130 children, with the mere assistance of one laborer
and a female servant, not only cultivate ten acres of land
most productively, so as to yield from 125*l.* to 140*l.* net
profit per annum, but all the work of the establishment,
including dairy, washhouse, cooking, baking, needlework,
and every description of house work, is done by the children.
Both girls and boys will accurately describe the best
modes of doing the kinds of work to which they are thus
practically inured, and which in a very short time they
learn to perform in the most creditable manner. Even
boys of eight or nine years are made useful in the lighter
employments of the ground, and many at this age can fork
and even dig with great ease. But this is not all. I have
carefully inspected and watched this school for many years,
and although half the day is usually spent in labor, so
far is this from injuring the school work, that I can confidently assert that very few National or British schools
can produce a larger proportion of thoroughly well educated children in every single branch of really useful
learning for their rank in life. The school has the benefit
of two admirable teachers—one, Mr. Garland, who nearly
confines himself to industrial superintendence; and the
other, Mr. Roach, to the school teaching. There are two
schools, one upper and one lower, but both are mixed
schools, the latter instructed by a schoolmistress. I am

persuaded, after many experiments in workhouse schools, that this plan answers best.

It is seldom possible to unite all the requisite qualifications for the outdoor and indoor work in the same man. It would often overtask him, even if he did unite them. The schoolmasters whose boys are thus industrially trained, are universally of opinion that their mental powers are greatly improved and sharpened by their outdoor work, and I do not know of a single instance out of thirty or forty such schools, where the master would, if he had the power, drop the industrial training. I think it needs no process of reasoning to show that the practical application of much that is or ought to be taught in the school-room, must powerfully tend to give it a reality, and impress it with tenfold more effect on the child's mind. It is also an invaluable opportunity of watching the character of the children, and exercising moral culture. In fact, moral and industrial training go hand in hand.

The necessary restraints of a school-room prevent anything approaching to complete moral training within its walls; and yet how important is this as an element in the great work of education, if its object be to improve the character of the mass of the people! I am far from depreciating the value of mental culture as an agent of moral elevation, but we must remember the power of this agent is greatly limited, while that of moral and industrial training is equally extended, by the proportion between intellectual faculties and bodily powers. So long as the abilities of the hand vastly outnumber the abilities of the head among our Anglo-Saxon folk, I submit that no schooling for them deserves the name of education which stimulates the intellects and neglects the physical agencies of moral welfare.

The experience of industrial training as productive of those priceless results has been amply proved — not in one class of schools or one phase of children alone — but alike among schools for the children of independent laborers, for paupers, and for criminals. I cite the National Schools at Hagley and Painswick, Glasnevin, Parkhurst, Red Hill, Mettray, and a large number of workhouse schools in this country as well as Ireland, as proofs that I am advocating no doubtful experiment, that I am eulogising no tentative theory, but a well-tested and established success. I could multiply evidence from persons who have witnessed both systems successively tried under their own eyes, almost *ad infinitum*, and bearing universal witness that, alike in moral improvement, mental vigor, facility of scholastic attainment, bodily health, and actual increasing industrial power, there is no question as to the superiority of a system which divides the day between bodily labor and literary learning, over the exclusive routine of book schooling. I will confine myself to the mention only of the convincing Reports of the Irish Commissioners on the National Agricultural Schools of Ireland for 1855, where so admirably useful and popular have farm schools proved, that they have increased from 92 in the year 1852, to 165 in 1855.

I have just been favoured with the following letter from Dr. Kirkpatrick, Chief Inspector of those schools :—

" Albert National Agricultural Training Institution,
" Glasnevin, Dublin, 18th June, 1857.
" Sir,
" Your letter of the 15th inst., addressed to ' The Secretaries of National Education, Ireland,' having been referred to me, I now beg leave to direct your attention to the accompanying documents, which, I trust, will satisfy you that a proper system of combined literary and agricultural or industrial instruction is calculated to produce the very best results, as regards alike the physical and mental condition of the children who partake of such training.

" I am persuaded that there can be no more appropriate exercise for schoolboys than light farm or garden labour, which, instead of retarding, promotes the acquisition of ordinary school and other useful knowledge; and in corroboration of this statement, which is indeed founded upon personal observation, I beg to direct your attention to the accompanying letters* from Messrs. Donaghy, Brogan, McDonnell, and Healy, all of whom were for *several* years engaged, and very successfully too, in carrying out this combined system of literary and industrial instruction in the National Agricultural Schools in this country. Had time permitted (I am just setting out on a tour of inspection), I could have collected a large mass of testimony on this very important subject, which, in my opinion, has not hitherto received that attention and patronage which it merits.

" I requested that the secretaries would forward to you a copy of my last Report on National Agricultural Schools, and I marked several passages which had a prominent bearing on the subject of your note. I trust you have received the volume, and that you have noted the opinions expressed by persons so well qualified to do so as Lord Monteagle, the Rev. Messrs. Brady, Ward, Payne, Callan, &c.

" I have the honour to be, Sir,
" Your obedient Servant,
" THOMAS KIRKPATRICK, M.D.
" Inspector of National Agricultural Schools, Ireland.

"P.S.—Allow me to call your attention to my 'Evidence before the Select Committee of the House of Lords on the Practical Working of the System of National Education in Ireland,' August, 1854.

" To J. C. Symons, Esq.,
" H. M. Inspector of Schools, &c. &c."

If industrial schools in England were so managed that the parents should benefit by the proceeds of their children's labour, I am confident that every objection on their parts would vanish, as I found the case with the parents of the children at Hagley by personal inquiry of themselves. And not only have the children from that school distinguished themselves in the recent competition for prizes awarded only to attainments, but the utility and merits of that industrial school are so well appreciated by

* See Appendix.

the parents, that the average duration of attendance there greatly exceeds the usual amount in most other schools. And this brings me to the practical bearing of this question. The moment we can convince the parents of the working class that the time their children spend at school —though it does not pretend to make them skilled laborers—has a practical effect in preparing them for labor-life, and is, by furthering their aptitude for it, enhancing its future gains—from that moment education assumes a new value in their eyes. It presents itself in a totally different aspect. It enlists the strongest aspirations of the laborer's heart in its favour, which mere scholastic education, such as it now is, arrays against it. If well-chosen industrial training were annexed to each common school, and were it rigidly required that much of the instruction in school should have a practical and special bearing on the pursuits of industry and the needs of the laborer, such instruction being adapted to the character of each district, we should have but little longer to deplore the sparse attendance at our schools. In a word, we should studiously adapt education to the class for whom we design it. This done, we should have small reason to seek by other remedies, whether in half-time systems, or prize schemes, to induce poor parents to fill common schools. The poor are shrewd judges of the value of what they buy, and they estimate schooling by the same test. Give it a money value and they will be ready customers. I am well aware that loftier motives ought to animate the people, but they do not; and we must condescend to adapt our tools to our materials.

There is no compromise in doing this. We have a noble array of philanthropists in this country : but unfortunately they mostly walk on stilts; their aims are above their objects, and they stride over the people instead of walking with them. The Prussian Government has striven to amend this error in its schools. The three edicts of 1854 enforce the practical instead of the scientific and purely literary tenor of their former teaching. Stahl's canon prevails—" Die Wissenschaft muss umkehren."

I would that we so far followed their example as to enforce sound instruction of a useful kind among all classes of scholars, in each of our common schools. If this were but done, how much formidable prejudice and obstructive apathy would disappear before the simple process of " setting our house in order !" Like most of the enmities and evils which mankind wastes so much of its energy in combating, the *fons et origo* are, like the remedy, within ourselves.

Great and cheering has been the progress of education, and especially of the general interest in its furtherance, and it is nowise a matter for wonder or despondency that so swift an advance from the stagnation of the past to the activity of the present should be attended by the mistakes incidental to our very zeal in the cause. But we must look our defects fairly in the face. We are applying our stimulants to a kind of instruction suited only to the forward intellects of hundreds, instead of adapting knowledge to the wants of the millions. Our schools are not what the people need; and that is why the people slight our schools. The remedy is to make them with all speed what Colman justly calls " one of the most valuable institutions of a community,"—SCHOOLS WHICH TRAIN MINDS AND BODIES, NOT FOR LITERARY LEISURE, BUT FOR THE ACTIVE AND BUSINESS PURSUITS OF LIFE.

APPENDIX.

EXTRACTS FROM MINUTES OF EVIDENCE BEFORE SELECT
COMMITTEE ON NATIONAL EDUCATION—IRELAND.

Extracts from the Evidence of Dr. Kirkpatrick, Inspector
of National Agricultural Schools.

"9514. Do you find that those who attend the agricultural
school are upon a par with the other children in the national
schools, with respect to literary education?—Not only upon a
par, but superior to them, generally speaking.

"9515. Is there any selection made in consequence of the
ability of the children to be employed in the agricultural
school?—Not on account of ability merely; on account of
their age also.

"9516. To what do you attribute their superiority in point
of literary education?—I think that industrial training is a
relaxation to the mind, and that the alternation of literary and
agricultural studies tends to promote the literary attainments
of the pupils. We invariably find that to be the case in all
the schools throughout Ireland with which I am connected.

"9517. Lord MONTEAGLE of Brandon.—Can you mention
the cases of any particular boys who were at once eminent in
literature and in agricultural training, and state what their
position now is, as the result of the education which they received at Larne?—I can. The following table shows the
destination of young men who were educated at the Larne
Model Agricultural School since 1848:—'11 were taken to
the National Model Farm, Glasnevin; 12 became teachers of
national schools; 3 went to college; 6 were appointed clerks;
8 emigrated to America; 22 went to sea; 22 were appointed
to different trades. The following important situations are
filled by pupils from the Larne School:—agriculturist to the
Munster Model Farm, Cork; agriculturist to the Bailieborough
Model Farm, Cavan; agriculturist to the Ballymoney Model
Farm, Antrim; agriculturist to the Lismore Union, Water-

ford ; agriculturist to the Clonmel Union, Tipperary ; agriculturist and schoolmaster to the Belfast Union, Antrim ; agriculturist and schoolmaster to the Piltown Agricultural School, Kilkenny ; agriculturist to the Kilwaughter Model Farm, Antrim ; assistant-chemist to the Chemico-Agricultural Society of Ulster.' Professor Johnson was so much pleased with the answering of the boys in Glasgow, that he proposed to me to take one of the five boys as an apprentice. A young man, who is now assistant to Professor Hodges, in Belfast, was for four or five years with Professor Johnson. A pupil, educated at the Larne School, is prosecuting his professional studies at the Queen's College, Belfast, with the most marked success, having taken a scholarship in the School of Agriculture during his courses, and the premium of 30*l.* from the Queen's University. It is not only that they hold these situations, but it is their exemplary conduct, also, which is worthy of notice. Several of those young men, from the humblest classes of society, are now filling important and responsible situations, and their conduct, in every respect, is most praiseworthy and gratifying.

" 9654. Lord MONTEAGLE of Brandon. — Have you been able to observe any beneficial consequences in those workhouse schools arising from the introduction of agricultural labour among the paupers? — Yes ; the amount of good is very great indeed.

" 9655. Viscount CLANCARTY. — Do you find that there has been a demand arising for the labour of the persons who have been trained in those workhouse schools, and that the result is very gratifying in that respect? — Yes.

" 9656. Have you had testimony to that effect? — Yes ; since I came to London I have received a very interesting letter* bearing upon that point ; it is from the Rev. Robert Park, Presbyterian clergyman in Ballymoney, in the county of Antrim ; it is dated June the 23rd, 1854. ' My dear sir,— Some years since, the Rev. Dr. Begg of Edinburgh, visited with me the Poor Law Union Workhouse in this town ; he was struck particularly with the arrangements for the instruction of the boys in trades, and for their training in agricultural pursuits. When last I met him in Scotland, he inquired as to the success of the experiment, and it gratified me much to be able to report favourably. Aware of your deep interest in these arrangements, especially with relation to agriculture, I beg

* This letter merits particular attention.

to mention some of the grounds upon which that report was given, confining myself to the department with which you are concerned. The first and obvious is, profit to the union. You are aware that the farm connected with the workhouse here is very limited, extending only to thirteen statute acres; nearly the whole of the work in its cultivation is done by the boys, aided by a few infirm old men; there is not a single able-bodied pauper in the house. These boys were, during the last year, thirteen; their average age, 11 years. Yet I find from the "Ballymoney workhouse farm account, from the 25th of March, 1853, till the 25th of March, 1854," that the balance in favour of the union is 144*l*. 2*s*. 8*d*.; I know that this large sum is due mainly to the excellent system of cropping pursued by the master of the workhouse, and to his judicious management of the stock and farm produce, for which, by the way, a handsome gratuity was awarded him last year by your Board; but without labour this system could not have been carried out; and of this labour the greater part was by boys, who under different circumstances might have been a charge upon the public, and a curse to society. The boys themselves are much benefited in their health. *I have no hesitation in saying that the open air exercise on the farm is a corrective of the injury to the constitution from the confinement necessarily consequent upon the workhouse system. The more robust appearance of the boys so employed, compared with girls of the same age, who are more within doors, strikes every eye. But this health is not obtained at the expense of their literary progress.* The boys employed on the farm are obliged to attend school three hours each day. They are there taught the elements of a useful education, and receive occasionally, through the excellent publications of the National Board, lessons on the science and practice of agriculture. The alternation of farm labour and school business prevents the mind and body from being too much fatigued by either employment, and prepares them to receive greater advantages from both. Their useful preparation for after life is not to be overlooked. I have often admired the expertness of the boys in the use of their implements; their quickness to receive, and their readiness to carry out, directions in farm business; their anxiety to make themselves useful in the different departments of field labour, and their efficiency in its general employment. These must tell favourably on their position in more mature years. The result of an experiment of last year has gratified me exceedingly.

A small portion of ground was allotted to each boy, which he was to cultivate, crop, weed, and manure, being supplied of course with the necessary seeds and manure. It was to be a voluntary exercise; a small sum which you were kind enough to appropriate as rewards for the most efficient management, being the only pecuniary inducement. The boys have been taught something of personal independence and of self-reliance, have been stimulated to diligent persevering exertion, and have been encouraged in friendly rivalry to excel in what must be useful in after life; whilst a moral advantage has followed. Instead of their leisure time being devoted to idleness, and its necessary facilities for evil, it has been employed in the formation of habits, whose influence may tell upon many succeeding generations. There has been some advantage to the farming class in the district. I do not ascribe altogether to their training, that the workhouse boys have been, and still are, anxiously sought after as farm servants. Labour is at present hard to be obtained, and from every quarter is the supply sought; but I have no doubt this preparation commends them to many, and awakens greater anxiety to obtain their services; and so far, I believe, they have given satisfaction to those by whom they have been engaged. I do anticipate still greater beneficial results, when the agricultural model school in progress of erection, and whose grounds adjoin the workhouse farm, is in operation. Upon the whole, I would be delighted were the system of agricultural training, which is carried out in the workhouse, extended to the children of our small farmers generally. Whilst I remark some progress in the management of their holdings, there is still much required to raise our district to a level with other portions of the empire. As confirmatory of the views I have above referred to, I take leave to add a copy of the report of one of your agricultural sub-inspectors, given this day :— " The management of the Ballymoney workhouse farm, for system and efficiency, is almost beyond praise ; and to any person feeling an interest in the welfare and industrial progress of this country, an examination of it would afford unmixed satisfaction. The boys, thirteen in number, whom I examined in the agricultural class, evince a very fair amount of improvement, considering their age and literary attainments, and they seem perfectly to understand the routine of management in which they are required to assist, and the value of the excellent industrial training they receive."

" ' To Dr. Kirkpatrick, &c. &c.' "

Extracts from the Evidence of E. Senior, Esq., Poor Law Commissioner.—June 30th, 1854.

"9421. As those children reach the age which, by the law, is termed able-bodied, is it not of the highest possible importance, both to the public at large and to the children themselves, that their treatment in the workhouses should be such as to enable them to earn an independent livelihood?— Certainly.

"9422. How do you think that that object can be best attained through the instruction of the children in the schools? — By training them to habits of labour early : agricultural labour appears to me the best suited to rural districts. In the case of large towns, that is more difficult; but even there that difficulty may be overcome; for instance, in Belfast and in North Dublin, and other town unions, they have a portion of land attached, and the children are well trained.

"9423. In your evidence yesterday, you stated that the result of your experience enabled you to inform the Committee that such a combination of industrial training, with intellectual training, was equally good for the physical and intellectual well-being of those children? — Certainly ; it is calculated to advance both.

"9424. Have you been able to observe whether, in those workhouse schools where industrial training has been introduced, there has been greater facility manifested in discharging the youth on their reaching the age of 'able-bodied,' than in other cases?—Certainly ; there is a marked difference.

"9425. In that respect the system has the further good effect of a diminution of the rate?—Certainly ; I was very much struck by it in the Belfast Union, the school of which I had almost the local management. In that union, in its earlier stages, the children obtained a bad character as not turning out useful servants. The guardians, with great liberality, built what may be almost called an additional workhouse. They took increased pains to train them, and the result was very satisfactory. I had an opportunity of ascertaining how they turned out in life after they left the workhouse ; and at the last date of my information, not 5 per cent. came back to the workhouse from any cause whatever, including sickness, which, seeing that there was everything against them, both the taint of pauperism, defective physical formation, and hence liability to sickness, is a very favourable result.

"9426. Have the Poor Law Commissioners acted upon the convictions which you have described as being your own individual opinions, and adopted any measures to give effect to such convictions?—They have, in communications addressed both to Boards of Guardians and to Inspectors."

"Glasnevin. June 18, 1857.

"I had charge of the Larne Model Agricultural School for a period of seven years. It was a National School, having seven statute acres of land attached. The instruction afforded to the pupils was of a mixed nature—literary and industrial.

"The result of this mixed teaching was very marked, and in the highest degree successful.

"The following is an extract from an official Report of the Manager of this school relative to the destination of the pupils, who were thus trained during the period mentioned:—

14 were appointed teachers of National Schools.
14 were taken to the National Model Farm, Glasnevin.
4 went to college.
23 entered shops and trades.
29 were apprenticed to sea, having been instructed in the school in navigation.

"Many of the young men educated at Larne occupy at the present time important public situations, among which are the following :—

Agriculturist to the National Model Farm, Glasnevin.
Agriculturist to the Munster Model Farm, Cork.
Agriculturist to the Balieborough Model Farm, Cavan.
Agriculturist to the Athenry College, Galway.
Agriculturist to the Lismore Union, Waterford.
Assistant Chemist and Secretary to the Chemico-Agricultural Society of Ulster.

" One of the young men who went to college is now a candidate for one of the East Indian appointments.

" I am quite satisfied that no amount of mere *literary teaching* would have produced the results pointed out in the above statistics.

" Since my connection with the Albert National Training Establishment (two and a half years ago), it has been a part of my duty to examine the students on entering the Institution, and I have invariably found that the most intelligent and best educated young men were those sent from the *Agricultural Schools.*

" JAMES MACDONNELL,
" Head Master, &c.,
" Albert National Training Establishment,
" Glasnevin.

" To Dr. Kirkpatrick."

Copy of a Letter from Mr. Brogan, Sub-Agricultural Inspector, and formerly Teacher of the Clones Workhouse Schools and the Belvoir National Agricultural School, County Clare.

" Margretta Place, Glasnevin, Dublin.
" June 17, 1857.

" SIR,

" In reply to your inquiry as to the effects of industrial training on the pupils attending the agricultural schools in connection with the Board of National Education, I beg to submit the following observations :—

" My first experience of the beneficial results of combined literary and industrial instruction, was at the Clones Workhouse, County Monaghan, where I undertook the joint duties of schoolmaster and agriculturist in February 1848, at a time when our workhouses were filled to overflowing, pauperism having then attained its maximum. At my entry, the school was in a most disorganised state ; for months previously there had been no attempt at teaching, or even preserving discipline. Having never previously entered a workhouse, I was so appalled by the state of the insubordination I witnessed, as well as by the haggard and miserable appearance of the boys (a large proportion of whom were under medical treatment from diseases incidental to their neglected condition), that I was giving up, in despair of being able to effect any improvement in them. I took heart of grace, however, and began to work in earnest. Three hours each day (ten till one o'clock) were devoted to *literary* instruction in the school, in which I at once established the 'monitorial system,' and four hours (two till six) to *industrial* work on the farm, in which every boy who was able to be of the slightest use was engaged. I got the guardians to allow them an increased dietary; and it was surprising the change which a few months'effected in their physical appearance. From being pale cadaverous-looking beings, whose miserable appearance would excite the pity of the beholders, they became cheerful and healthy. Nor was the change in their moral nature less marked than that in their physical appearance. From being notoriously vicious and insubordinate, they became quiet and obedient to my directions, whether in school or when working in the farm. Neither was the progress in the school in any way retarded by the industrial employment outside, as a reference to the Reports of their district inspector (A. T. Osborne, Esq.) will, I believe, fully testify.

"I did not remain longer than half a year at Clones, but still long enough to witness, with intense satisfaction, the gratifying results achieved under the new system then introduced.

" My next engagement was as teacher of the Belvoir Model Agricultural National School, County Clare; and although the very different moral and physical condition of the pupils I had there to deal with, as contrasted with that of those recently under my management, did not afford scope for the realisation of the same striking results, still I found it to work very effectively, and to be beneficial to the pupils in many respects. The hour usually allocated to 'recreation and amusement' was employed by the pupils in assisting me in my various operations on the model farm attached; and I never could observe that the boys evinced any reluctance to thus employing the time; on the contrary, they seemed eager to accompany me, and to work by my side, until, at the expiration of the hour, we all returned to school together, and resumed the literary occupations with increased zeal and energy.

"I cannot imagine how such a system could have any other than a beneficial effect on the habits and progress of the pupils trained under it. We all know that there is a large amount of vital energy or animal spirits in boys—that if left to themselves, it will evaporate uselessly, most probably mischievously, as we often witness the harm they do when romping about idly. Now it seems a very judicious idea to give vent to this extra energy in a *useful* way, and thereby not only keep the children from evil, but further teach them many useful things, and lay down in their young minds the foundations of industrious and provident habits.

" Again, under a good-tempered and judicious teacher, this industrial work may be made rather *amusement* than drudgery to them.

" The waste time and waste energy of our schoolboys might be usefully applied, if their teachers will only, by skilful management, overcome their natural reluctance to give up 'play' for useful work, which generally involves less physical exertion than the former. I would certainly, in all schools for the poor, substitute *digging* for *jumping, hoeing* for *somersaulting, weeding* for *swinging,* &c., and thus institute a system of *industrial gymnastics,* the superior physical and moral effects of which would soon manifest themselves, as it already has in our agricultural schools here.

"I am your obedient servant,

" M. BROGAN,

"Sub-Agricultural Inspector.

" To Dr. Kirkpatrick."

" Ruthville, Philipsburgh Avenue, Dublin.

"June 19, 1857.

" DEAR DOCTOR,

" In reference to the subject of the enclosed note, I beg to say that, from an experience of sixteen years, I am most decidedly of opinion that combined literary and agricultural education, instead of impairing, strengthens both the mental and physical faculties of youth. In giving expression to this opinion, I do not mean to convey the idea that young persons should be *overpowered* with severe or prolonged labour ; but that their in-door instruction, and out-door practical training, should be so alternated and adapted to their mental and bodily capacities as to prove agreeable and pleasant rather than troublesome and irksome. By attending to the points referred to, injurious consequences can in no way result from the system, but immense advantages be gained. Young lads trained in this way not only acquire a knowledge of farming operations, based on correct principles, but also habits of industry, forethought, and regularity in the performance of their duties, which, except in very rare cases, they never lose in after life.

"I am, dear Doctor,
"Yours very faithfully,
"JOHN DONAGHY,
"Sub-Agricultural Inspector.

"Thomas Kirkpatrick, Esq., M.D., &c."

Juvenile Delinquency, in its Relation to the Educational Movement. By MARY CARPENTER.

[This Paper is here considerably abridged, and in order to confine it within the required limits, it has been necessary to omit many statistical details, mentioning simply results.]

THE Educational Movement has hitherto been considered as regarding the "Working Classes" of the community only, *i. e.*, those who are productive members of it, and who have sufficient enlightenment and moral character to desire education for their children. Those from whom juvenile delinquency chiefly springs, — the actually dangerous, because dishonest, and those perishing and ready for crime, whom preventive measures may and can rescue, — have been until lately by all, and are still by many, considered aliens and outcasts, on whom the public money granted for education ought not to be squandered. We believe that the two classes are inseparably connected with each other, and *that both for the benefit, direct and indirect, of the working classes*, and *as their own inalienable right*, a fair and sufficient share of the public money ought to be applied to their educational training, and applied in such way as may best meet their real wants.

None more than the children of the Working Classes suffer from the proximity and continual contact of the lawless and untaught children who form the million that cannot be accounted for, when an educational census numbers the children of England, and finds so many in schools, so many at work, so many at home, and the

rest?—Where ? These wretched young creatures infest
the streets, tempting or tormenting the steady ones on
their way to school, luring them from it, if possible,
drawing them on to steal, or stealing from them ; or they
diffuse a subtle, unseen, but sure poison in the moral atmosphere of the neighbourhood, dangerous as is deadly
miasma to the physical health. Hence, one after another
of the children of the labouring classes are drawn into the
vortex, and we find them degraded in rank, and supported
by the public in Reformatories. Their existence constitutes also a very important cause, though one not hitherto
understood or generally recognised, of the early age at
which children are removed from school ; for they lower
the educational status of the common schools,—as could
easily be demonstrated, did space permit, — and by throw-
ing into the labour-market of children a number of young
persons quite ignorant, but clever and energetic, whose
strong muscular force and restless minds may be made to
do good service in the hands of a sagacious employer,
learning is at a discount, and parents early remove their
children from school to earn money likewise. Educate
the lower class, and the higher must improve to sustain
their position.

But not only should society *desire* education for this
" perishing and dangerous " class in simple self-protection
from much pecuniary cost and moral injury. These
children, sunk in ignorance and Egyptian darkness, destitute of all that can profit for the life that now is or that
which is to come, have a strong *claim* on those who possess
treasures surpassing gold that perisheth, — a claim impressed by the Heavenly Father on all His creatures, by the
Saviour on all who bear His name and own His sway.
Words are not needed here to enforce that claim, since it
has been so powerfully set forth by His Royal Highness
the Prince Consort in his concluding sentences, and una-

nimously received from him as the voice of this Conference.

We shall regard it as assumed that ignorance and crime coexist to a very great extent, though they are far from being inseparable; and we shall not here attempt to prove the amount of this ignorance in England. The public has been long acquainted with the " Moral Statistics of England and Wales," by the late Joseph Fletcher, Esq., Her Majesty's Inspector of Schools; the reports of various gaol chaplains, especially Rev. J. Clay; the works of Thomas Beggs, in his " Essay on Juvenile Depravity ;" Plint on " Crime," and many others. Yet even these may fail to impress us so strongly with an idea of the ignorance actually existing in our large cities, as the fact, that during only nine months, ending September 30th, 1856, in the town of Liverpool, there were apprehended 19,336 persons, and that of these only 3·00 could read and write well enough to be available for any useful purpose (Vide " Liverpool Police Report"). Half of the remainder had a little imperfect knowledge ; the rest were profoundly ignorant.

Before proceeding further, let us consider what this ignorance actually means. It is not a simple deficiency in intellectual training; not a want of certain kinds of knowledge which are very useful in the ordinary business of life, and which may be made highly available either for good or for evil. This is not the blighting, poisoning ignorance which is at the root of all the criminality which infests our land; nor is any *head-knowledge*, even of the sacred Scriptures, that without which " it is not good for the soul to be." The ignorance which has been here slightly indicated by decimal figures, and by mention of the " beggarly elements" of reading and writing, is a practical ignorance of man's immortal nature and destiny, — an ignorance which degrades below the brute creation, that does fulfil, after its kind, the end for which the Creator gave existence, — which chains to sense and debases by sensual indulgences, — which makes men hunger only for the bread that perisheth, and not for that which is the nutriment of true life, — which makes them thirst only for that which stimulates to maddening frenzy, preventing them from receiving the waters of life. Such is, in faint and few words, the meaning which is really hidden under the simple word "*ignorance*," but which is too often lost sight of in our anxiety to convey rudiments of book-learning, which we most falsely suppose will be an antidote to crime. And the effect of such ignorance is, not only that the individuals labouring under it are utterly unfit to hold any useful social position in the State, — not only that they are without such *practical* acquaintance with the laws of God and man as will withhold them from the crime into which they are continually led by the desire of sensual gratification, — but that they live in a state of entire isolation from the comparatively virtuous and respectable portions of society, and, consequently, more or less in absolute antagonism to it. This condition of things necessarily perpetuates itself. The state of isolation which must be adopted by the grade above for simple self-protection, cuts off the class of which we are speaking from all the civilising influences, the importance of which is increasingly felt in our country by those to whom God has given the talents of wealth and enlightenment. Thus, while for those truly and emphatically called "the people," whose character and education enable them to appreciate these, there are numerous plans adopted for their benefit, nothing has yet been done by the country towards acting on the very class which most of all requires to be raised. We have learnt by this time the lesson, that however necessary gaols and police forces may be, and *are,* for the protection of the community, they *cannot,* by their very nature, do anything towards raising the condition of these outcasts of society ; and however valuable and *essential* in the present state of things are all the refuges and asylums which have been originated by Christian love, and must be sustained by an immense cost of labour and money, if we could rescue only a few, and hold out a way of escape to all,—yet these are merely palliatives, affecting individuals, and *do not strike at the root of the evil.*

This evil really lies in a simple inability, or, more commonly, a profound selfish apathy, on the part of parents respecting the education of their children,—an apathy springing from a moral and spiritual degradation which must involve the child's being brought up in a manner *utterly unfit to enable him to discharge aright the duties of life.*

Such being, then, the presen⊥ position of a large proportion of our rising population, we must consider how we are to apply the remedy.   And, simultaneously with our efforts of a directly educational character, let us endeavour to act on various evils existing in all our large cities, which are both the cause and the effect of crime and ignorance.   Let us remove or suppress the schools of vice, filled with far more skilful and powerful teachers than are to be found in seminaries of learning.   When we study such Police Reports as those already quoted of Liverpool, and learn the number of pest-houses known and allowed, because not put down, and daily shedding their Upas influence over the population, we wonder that so little rather than that so much vice exists.   It is stated in the last Report, that there are in Liverpool 1,445 public houses, and 896 beer-houses, and we know but too well that the consequences of drunkenness are not confined to adults, but extend to the children ; there are no fewer than 714 houses of ill-fame, ready to ensnare the young girls who have not sufficient parental guardianship; there are 431 "marine stores" so called, but in reality places where the products of all kinds of pilfering may be safely disposed of without unpleasant questions being asked; and 271 old-clothes shops, places of a similar description. Besides these, we have a MS. report of 46 houses well known to the police as harbours and training schools for young thieves, truly described as " second hells," where the instructors in crime, most frequently themselves escaping legal detection, gain their livelihood by leading on the young to destruction. What wonder, then, that in a house to house visitation of the homes of 91 juveniles in Walton Gaol, July 14, 1856, none were found to have homes where they could be instructed and guided aright; many had fallen into the snares of some old " queen of demons," as she was not unaptly designated, and many, to escape from drunken homes, had sought refuge in them. Every auxiliary that can be devised by the wisdom of the State, or carried out by Christian benevolence, is needed in this work of regeneration. Yet these are simply auxiliaries; no external means can cure the evil until the spirit is changed and better desires are infused into the heart, and to begin with the children is the only certain and effectual course.

The duty of the State to aid in this work, and the principle on which such aid should be given, were recognised by the Government in the Juvenile Offenders' Act, 17 & 18 Vict. c. 86., passed three years ago. The needful power and pecuniary aid, with due inspection, under certain conditions, were given to institutions under voluntary management, for the reception of children who had become injurious to society by criminal practices. Reformatory schools are now also aided by the parliamentary grants entrusted to the Committee of

Council on Education, under special minutes. These
schools have been multiplying even more rapidly than
the demand for them has increased. A perceptible effect
has been produced on the criminal juvenile population
of every place where they have been fairly tried. In
Liverpool there was an actual diminution of nearly 150
convicted children, chiefly girls, in one year. The chief
constable of Newcastle gives a strong testimony to the
same effect, and Mr. Baker, who has aimed, in his Hardwicke Reformatory, to clear the county of Gloucester,
including Cheltenham, a place very prolific of crime, of
skilled and determined thieves,—an attempt which four
years ago was deemed Quixotic,—has now so fully accomplished his object, that he is able to turn his attention to
Bristol, where the old system of frequent commitments to
Bridewell still continues, and with the well-known results.

Educational returns, obtained from the chief Reformatories which have been established since the passing of
the Act, present the following results. Out of 1,174
children, only 259 (between one-fourth and one-fifth) had
such knowledge on entering the school as would enable
them to read their Testament, and thus learn their duty ;
369 had a little preparatory training, while 554, nearly
one half, were in profound ignorance. The educational
status of the Reformatories varied greatly with circumstances. At Hardwicke a very large proportion were fairly
educated, but they proved to be lads belonging to the
better class of society, who, as we have before shown, had
been dragged down by the lower criminal class. Indeed,
where it has been possible to analyse the returns of other
schools, it has been found that scarcely any were able to
read the Testament except such as had belonged to a
superior class of society, or had been taught during frequent imprisonments. In some of the schools, the proportion who had received a small amount of available

information was not one-fifteenth of the whole! Such, then, being the condition of the juvenile delinquent class (for we have already shown what this ignorance indicates), how can we remedy it? It is evident that these children had received all the education they would have, for only about 40 were under 10 years of age, and a large proportion were between 14 and 16. But this ignorance is not the effect of inability to find schools, for we learn from the returns, that very few children profess to have been at no school at all, and the attendance ranges from twelve months to five years. What effect this schooling had had, may be judged from the fact, that one boy, who could barely tell his letters, professed to have been at school for six *years* (six *weeks* would have been nearer the truth); and in a large class, of which only one had not been at school, a single lad alone had ever heard of the Fall of Man before coming to the school.

All these children belong to that extensive class of whom we have already spoken, where the parents, either from extreme poverty causing a precarious mode of life, or vicious habits causing utter recklessness, do not take the slightest concern for their children's true welfare. Where this evil has been great, it has been grappled with by Reformatories; but these can no more prevent crime and remove ignorance in a district, than can a hospital spread a healing influence through an infected locality teeming with pestilence. The numbers of actually convicted children in a locality is small in comparison with those known to the police, as indicated by the number of apprehensions. In Bristol there were 552 of these in one year; in Liverpool, 1,444. The children who are preparing to constitute our criminal class cannot endure the regular restraint and control of any school; no allurements of food or clothing will induce them to forfeit their Arab and lawless liberty voluntarily. But society, which will have to bear the burden of the necessary consequence of such ignorance and license, surely has a right to *require* that young persons, *so* growing up, shall be led by the hand of the law to a school where, while food is supplied, the means of earning such bread honestly is also communicated, as well as the knowledge of the laws of God and man.   Such right is asserted in the Bill now before Parliament, formerly introduced by Sir S. Northcote, now introduced by Mr. Adderley.   The soundness of the principle has for many years been demonstrated in Scotland by Sheriff Watson and his coadjutors, and is now supported there by the Dunlop Acts.   It has been asserted, within the last two years, by the Government of the Commonwealth of Massachusetts, in passing a bill to establish a reform school for girls (that for boys having for some time existed), wherein it is enacted that if it is proved to the satisfaction of the judge that a girl's " *moral welfare and the good of society* require that she should be sent to the said school, he shall commit the said girl to the same." It is hoped that England will not be behind Scotland and the United States in *comprehending the true nature of liberty.*   " Whoso sinneth, is the slave of sin."

But let us suppose that all the children are within the walls of Reformatory or Industrial Feeding Schools who ought to be there, will juvenile delinquency be in the course of extinction?   *Most certainly not!*   Some of the recruits will spring, as already shown, from the ranks of those who ought to have been in a very different position in society,—boys and girls whose bad home influences, or peculiar character, have been lowered into the ranks.   But the bulk of them are those who are growing up, owing to the vice or extreme poverty of their parents, without any *true education.*   This is well known to all who have practically studied the subject ; and the vast discrepancy existing between the numbers of children in any large town, and the number of those attending schools, proves to us the existence of such a class. They neither *can* attend our common schools for want of suitable clothing and the means of payment, nor *would* they do so if these were provided. Besides, experienced British schoolmasters have assured me that the simple presence of such children in a school is a decided injury, in lowering both the educational and moral tone. The experiment has been tried in an admirable school situated in a very low neighbourhood. The master admitted any of this class who could be induced to come; but found the disadvantage to the school more than counterbalanced the gain received by the boys, whose wild nature with difficulty submitted to restraint.

It is evident that a mass of irregular, ill-clad, low children, as the nature of their homes necessarily makes them, would be an injustice to the offspring of respectable working people, whose frequent local proximity to these would make them anxious to preserve their children from habits of intimacy which might prove most injurious. But were they admissible, do the common schools actually meet the wants of the class contemplated? The instruction, chiefly intellectual, and every year reaching a higher standard, under the fostering care of the Committee of Council on Education, is little calculated alone to fit them for life. Do they not want still more, moral and religious training, the inculcation of virtuous habits, and a love of labour? To these, intellectual instruction may indeed be subsidiary, but it is the means, not the end. It is clear that no mere schools can meet the wants of this class. Earnest Christian action on the parents, as well as the children, and the appliance not only of instruction but *education*, is needed.

Now, to meet the wants of this class of children, who are swarming in all our large cities, and infesting our streets, and not only growing up to crime themselves,

but luring in those who would otherwise be attendants
of school, it is evident that no merely mechanical means
can suffice, and that the devoted work of Christian people
is needed, who would strive in every way to discover the
true method of meeting the difficulty. And it is necessary, while doing everything possible to promote the
spiritual welfare of these poor children, that care should
be taken not to foster the improvidence and vice of their
parents, in whom simple poverty is *seldom* the chief or
only cause of this moral destitution. To afford education
solely, is practically found *not* to foster improvidence in
this class, since *accepting* it only for their children often
involves considerable self-denial, and does not directly
conduce to their own benefit. Now, to meet this great
want, Ragged Schools were first established, at first ex-
perimentally and very imperfectly; but with increasing
experience, the machinery has been improved, the work
extended, and very striking results have been obtained.
The last Report of the Ragged School Union states that
there are no fewer than 100 day-schools connected with
it, containing no fewer than 14,700 scholars. Doubtless
many of these schools are of a low educational rank, and
might be greatly improved were the means of making
them so afforded. But with all their disadvantages and
deficiencies, it is no slight benefit to have transformed idle
ignorant children into those who know how to acquire an
honest living, and desire to do it. In the course of the
last year, the shoe-black brigades earned no less than
2,981*l.* for their own support; 1,260 scholars were put
out into situations; in 46 of the schools there are no fewer
than 10,117 depositors in the Penny Banks, and the sums
paid in during the year have amounted to 3,439*l.* It is
evident that an immense amount of very varied voluntary
work, independently of the ordinary school training, must
have been needed to effect this, and that the results on

the class attending must be highly beneficial, not only in raising an unproductive class to be productive, but in the direct repression of crime. Mr. M. D. Hill, in his recent work on this subject, states that while in the Bristol Ragged Union Schools there were 26 imprisonments of children attending the schools in 1849, during the last five years there have been together only three; in the St. James' Back Ragged School for many years no child in attendance has been in prison, though near its commencement there were 25 in one year. And yet a careful inspection will satisfy any experienced observer that the children attending are actually those who could not attend the ordinary day schools, and most of whom would be in the streets without such agency.

Such schools must necessarily be very expensive: with a sufficient staff, more than twice as much so as ordinary schools, where the pence of the children supply a considerable income, and where pupil teachers, paid by Government, supply the place of adult assistants. Besides, no ordinary teachers will be required. While creeds and formulas, and *mere* Scripture knowledge will be of little value, yet the spirit of religion should be deep in the teacher's heart, and infuse itself into his teachings. He must endeavour to gain a hold in the children's *hearts*, to make them *feel* that they are no longer aliens and outcasts, and that no man careth for their souls; and this must be done, not by formal lessons, but through the medium of daily intercourse, in all " the patience of hope and the labour of love." The intellectual training will be such as rather to aid in the moral discipline, to excite a desire of knowledge, and to give the power of reading and enjoying books of a healthy and interesting character rather than in the communication of ordinary school details; and industrial occupation must form a prominent part of the day's routine. These, and provisions for cleanliness and sanitary discipline, for innocent amusement and exercise, the aiding to obtain work on leaving school, with many other auxiliary plans which experience will suggest, must form part of a Ragged School.

Now it is evident, that if any school deserves and needs a full share of the Parliamentary Educational Grant such an one as this does. The Ragged School is the only barrier to the country against the continual increase of ignorance and degradation,—the only refuge of that large portion of the population whose children, not yet condemned to the Reformatory or sunk into the Work-house, are struggling on to secure from day to day a precarious support, or who are utterly careless about their moral and spiritual wants. It is evident also that the Minutes of Council adapted to the British and National Schools are perfectly inapplicable to these. No certificate *can* test the fitness of a master; no young pupil teachers can be trained in *these* schools; no capitation grants can be made for children whose parents pay *nothing* for them; and no returns of the number of children who can read, write, or cipher, can give a correct idea of what has been done in the school. In fine, considerable latitude must be allowed to zealous and judicious managers, and free scope to devoted teachers, especially in their religious instruction. With such help as can be given to Ragged Schools by pecuniary grants, and the experienced inspection of the Committee of Council on Education, Ragged Schools may be made to supply the need existing in the country; but without such aid they must struggle feebly on, fail efficiently to do their work, or sink, and the children grow up as before untaught. Devoted *voluntary* workers *only* can draw within the bonds of society these unfortunate children, but the hands of these workers must be strengthened by such help as the State can give. The Minute framed for Reformatory and Ragged Schools, June 2nd, 1856, would fully answer the end proposed; but unhappily a test recently imposed confines the application of that Minute to schools for convicted or vagrant children, which Ragged Schools are not necessarily, though they do not exclude such. Surely this Conference will direct its attention to the condition of those schools for a portion of the population whose well-being is so closely allied with that of the working classes. Nor will this Christian country forget the words of the Saviour, " Inasmuch as ye have done it unto one of the least of these my little ones, ye have done it unto me."

On the Proposed Middle Class Examinations as a means of stimulating the Education of the Lower Classes. By W. L. SARGANT, Esq., of Birmingham.

THE subject appointed for discussion by this section especially, is the question what means can be adopted to induce parents to keep their children longer at school. In the opinion of many persons, the most effectual of all means would be to improve the quality of the instruction given. Among the middle classes, it has been observed, the addition of French and German to the old classical course, has had the effect of retaining boys at school longer than was customary before. There is no doubt that the same rule applies to the working classes. It is notorious that inferior and neglected parish schools are generally half empty, while the really good schools in the same neighbourhood are overflowing with pupils.

The question then is, what mode can best be adopted for imparting additional excellence to the school instruction of the country. I am afraid that it is not of much use to try to raise the quality of the instruction of the lowest classes, unless we can first do as much for the middle classes. The different ranks of society run so much into each other, that one cannot be raised without the other.

On this ground I have been permitted to bring before this section a short account of the move now being made by the Universities to further the education of young persons in the country at large. The object proposed by this Conference is, no doubt, to inquire into the education of the working classes; whereas the new university scheme professedly relates to the middle classes. But in towns, at least, the different classes of society so run into each other that it is impossible to separate them. A large proportion of the pupils of grammar schools, if they are not actually the sons of mechanics, are the sons of persons only just above that position.

I am not, I confess, one of those who believe that the education of the true middle classes is more in want of improvement than the education of the lower classes and who think that the kibe of the employer is galled by the clouted shoe of the mechanic. To say nothing of the formation of manners and of character, the greater part even of instruction which most men acquire is learnt at home. A boy of the better classes knows more when he first goes to school, than the son of a mechanic when he leaves school. But among those people who have risen from the ranks, this is not true. A man and his wife who themselves never received instruction, are, of course, quite unable to teach their children. They send them, at nine or ten years old, to schools where hitherto it has been too much assumed that the pupils, on entrance, are already instructed in the elements of an English education. The result is that many boys grow up with some knowledge of the higher departments of literature and science, but with an unhappy ignorance of the rudiments of instruction. The Government examinations besides, have shown us that this disgraceful want of elementary instruction is not altogether confined to this class of persons.

The scheme before us is intended to remedy this crying evil. It has been constructed with great care by the Rev. F. Temple, one of her Majesty's inspectors of schools. Mr. Temple, after anxious deliberation, and much consultation with his friends, determined on propounding his plan to the public. He agreed with his brother inspector, the Rev. H. W. Bellairs, that Birmingham should have the honour of bringing the scheme into the world. An Educational Association had been formed in that borough some time before, for the purpose of improving the elementary schools, and of furthering education generally. To a committee of this society, Mr. Bellairs explained Mr. Temple's propositions, on the 15th April last. He read the following letter:—

"*April* 11, 1857.

"MY DEAR BELLAIRS,

"The education of the Middle Classes in England appears to me to suffer from two causes : the schoolmasters have no guide to direct them what subjects they should teach, or how they should teach those subjects ; the parents no guide to direct them what schools they should prefer.

"Every one who knows anything of education knows how fatal the former deficiency must be. Without any definite aim, or, if he makes an aim for himself, without any recognised *means* of testing his own methods of attaining it, the schoolmaster in this class of schools flounders from one mistake into another, or persists year after year in a false system, depending for his bread, not on hard work and honest endeavour after excellence, but on plausible appearance and skilful puffing. The parents, meanwhile, though they certainly know enough about (if not of) education to desire it for their children, are constantly misled into preferring showy useless acquirements to solid knowledge and real cultivation.

"These difficulties would at once disappear if some Body capable of commanding the confidence both of teachers and parents were to undertake the task of guiding and testing the work done in these schools.

"I think that the University of Oxford might do this, and do it well.

"I should propose that the University should appoint a Board of Examiners to examine all boys, from whatever rank, and however educated, who might choose to present themselves, and should grant to all who passed, some such a title as that of Associate in Arts. (A.A. to rank as it were below our present B.A.)

"This examination should have two grades; one taking a standard fairly within the reach of boys of 15 for Junior Associates; the other taking a standard to correspond with the age of 17 for Senior Associates.

" The examination should consist of —

" 1. A preliminary examination in

"*a*. Writing from Dictation, Arithmetic, Parsing, General Geography, for all.

"*b*. Religious Knowledge for those whose parents did not object.

" 2. Four schools —

"*a*. The School of Languages; to include French, German, and the Elements of Latin.

"*b*. The School of English; to include English Literature, English History, and Geography.

"*c*. The School of Mathematics; to include Practical Mathematics and Drawing.

"*d*. The School of Physics; to include the Elements of the Mechanical, Chemical, and Physiological Sciences.

" Every candidate should pass through the preliminary examination, and also one of the schools.

" Honours should be granted in a Class List of those who did well; a pass without honours to those who did satisfactorily, but no more.

" The examination should be held annually in Oxford. But an Examiner should be sent down, with the same papers as were being set at the same time at Oxford, to any place where the gentry and local authorities desired it, and were willing to pay the additional expenditure incurred in hiring rooms for the examination.

" Every candidate should pay a fee (say 5*s*.) for admission, and every candidate who passed should pay an additional fee (say 2*s*. 6*d*.) for his *testamur*.

" Yours ever,

" F. TEMPLE."

This letter seems to me to explain with clearness and precision the objects aimed at, and the means proposed for attaining them. The details were given merely for discussion, and not with the idea that they would be adopted without alteration.

The Birmingham Committee at once appreciated the importance of Mr. Temple's scheme, and passed a resolution pledging itself to support it. At a meeting subsequently, of the whole association, this resolution was approved. Memorials were then signed by a number of the clergy, magistrates, and other principal inhabitants, praying the University of Oxford to take the matter into consideration.

About the middle of May this, with other memorials, was laid before the authorities of Oxford; a committee of the Council was appointed to consider the subject, and a Statute was passed through the first of the three governing bodies. The particulars are thus given in the "Times" of 30th May, under the head of University Intelligence.

"The following is a more exact abstract of the new statute on the subject of middle-class education than our space permitted us to give yesterday :—

"The preamble recites the fact of numerous applications having been made to the University to bring into connection with it by a system of examinations classes of persons beyond its bounds engaged in studies of a liberal character.

"Clause 1 enacts that two examinations of such persons shall be held annually, either in Oxford or elsewhere, as may seem expedient,—one of older students between the ages of 15 and 18; the other, of younger students, who have not completed their 15th year.

"Clause 2 fixes the subjects of examination, which are (1) the Rudiments of Religion for those persons whose parents or guardians do not object; (2) English Literature; (3) History; (4) Languages; (5) Mathematics; and (6) Natural Science.

"Clause 3 enacts that *Testamurs* shall be given at both examinations to all who satisfy the examiners; and that the title of Associate in Arts shall be conferred on those who obtain a *Testamur* in the senior examination.

"Clause 4 provides for the appointment of a delegacy to nominate the examiners, and to fix the time and character of the examinations, the number of the classes, &c. The delegacy proposed consists of twenty-one members ; viz., the Vice-Chancellor, the proctors, six persons named by the Hebdomadal Council from their own body, six persons elected by Congregation, and six nominated by the Vice-chancellor and proctors. The delegacy is to be appointed for three years.

"Clause 5 gives the delegates the power of requiring from the candidates a scale of fees sufficient to defray the expenses of the examinations.

"Clause 6 imposes on the delegates the duty of making an annual report to the University.

"The statute is accompanied by the report of a committee of the council appointed to consider the subject, consisting of the Vice-chancellor, the Provost of Worcester, the Masters of Pembroke and Balliol, the Principals of Brasenose and Magdalen Hall, Professors Pusey and Daubeny, Mr. Michell, Mr. Gordon, and Mr. Mansel. This report is followed by a number of documents, chiefly memorials from places of importance in favour of such a scheme as that proposed. The most important are two from Birmingham, — one from the Educational Association, the other signed by eighty-one of the most influential inhabitants ; one from Cheltenham, with forty-six signatures ; one from Gloucester ; one from Leeds, signed by the trustees and masters of the Grammar School, and by many clergy of Leeds and of the neighbourhood ; one from the Hants and Wilts Education Society ; one from the Warwick and Leamington Schoolmasters' Association ; and one from the Examination Committee of the West of England Prize Scheme. These memorials are preceded by two letters from the Rev. F. Temple to the Master of Pembroke, suggestive in all the main points of the scheme to be proposed to Congregation."

It was never intended that this move should be confined to Oxford. Mr. Temple, being a member of that University, and naturally possessing more influence there, began where he thought himself more secure of success. But when the first step had been fairly taken, it was suggested that a similar application should be made at Cambridge. The Council of that University consented to receive a deputation from the Educational Association, and on the 29th of May, five gentlemen, including Mr.

Temple, had an interview with the Council at Cambridge. Before this time, a pamphlet on the subject had been printed and circulated among the members of the Council. A few days afterwards the Council met again, and made the following report :—

"June 1. The Council of the Senate beg leave to report to the Senate that they have received a deputation from Birmingham, consisting of the Rev. E. H. Gifford, Mr. J. T. Chance, Mr. W. L. Sargant, the Rev. H. W. Bellairs, and the Rev. F. Temple, on the subject of middle-class education. They have also received the subjoined memorials on the same subject. They are further informed that a scheme has been prepared by the Hebdomadal Council of the University of Oxford for the purpose of establishing a system of examinations to be conducted under the authority and direction of the University, either at Oxford or elsewhere, and of conferring certificates or some title of proficiency upon those candidates from schools of a middle-class character who may pass the examinations with credit. The council are of opinion that a scheme of a similar nature might advantageously be adopted by this University ; and accordingly they recommend that a syndicate be appointed for the purpose of conferring with the persons who take an interest in the matter, and of preparing, in the form of a report to the Senate, the details of such a scheme as they can recommend for its adoption. (Signed) H. Philpott, Vice-chancellor, Robert Phelps, W. Whewell, G. E. Corrie, William Selwyn, E. Harold Browne, J. Grote, W. H. Bateson, G. E. Paget, W. G. Clark, F. France, Francis Martin, J. C. Adams, Charles Hardwick, W. M. Campion."

It is hoped, from the desire shown on these occasions, by a large party in both the old Universities, that measures similar to the one proposed will be hereafter adopted. The advantage to be derived seems to me quite manifest. I have for the last ten years watched with great care the proceedings of a particular school which is attended by boys of the classes I have mentioned ; some of the boys being sons of well educated men, others being sons of persons of indifferent education. I believe the school in question to be one of the best in the kingdom, whether for boys intended for trade, or for the London University.

The Latin and Greek are good, though without those fopperies which consume the time needful for other pursuits. The Mathematics are excellent, and leave nothing to be desired. The French and German are beyond the common run, as is the Drawing also. Still there are deficiencies of a rather grave kind, and such deficiencies as the proposed scheme is exactly fitted to supply. I will not say that the boys cannot spell correctly, though perhaps it is too readily assumed that that ignoble part of learning is given at home. But if we come to English Grammar, General Geography, Modern History, there is considerable ground for finding fault. Even the modern languages would be far better taught if the resident masters had constantly before their eyes the fear of an examiner's approval or censure. The severest sense of duty will hardly keep a master so well up to his work as the hope or fear of distinction or disgrace.

On the other hand, it is said that there are many commercial schools of a very inferior character, in which Latin and Greek are unknown, and where, therefore, there is plenty of time for instruction in modern learning. It is suspected, however, that in some of these academies, much of this time is thrown away by an injudicious course of instruction.

My own observation has led me to this conviction, that a boy who remains at school till seventeen, may, with ordinary ability and application, become a fair Latin scholar, may acquire a considerable knowledge of Greek, may learn as much French as will enable him to read it with facility; may know enough elementary German to enable him to pursue it afterwards if he pleases, and may unite all this with a sound English education. But this proficiency will not be generally attained, until some test is applied to the boys who leave school; and this test the proposed examination supplies.

This scheme has received the support of very different parties, both in the Universities and in the press. It has, of course, also met with objectors. It has been said that to give a degree to a boy would make him conceited. This objection is on a par with Pope's hackneyed couplet :—

> " A little learning is a dangerous thing ;
>   Drink deep, or taste not the Pierian spring."

The answer is obvious. Give a little learning to every one, and none will be puffed up by it; let boys of seventeen generally have a degree, and it will become a disgrace to be without it rather than a subject of vanity to possess it.

Then it is said that if all possess the degree it ceases to be worth contending for ; better, therefore, to give it only to those who do unusually well in examinations. The answer is obvious. You inflate the vanity of the few, and leave the many to accident; you encourage an ambitious master to coach up his clever boys, and to neglect the dull boys, who especially need his attention.

An appeal has been made to the public against Mr. Temple's scheme, on behalf of the College of Preceptors and of the Society of Arts. The ground, it is said, is already occupied by these institutions, and the present proposal is a poaching on their manor. For my own part, I think there is room for all, and I welcome all these attempts as aiming at the same object. The College of Preceptors has been in existence some years; but though it may claim the whole educational field on the ground of prior discovery, it certainly has at present actually occupied and cultivated only a corner. The Society of Arts appears to me to have another field peculiarly fitted for it. The scheme before us proposes to deal with boys under 18, and abandons to the Society of Arts that large class, who have received an imperfect education, and who, as adults, try to supply the deficiency by attending mechanics' institutes or people's colleges.   But even if this were not so, I hardly think that much toleration would be shown to a claim of vested interests.

A newspaper of large circulation has put out an objection, that it is insulting to the public, on the part of the Universities, to offer the inferior degree of A.A. to the commonalty, while they reserve their choicer B.A. for their more aristocratic residents.   The whole statement indicates much carelessness on the part of the writer. The comparison of the two degrees is essentially false, since the A.A. is offered to boys under 18, the B.A. cannot be well obtained under 21.   A boy may hereafter get his A.A. at school, and then go to the University to read for his B.A.; nay, it is perfectly conceivable that hereafter, if this scheme should be generally adopted, the Universities may require from every candidate for admission, that he should have obtained the school degree of A.A.   At any rate, it would be absurd to offer a school boy of 18 the same degree that is now conferred on young men of 21 or 22, after three years' residence.

At the Universities themselves, the objections are of a different kind.   To say nothing of the religious difficulty which meets us at every turn in educational matters, some fear is felt of any thing that may tend to lessen the practice of residence at Oxford or Cambridge, on the part of the ordinary students.   I should myself deeply regret any such tendency.   I feel that in the formation of the character and the manners of our educated classes, a residence in an University is of high importance, and that this practice would be ill supplied by substituting private tutors, and still worse by sojourning in foreign universities.   Whatever spicy pictures may be drawn by romance writers of the habits of undergraduates, I believe that in no country are a thousand young men thrown together with less dissipation and vice than in Oxford and Cambridge. It is a matter of astonishment to Mr. Emerson that in both those places a duel should be a thing unheard of.

One other objection, and I have done. Some persons affect to look with alarm at the threatened extension of university influence. Now if it were proposed to apply to Parliament to grant any new powers,—if it were proposed to confer a monopoly on these learned bodies, to prevent any other body from either teaching or examining, — we should have reason to cry out against such a proposition. But if the Universities offer to do what, from intellectual fitness, and long-proved impartiality, and great experience, they are peculiarly fitted to do,—and if the public accept their offer, I cannot see any ground for jealousy. Every one who confers a service on another obtains a certain influence over him ; every one who is of service to the public obtains a certain influence over the public. But such an influence as this, which is measured strictly by the services rendered, I cannot grudge to any person, nor to any body corporate. I am not aware of anything to alarm us either, in the character of our university men. In running over the schools and colleges supported by gentlemen not belonging to the Church of England, I find many instances in which the masterships are filled by graduates of Oxford or Cambridge. Such men are trusted by those who differ from them in creed, because it is well known that there is no danger of any attempt to make proselytes. Surely those who are trusted to educate, may be well trusted to conduct an examination.

I am glad to find that since I wrote this paper, the statute has gone through all its three stages at Oxford, having been passed finally by Convocation, with an over-

whelming majority, though the granting the degree of
A. A. did not meet with such decided favour as the general
provisions.   Cambridge, too, has done all that time permitted, by appointing a Syndicate, or what the world calls
a Committee, to arrange a scheme for consideration next
term.   Everything now depends on the wise execution of
the measure, and on the hearty cooperation of the country
at large.

Indirect Compulsory Schooling: a Scheme submitted to the Educational Conference. By the Rev. J. B. OWEN, of St. John's, Bedford Row, London.

I WOULD not have ventured to submit any suggestion on this important occasion, except for the fact that I appear rather as the amanuensis of another person than as embarking upon any theory of my own. The practical experience of the individual whom I represent entitles him to be heard. In the first instance, some objections may be urged against Sir John Pakington's Bill, dated February, 1857. With the deepest respect for the Right Honourable Baronet's sincere intentions, it may be remarked that his visit to Manchester seems to have synchronised with his adoption of the Manchester scheme, which at all events is identical with his own. The objections to the former scheme, and consequently to its embodiment in the Right Honourable Baronet's, seem to be, 1st. That its provisions, being applicable only to corporate cities and boroughs, are not commensurate with the demands of the country. 2nd. That the adoption of the bill being discretional with such cities and boroughs, any advantages supposed to be involved in it, are contingent upon elective caprice and popular prejudice. 3rd. That the election of the School Committee being vested in ratepayers, is obnoxious to the mischance of an inefficient and prejudiced Board of Supervision. 4th. The bill being based upon rates, seems open to the abstract objection, that all compulsory levies are *primâ facie* unwelcome, and hence any system so supported is disparaged by an *â priori* unpopularity, and therefore not likely to attract much public co-operation. Certain details of the measure are further questionable, as the indiscriminate choice of the governing body, affording too slight a guarantee of competence; the rule of a third of the number retiring annually, who, though reeligible, are liable to rejection; and, if so, exposing the school to the mischiefs of a shifting supervision, or to the alternative of a permanent misrule. Any improvement, however excellent in itself, happening to be unpopular, would be periodically set aside by the non-election' of its projector, the tendency of which would be to discourage improvements, and retard educational progress. Generally, any legislative measure which supported education by rates would naturally tend to cheapen education,—to keep down the rates, instead of to raise the style of teaching.

Lord Kinnaird's Bill, dated 14th May, 1857, in my humble judgment, is a step in the right direction. It proposes an extension of the existing factory plan to " all trades, handicrafts, works, and businesses, whether in towns or villages."

The defects in his Lordship's Bill appear to be:

1st. The limitation of its certificate to reading—writing at least is an indispensable addition, as implying probably a longer period of educational influence. Reading and writing are the arms and legs of education, and nothing more; but if only part of the limbs of instruction be supplied, the child starts into life intellectually crippled.

If the child be unable to write, he can make no memorandum to refresh his memory, nor hold epistolary intercourse with his family, patron, or employer, or other desirable, and sometimes necessary correspondents.

Instances repeatedly occur where pupils, who have removed to their callings at distant places, have so confided in the advice, and realised the influence of their old teachers, that salutary impressions, originated under the blessing of God at school, have been perpetuated in their after life through the medium of correspondence.

2nd. Another defect in his Lordship's bill is the devolving the educational certificate upon magistrates, or ministers of religion, or schoolmasters, and even mistresses. With no disrespect to these or other local functionaries, the objection is, their possibly vague and indefinite educational status as a body : while in individual instances they may be indifferent or opposed to educational advancement, or too much occupied to pay sufficient attention to any real examination of the child, or they may be influenced by feelings of sympathy for the parents, or other local circumstances. The inadequacy of a mere reading test may be illustrated by the old legal fiction of the benefit of clergy. A man on his trial for felony was usually put to read a certain Latin verse in the psalms, called " the neck verse," because on his ability to read it, his neck depended. A forensic cram, however, commonly enabled him to secure the clerk's exemption on the score " legit at clericus," and entitled him to benefit of clergy. With equal facility a child might be taught to read some hackneyed passage to pass muster for its certificate, but no such trick could be played with the mechanical act of writing. It is suggested that in every market town an officer may be appointed by the Vice-President of the Committee of Council on Education, on satisfactory evidence being produced of such officer's capacity. Any moderately educated tradesman, or clerk in the town, might be selected, much in the same way as local post-masters commonly are, who, having merely to judge of the ability of a candidate for a certificate in the rudimental arts of reading and writing, could be everywhere readily found. He should file the specimen of the writing on which he granted or declined his certificate in a book, subject to the revision of a district inspector, for purposes of reference in cases of complaint, whether for or against the certifier's decision. The expense might be defrayed by a fee of 1s. per certificate granted, of which sum 10d. might be the proportion to remunerate the certifier, and, the certificate being written on a twopenny stamp, the balance of 2d. thus readily collected, be credited to a general fund for the disbursement of the expenses of central offices of supervision.

Subject to these amendments, Lord Kinnaird's Bill has my warmest support. It would then generally embody the proposal of this paper, which, with the great advantage of simplicity of operation, is briefly this : " to impose a penalty on every person employing any one who being under 10 years of age, at the time of passing of the Act, has not a certificate of ability to write from dictation a simple sentence, and read with ease a simple narrative." The above certificate to be given by some such officer as above described, for the fee above mentioned, and, if lost, to be renewed at a like charge. The employer also to be obliged to take some specimen of the person's writing, say his name, age, date of certificate, &c. It is obvious the opportunity of appealing to such a law would give school managers great influence with the parents of idle and irregular children now under 10 years of age. They could say to them, what they cannot say now, " Your child will never get employment till it can read and write." The employer should be exempt from penalty if he provide, at his own expense, instruction at school for his employés at least three hours a day for five days in the week. This plan indirectly, but effectually, meets the case of parents employing children to assist a little at home ; for though they incur no penalty at the time, they will see that ignorance must preclude their getting employment afterwards.

It is well known that the attainments of a large number of children on leaving school are so imperfect, that they are often lost in a few years or even months. This plan will operate as an inducement to young persons to keep up their power of reading and writing, inasmuch as, in case of loss of the certificate, they will have to be re-examined; and, moreover, on each change of place they will be required to write.

It has been suggested that the restriction above referred to must not be applicable all through life; and perhaps it will be sufficient if limited to persons under 21 years of age.

A certificate from the examiner, of natural inability to learn, would exempt from the penalty.

The painful pressing critical question of popular ignorance, with its invariable concomitants of vice and ungodliness, cannot, with impunity to any of the great interests, duties, and responsibilities of society and government, be longer postponed. There are dangers to be intercepted, and difficulties to be surmounted, which demand earnest and immediate grappling with, and a conscientious conviction of the possibility of success, under the blessing of God, upon the diligent use of well-advised means.

Two facts may be noticed in connection with the subject: —

1. There are in this country myriads of children growing up without any adequate instruction.

2. Existing school buildings are not sufficient to receive all the children who ought to be in school.

From these two facts a conclusion is drawn, which is the foundation of most of the efforts and plans of the *theorists in education,* who have the ear of the country both in and out of Parliament; namely, that if a sufficient number of schools were provided and could be maintained, the problem of National Education would be solved.

This conclusion is, unfortunately, a mere groundless assumption, the fallacy of which may be proved from numberless instances of good schools which are not filled.

The practical difficulty of providing for the maintenance of schools, when built, has caused the failure of all schemes for the extension of National Education.

While, then, the *theoretical educationists* are occupied with devising plans, which, if successful, would probably issue in disappointment, it may be well to view the question in another aspect.

Managers and Inspectors of schools throughout England concur with scarcely a dissentient voice, that the great educational want at the present moment is not so much the want of additional school rooms, as the means for bringing children into existing schools, and retaining them there for an adequate time.

Prodigious efforts have been made within the last fifteen years to raise up a staff of able earnest teachers for juvenile schools; success has crowned those efforts. Teachers are dispersed by hundreds and thousands over the country, but they are to a great extent surrounded by mere infants.

Is the case hopeless? With the deep-rooted feeling of Englishmen on the subject of individual freedom of action, any attempt, by direct legislative enactment, to compel all parents to send their children to school may be regarded as impossible.

Can the object be accomplished indirectly? To expect that any scheme to enforce the attendance of all children of any prescribed age will at once be effectual, is visionary. Any plan for this purpose can only be an experiment.

Lord John Russell, in his Educational Resolutions of 1856, proposed to meet the case by requiring *employers of children*, between nine and fifteen years old, to furnish half yearly certificates of attendance at school, and to pay for their instruction.

Let it be borne in mind that the leading object of his Lordship is to lay hold of that vast mass of children (according to the last census, 2,250,000), who are neither at work nor at school. Lord John Russell's proposal would not reach these children. It is possible that a majority of these children who are at work, but who ought to be at school, do not remain half a year at a time with one master. Lord John Russell's proposal would not reach them. Though it is comparatively easy to legislate for a few factories over which inspectors are appointed, the difficulty of carrying the law into effect, even in reference to those children, may be judged of from the number of precautions necessary to prevent evasion. To enforce such a law on the employers of single children over the whole country is impossible : I therefore fall back upon the plan already proposed, in reference to which Archdeacon Wigram observes in a private letter to a friend — " I do not feel that we have solved the problem yet, but I have not seen a nearer approximation to the solution than Mr. Jos. Allen has made, and I feel confident that the discussion of it must do good." It is submitted, that the scheme proposed involves nothing anti-ecclesiastical on the one hand, nor sectarian on the other, but simply makes indirectly compulsory an universal popular education, which would help to fill all kinds of existing schools, and, by their need, multiply their number. The objection to the proposal, in some minds, may be its apparent interference with the liberty of the subject. This may be met by the reply, that great social benefits are usually unattainable except by some corresponding infringement of individual liberty; the public sooner or later submit to regulations which really promote their own interests. For instance, compulsory vaccination, and the penalty for exposing the public to contagion, by persons suffering from small-pox being found at large, may seem arbitrary invasions of individual rights; but the terrible evils of the malady, avoided by adherence to the statute, disarm popular objection to its provisions, and if it were otherwise, would still justify the legislative interposition. The compulsory registration of the birth, and the date and cause of the death of members of our family, might appear to be matters with which the public have no concern; yet, as in many indirect or possible contingencies, the public interest may be involved in the registration, the law makes it imperative on pain of fine for its neglect. Though they had to encounter much ignorant deprecation at first, the common sense of the public has long ago endorsed both bills, without further protest on the score of the liberty of the subject. The laws of quarantine, in all maritime countries, are another illustration of the necessity of individual restraint, with a view to the protection of the public. The plastic season of youth is the moral quarantine of life, through which the public safety, as well as individual interest, require a child to pass if we would secure some guarantee for averting moral contagion.

The proposal, in a positive view, affords —

1st. All practicable liberty of conscience: the child may be trained at home, or in other private house; in a church school, chapel school, or Jew school, under a dame or dominie, with or without inspection; it leaves it discretional where you teach, but insists on the child being taught somewhere.

2nd. The minimum of education required is moderate. It does not exact astronomy nor geography, algebra nor Euclid, chemistry nor philosophy, arts nor sciences, dead languages nor living ones, except the mere ability to read and write the vernacular.

3rd. Reading alone is an inadequate stipulation, because it secures no check whatever upon the rigour or indulgence of the certifier in the shape of a test cognisable by other persons, such as a MS. sample affords; because, as between servant and employer, the power of executing written directions or orders, in the way of business, is precluded; because the exclusion of all but oral intercourse suspends, if not ultimately obliterates, anterior educational influence, except from intrinsic sources; and because there is supplied no aid nor exercise to the memory, conservative of antecedent facts and acquirements.

4th. The scheme suggested gets rid of the rate difficulty, either by causing the people to find for themselves the means of teaching their children, or by conciliating their objections to a rate that would pay for an imperative education, which otherwise they must provide at their own charges. The working classes will submit to the education if the law insists upon no employment without it. They would either make it a constructive trade charge on their several callings, or submit to a school-rate in preference.

5th. Few places, however remote, would be beyond the reach of some school comparatively or entirely free; and if otherwise, the minimum of education required is so low as to be within the means of the poorest. At all events, where such schools do not now exist, this law would compel their provision, as having become one of the necessaries of social life.

6th. If a stray illiterate were found, who could not be taught in any other way, he might be consigned to the union school, and as his escape from the union, and the relief of the rate-payer, alike depended upon his easy acquirement of reading and writing, it would be the interest of both parties to terminate the disqualified pauper in the enfranchised scholar.

7th. Prizes and certificates of merit are desirable as supplemental stimuli, but do not obviate the necessity of the scheme suggested as a general exaction. They increase the degree and quality of instruction; this determines a certain prescribed minimum.

8th. In any case, the question of a rate is distinct from that of a school. It is believed, however, that the scheme which necessitates some school would tend to simplify the question of its support.

I venture, in conclusion, to invite serious attention to a few leading educational facts, extracted from a sensible letter in the " Daily News " of February 5th, 1857.

By the census of 1851, there were in England and Wales 15,518 day schools, of which, according to the Minutes of 1855-6, only 4,800 were under inspection. Exclusive of grants for building and other extras, which amounted last year to 119,079*l.*, the maintenance of these 4,800 schools cost the country 250,523*l.* The majority of the remaining 10,718 schools, not under inspection, from inability to meet the requirements of the Committee of Council, are notoriously inefficient. Calculating from the cost of maintaining the 4,800 schools under inspection, the cost of similar aid to the 10,718 schools uninspected would be 557,511*l.*; and to bring them within the rules of the Committee would cost as much more, or 1,365,545*l.* in all.

The quality of schools being quite as essential to educational effect as the quantity, the condition of more than two-thirds of existing schools shows the fallacy of boasting that one in eight of the population is under instruction because that proportion is in school. It is not probable that Parliament would vote such large sums, which would amount in all to about two millions annually, subject to continual increase in proportion to the growth of the population.

All these facts, chiefly drawn from reports presented to the Committee of Council, combine to prove the immediate necessity of some efforts being made by all classes of religious believers to suspend the obstructive conflict of doctrinal theories, and divert the current of internecine zeal into the earnest elaboration of some practicable system by which the school-door may be more widely opened to the illiterate millions of England.

" Will an Improvement of the Dwellings of the Labouring
Classes have any Influence upon the Value which they
attach to the Education of their Children, and can any
Use be made of the Electoral Franchise in the same Direc-
tion?" By the Rev. EDWARD GIRDLESTONE, Canon
of Bristol.

IN order to constitute a school really efficient for the purposes of education, three things are requisite. These are,
adequate school buildings, competent teachers and appliances for teaching, and a sufficiency of scholars of a sufficient age and for a sufficient term. There can be no
really efficient school, except by a combination of these
three elements. The progress of really effective education has been much retarded by inattention to the necessity of this combination. Reports have been issued by
societies and statements made by individuals, which,
simply because they have ignored this necessity, have
grievously misled the public mind. It has been pro-
claimed, and with truth, that a very large number of
school rooms has been built, a very large number of
teachers employed, and a very large number of children
assembled in the school rooms. As a necessary result of
all this it has been assumed, that education must have
made a satisfactory progress. Meanwhile, the plain un-
deniable matter of fact is, that the progress, neither positively, nor in comparison with other countries, either has
been or is satisfactory. The fallacy lies in inattention to

the necessity of the combination already referred to. It has been forgotten, that in a large proportion of the school rooms so much boasted of, there has been an entire absence of efficient teachers and proper books and other appliances for teaching. It has been forgotten likewise, that in all such badly taught and badly furnished school rooms, and in a large proportion even of those well taught and furnished, the scholars have been few in number as compared with the population, infants in age, many only Sunday scholars, if daily scholars, irregular in attendance and early taken away. The difference between the presumed and real progress of education is thus easily accounted for. The mystery is readily cleared up. There is in truth as much difference between a *school room* and a *school*, as between a clock-case and a clock. The clock-case may be very pretty to look at, and it might by the ignorant be assumed, that if the country were covered with such good-looking clock-cases, time must be kept. In order, however, to time being really kept, there must, besides the case be the spring, and all the various wheels, axles, levers, without which there may be indeed a clock-case, but cannot be a clock. In like manner, in order to the population being really educated, there must be not school buildings alone, but competent teachers, competent appliances for teaching, and a right proportion, not merely of the infants, but of the youth of the country, regularly under tuition and for a sufficient time. In practice nothing misleads so widely as an ambiguous use of terms. The sooner we accustom ourselves therefore to distinguish accurately between school buildings and schools, the better. The one is a mere shell and nothing more. The other is a shell with the kernel in it.

Now it cannot be doubted that we still want, and, as the population increases, shall continue to want more school buildings. This cannot, however, be considered at the present time a very urgent want, and may safely be left to be supplied by the existing agencies, such as the government, and voluntary aid, contributed either locally or through the National and British and Foreign School Societies. Equally certain is it, that there is in existing school buildings a wide field open for improvement, both as regards teachers and appliances for teaching. Considering the difficulties with which the administration of the only other alternative, a local rate, is beset, it is much to be desired, though not by any means yet certain, that this want, far more urgent than that of school room, and chiefly arising from deficiency of funds, may also be supplied by existing agencies; by some further relaxation, for instance, of the rules of the Committee of Council in the case of poor districts, and by a more liberal support of the Church of England Education Society, which, in the matter of raising poor schools to the mark at which they may be brought under inspection and share in the public grant, may be considered as the almoner of the richer for the benefit of the poorer districts. Be this however as it may, there is still the third element of a *bonâ fide* school to be provided for, namely a sufficiency of scholars of sufficient age and for a sufficient term. It is taken for granted, that the absence of this sufficiency is one of the most urgent educational difficulties of the present time. The returns of the last census, the Reports of Her Majesty's Inspectors, and other statistical information, to which reference has probably already been made in other sections of this Conference, must be considered sufficient evidence of this. It is taken for granted also, that, just as the whole education question in the aggregate is not likely in this, as in more despotic countries, to be solved by any one large, comprehensive, arbitrary, and Procrustean measure, but rather by a combination of agencies, some compulsory, some voluntary, some public, some private, all, however, dovetailing into each other; so in this particular detail of that question, success must be looked for from a combination of several agencies, from a group of schemes rather than from one scheme only. That is to say, in order to overcome that indifference on the part of the parents which is the chief cause of small and irregular school attendance, and so to enhance the value of education in the estimation of the labouring classes as to ensure a larger number of older pupils for a longer time, we must not only make the schools efficient, which is the first and most important step; not only adopt half-time schemes, whether compulsory or voluntary; nor yet prize schemes alone, nor industrial training, nor civil service competition, nor improved factory education alone; but a combination of all these, and of anything else of like sort and tendency. Such then being the case, though the two agencies to which attention is now called, namely, an improvement of the dwellings of the poor, and the prospect of obtaining the electoral franchise, may not singly, and as compared with the other more direct inducements above mentioned and already discussed in this place, be considered as likely to be very effective, yet, as a part of a whole, as units in a group, they may perhaps indirectly have some, if it be only a little weight, and are at least worth a few minutes' attention.

" Will, then, an improvement in the dwellings of the labouring classes have any influence upon the value which they attach to the education of their children?" This question shall be answered on the authority of a twenty-five years' experience, amongst a widely-scattered rural, but manufacturing and mining population in Lancashire, gained in the general supervision of a parish of 25,000 souls, and the actual pastoral care of a district of 5000, in which there were six daily schools. The six sets of school buildings were all good of their kind. So, also, were the school furniture and appliances, and the several teachers. There was no want either of supervision or funds, and still less of endeavour on the part either of the clergy or employers, to enlist the sympathy of the parents, and lead them to value, as they ought to have valued, a really good education. Notwithstanding all this, however, these schools, though not certainly to the same extent as others less well organised and maintained, yet to a considerable extent, were rendered practically inefficient as regarded the real education of the population by the comparatively small number of scholars, and the irregular attendance and infantine age of those whose names were on the books. In other words, the parents did not value the education provided as they ought to have valued it. Poverty could not be pleaded. For the school fees were moderate, and, usually speaking, work was plentiful and wages good. There was, doubtless, the prevalent seduction of remunerative employment for children easily procured. This, however, would of course exercise its influence in all cases alike ; equally in the case of parents whose dwellings were, as of those whose dwellings were not, of an improved character. The question rather is, Whether this, and all other such like influences against children being sent to school and kept there, were found to be powerful in all cases alike ; or whether a difference was observed in the case of those who had well-built, roomy, and comfortable homes, and those who had not. It may be answered unhesitatingly, that, as a matter of fact, this difference did exist, and in a very striking degree. Not in all cases, but upon the long run, and to a considerable extent the labourers, whose homes were well-built, roomy, capable of comfort, and comfortable, did send their children to school in greater numbers, more regularly, and for a longer time, than those whose homes were mere hovels, incapable of comfort, and in some cases more fit for the residence of brutes than of men. The home comforts had evidently a softening and humanising influence on the inmates. They thought more about the future advantage of their children, less about their own immediate profit. The fathers were more steady, spent less at the public-house, had less need to eke out their own by the wages of their children, and were even inclined to deny themselves some necessaries in order to avoid doing so. The mothers were less apt to leave home either for employment or profit; had less need, therefore, of resorting to the school-emptying expedient of keeping at home the children of eight years old and upwards, to mind the house and younger brothers and sisters; were more clean and tidy in their own habits and tastes, and therefore valued the good habits acquired at school as much as they disliked the dirty and desultory practices acquired by roaming and playing in the streets and lanes. Considering the great power of home influence wherever there is scope for its exercise, that which has been above stated does not seem more than might have been looked for. The result is not at all greater than the agency would warrant an expectation of. There is nothing at all inexplicable in the matter. It would rather be surprising if the result were otherwise. Be this, however, as it may, the *fact* is so. Such, at least, is the result of an experience on a large scale and for a long term of years. Nor is there any doubt but that the experience of most persons, who have mixed much with the labouring classes, is the same. The improvement of the dwellings of the labouring classes is a question in every way much mixed up with that of the progress of education. The two questions exercise a reciprocal influence. It is acknowledged, probably on all hands, that the better men are educated, the more they will loathe small, dirty, crowded, dilapidated homes, and prize those which are the reverse of all this. Equally granted is it, that there is nothing which in childhood so much tends to neutralise, and afterwards to obliterate, the good, religious, moral, and refined tastes and habits acquired at school, as homes in which not only cleanliness, comfort, and order, but often even common decency is impossible. Let it be further granted, then, for this is all which is asked, that — unless the experience of those who have long mixed amongst the labouring classes be at fault—the improvement of their dwellings, the making them more roomy and airy, better ventilated and lighted, more consistent with habits of order, comfort, decency, and intellectual refinement,—in a word, more *homy*, will prove a not inefficient unit in a group of expedients, for inducing the labouring classes to value education for their children, and so helping to fill our schools. The possession of a comfortable home will also tend to make the working classes less migratory, and thus indirectly provide a remedy for another fertile cause of care in infant school attendance in London and other large towns. Educational societies, and societies for the improvement of the dwellings of the labouring classes, are twin sisters, engaged in promoting one and the same high and holy object. Those educationists do only half their work, who never follow the children from the school to their homes, nor help to raise the one to something approaching to the level of the other.

The first clause of the inquiry proposed at the head of this paper has been answered without any hesitation, because the very result which, theoretically, might have been anticipated, is borne out by matter of fact. As regards the second clause, there is not the same sure foundation to build on, and the whole subject is surrounded with much practical difficulty. Under present circumstances, however, nothing which can by the most remote possibility exercise even the slightest influence upon the solution of the great and important educational problem, must be either overlooked or shrunk from. It is certain that the franchise cannot be safely extended to any who are not educated, and whose homes are not improved. It may be, such is the reciprocal influence such things exercise, that the extension of the franchise may be made a stimulus to education. Without pretending, then, to any large amount of positive proof on the subject, it may indirectly, yet fairly be assumed, that the power of exercising the electoral franchise is one which all classes in this country highly value, and to attain which they are prepared to make considerable sacrifice. The great interest already taken by all who can read, and even by many who cannot read, in the political questions of the day; the pure political zeal with which many of the working classes, over whom the attractions of riot and excess, so seductive to others in the same class, have no influence, enter into the strife of a contested election; the sacrifices which are made to acquire that property qualification which the law at present makes the sole condition of a vote; the widely-spread interest always taken in the subject of parliamentary reform; our present experience at the other side of the Atlantic; the experience of past ages amongst the citizens of ancient Athens and Rome; all combine in leading at least to a presumption, that the electoral franchise is looked on as a prize worth trying for, and that consequently, if it could in any way be safely connected with education, it might take its place as one in the group of stimulants, by which it is hoped that an increased desire for education may be excited.

But how can the possession of the electoral franchise and education be associated, with due regard to the legitimate rights of property, and without prejudice to the spirit of that wonderful constitution, which, under God's blessing, has made and maintained Great Britain the happiest and most prosperous country in the world? This is indeed a very difficult question. Possibly it may not be capable of any solution whatever. At any rate it cannot be decided dogmatically. There is no reason, however, why it should not be well sifted and ventilated. There is no reason why an attempt should not be made to identify a great political prize with a powerful educational stimulant. If, likewise, parliamentary reform be, as it is said to be, looming in the distance, there is no reason why those who have the education of the people at heart, and are anxious that, before any new system is ventured on, the present system under every circumstance which can by any possibility minister to its success should have a fair trial, should not at least make an attempt to enlist such reform in their own cause. What harm, for instance, or rather what but good, could arise from its being enacted that no elector, though possessed of the legal property qualification, should be permitted to exercise the franchise unless able to write his name legibly in the poll book ; or even, if challenged, to produce a certificate from, say a magistrate or the parish schoolmaster, of ability to read fluently, write legibly, and of a knowledge of the first four rules of arithmetic? What danger could be apprehended from conferring the electoral franchise upon every certificated and registered schoolmaster, without any reference to property qualification at all? Supposing the project at present under consideration be carried out and extended from the middle to the lower classes, of some sort of honorary certificate being granted, either by the Universities or some other competent authority, to those who attain to a certain moderate amount of proficiency in various stipulated departments of practical knowledge and physical science, why should not the privilege of a vote be extended to the recipients of these certificates? Or, if it be thought that the number of votes thus created would be so large as to overpower, or improperly interfere with the legitimate influence which property ought to exercise in returning members to parliament, why should not such certificated persons be formed into a sort of collegiate constituency, in which should be vested the right of returning two, or four, or any other number of members deemed consistent with safety? Thus the educated among the labouring classes would be directly represented in the House of Commons in the same way as the learned amongst the higher classes are at present represented through the members for the Universities.

The above are merely suggestions. They are not intended as any thing more. On such a subject anything dogmatic would be out of place. They are merely roughly sketched outlines for statesmen to ponder on, alter, amplify, improve, and fill up or reject at their leisure. Neither is it contended that singly, or even perhaps in combination, the electoral franchise could be so made use of as to exercise any great influence upon the progress of education. It must not, for instance, be expected to be any thing like as great as that which would be the result of a general improvement of the dwellings of the labouring classes. At a time, nevertheless, when the question which presses more heavily than any other on the minds of all thoughtful persons is, How can the vast and increasing population of this great country be educated? — when the adoption of any general compulsory system, owing to religious and other difficulties, seems well nigh impracticable — when, at any rate, public opinion is clearly in favour of a further trial of the present mixed system of government and a voluntary agency—no influence of which it can even in the least degree be hoped that it may be brought to bear successfully on the solution of such a question, ought to be overlooked. The British constitution has, by the blessing of God, become what it is, not by any single act, but by a long succession of acts at various intervals, by combination, producing a whole if not perfect, at least more perfect than any thing of the kind which the world has yet seen. In like manner it is most probable that the educational system of this country will not be brought full-blown into the world by any single Act, in any single summer. It will rather steal upon us insensibly by a process of gradual development, and as the result of a group of measures. Some of these, like that at present under consideration, viewed singly, may appear at first sight small and unimportant. Viewed, however, as part of a great whole, no one of them is so small as to be unworthy of attention.

PART VI.

PROCEEDINGS AT THE EDUCATIONAL CONFERENCE.

—◆—

THE INAUGURAL MEETING.

THE Inaugural Meeting of the Conference took place, on Monday, June 22nd, at Willis's Rooms. The chair was occupied by His Royal Highness the Prince Consort, who entered punctually at three o'clock, and was very enthusiastically received. He was supported by the Bishops of Oxford, London, St. Asaph, Manchester, Sir J. Shuttleworth, Sir J. Pakington, the Right Hon. W. Cowper, M.P. Lord Ward, Earl Granville, the Bishop of Durham, Lord Brougham, the Bishop of Winchester, Archdeacon Sinclair, Sergeant Woolrych, Lord Calthorpe, Lord Ingestre, and other noblemen and gentlemen. Amongst the general visitors were the Dean of Bristol, the Hon. and Rev. Grantham H. Yorke, the Rev. Canon Miller, the Rev. Prebendary Burgess, Robert Owen, "the philanthropist," Mr. George Dawson, the Rev. J. F. Lingham, Archdeacon Thorpe, Mr. H. Chester, the Rev. J. Jackson, the Dean of Salisbury, Rev. H. Baber, the Rev. F. C. Cook, the Rev. J. P. Norris, the Rev. F. Fussell, the Rev. Canon Moseley, the Rev. W. Rogers, the Rev. Peter Marshall, Miss Carpenter, &c.

His ROYAL HIGHNESS, in introducing the business, spoke as follows:—

" Gentlemen, we have met to-day in the sacred cause of education—of national education. This word, which means no less than the moral and intellectual development of the rising generation, and therefore the national welfare, is well calculated to engross our minds, and opens a question worthy of a nation's deepest interest and most anxious consideration. Gentlemen, the nation is alive to its importance, and our presence here to-day gives further evidence, if such evidence were needed, of its anxiety to give it that consideration. Looking to former times, we find that our forefathers, with their wonted piety and paternal care, had established a system of national education based upon the parish organisation, and forming part of parish life, which met the wants of their day, and had in it a certain unity and completeness which we may well envy at the present moment. But in the progress of time our wants have outstripped that system, and the condition of the country has so completely changed, even within these last fifty years, that the old parochial division is no longer adequate for the present population, which has increased, during that period, in England and Wales, from nine millions to eighteen millions in round numbers; and where there formerly existed comparatively small towns and villages, we now see mighty cities like Liverpool, Manchester, Hull, Leeds, Birmingham, and others, with their hundreds of thousands springing up almost as it were by enchantment: London having increased to nearly two and a half millions of souls, and the factory district of Lancashire alone having aggregated a population of nearly three millions within a radius of thirty miles. This change could not escape the watchful eye of a patriotic public; but how to provide the means of satisfying the new wants could not be a matter of easy solution. Whilst zeal for the public good, a fervent religious spirit, and true philanthropy are qualities eminently distinguishing our countrymen, the love of liberty and an aversion to being controlled by the power of the State in matters nearest to their hearts, are feelings which will always most powerfully influence them in action. Thus the common object has been contemplated from the most different points of view, and pursued upon often antagonistic principles. Some have sought the aid of Government, others that of the Church to which they belong; some have declared it to be the duty of the State to provide elementary instruction for the people at large; others have seen in State interference a check to the spontaneous exertions of the people themselves, and an interference with self-government. Some, again, have advocated a plan of compulsory education, based upon local self-government, and others the voluntary system in its widest development. Whilst these have been some of the political subjects of difference, those in the religious field have not been less marked and potent. We find on the one hand the wish to see secular and religious instruction separated, and the former recognised as an innate and inherent right to which each member of society has a claim, and which ought not to be denied to him if he refuses to take along with it the inculcation of a particular dogma to which he objects as unsound; whilst we see on the other hand the doctrine asserted that no education can be sound which does not rest on religious instruction, and that religious truth is too sacred to be modified and tampered with, even in its minutest deductions, for the sake of procuring a general agreement. (Cheers.) Gentlemen, if these differences were to have been discussed here to day, I should not have been able to respond to your invitation to take the chair, as I should have thought it inconsistent with the position which I occupy and with the duty which I owe to the Queen and the country at large. (Hear, hear.) I see those here before me who have taken a leading part in these important discussions, and I am happy to meet them upon a neutral ground —(loud cheers)— happy to find that there is a neutral ground upon which their varied talents and abilities can be brought to bear in communion upon the common object, and proud and grateful to them that they should have allowed me to preside over them for the purpose of working together in the common vineyard. (Cheers.) I feel certain that the greatest benefit must arise to the cause we have all so much at heart by the mere free exchange of your thoughts and various experience. You may well be proud, gentlemen, of the results hitherto achieved by your moral efforts, and may point to the past, that since the beginning of the century, while the population has doubled itself, the number of schools, both public and private, has been multiplied fourteen times. In 1801 there were in England and Wales — of public schools, 2,876; of private schools, 487; making a total of 3,363. In 1851 (the year of the census) there were in England and Wales — of public schools, 15,518; of private schools, 30,524; making a total of 46,042; giving instruction in all to 2,144,378 scholars, of whom 1,422,982 belong to the public schools, and 721,396 to the private schools. The rate of progress is further illustrated by statistics, which show that in 1818 the proportion of day scholars to the population was 1 in 17; in 1833, 1 in 11; and in 1851, 1 in 8. (Hear.) These are great results, although I hope they may only be received as instalments of what has yet to be done. But what must be your feelings when you reflect upon the fact, the inquiry into which has brought us together, that this great boon thus obtained for the mass of the people, and which is freely offered to them, should have been only partially accepted, and upon the whole, so insufficiently applied, as to render its use almost valueless? (Hear, hear.) We are told that the total population in England and Wales of children between the ages of 3 and 15, being estimated at 4,908,696, only 2,046,848 attend school at all, whilst 2,861,848 receive no instruction whatever. At the same time an analysis of the scholars with reference to the time allowed for their school tuition, shows that 42 per cent. of them have been at school less than one year, 22 per cent. during one year, 15 per cent. 2 years, 9 per cent. 3 years 5 per cent. 4 years, 4 per cent. 5 years. Therefore, out of the two millions of scholars alluded to, more than $1\frac{1}{2}$ million remain only two years at school. I leave it to you to judge what the results of such an education can be. I find further, that of these two millions of children attending school, only about 600,000 are above the age of 9. Gentlemen, these are startling facts, which render it evident that no extension of the means of education will be of any avail unless this evil, which lies at the root of the whole question, be removed, and that it is high time that the country should become thoroughly awake to its existence and prepared to meet it energetically. To impress this upon the public mind is the object of our conference. Public opinion is the powerful lever which in these days moves a people for good and for evil, and to public opinion we must, therefore, appeal if we would achieve any lasting and beneficial result. You, gentlemen, will richly add to the services which you have already rendered to the noble cause if you will prepare public opinion by your inquiry into this state of things, and by discussing in your sections the causes of it, as well as the remedies which may be within your reach. This will be no easy matter, but even if your labours should not result in the adoption of any immediate practical steps, you will have done great good in preparing for them. It will probably happen that in this instance, as in most others, the cause which produces the evil will be more easily detected than its remedy, and yet a just appreciation of the former must ever be the first and essential condition for the discovery of the latter. You will probably trace the cause to our social condition, perhaps to a state of ignorance and lethargic indifference on the subject amongst the parents generally; but the root of the evil will, I suspect, also be found to extend into that field on which the political economist exercises his activity—I mean the labour market—demand and supply. (Hear, hear.) To dissipate that ignorance, and rouse from that lethargy, may be difficult; but, with the united and earnest efforts of all who are the friends of the working classes, it ought, after all, to be only a question of time. What measures can be brought to bear upon the other root of the evil is a more delicate question, and will require the nicest care in handling, for there you cut into the very quick of the working man's condition. His children are not only his offspring, to be reared for a future independent position, but they constitute part of his productive power, and work with him for the staff of life. The daughters especially are the hand-maids of the house, the assistants of the mother, the nurses of the younger children, the aged, and the sick. To deprive the labouring family of their help would be almost to paralyse its domestic existence. (Hear, hear.) On the other hand, carefully collected statistics reveal to us the fact that, while almost 600,000 children between the ages of 3 and 15 are absent from school, but known to be employed, no less than 2,200,000 are not at school, whose absence cannot be traced to any ascertained employment, or other legitimate cause. You will have to work, then, upon the minds and hearts of the parents, to place before them the irreparable mischief which they inflict upon those who are intrusted to their care by keeping them from the light of knowledge—to bring home to their conviction that it is their duty to exert themselves for their children's education, bearing in mind at the same time that it is not only their most sacred duty, but also their highest privilege. Unless they work with you, your work, our work, will be vain; but you will not fail, I feel sure, in obtaining their cooperation if you remind them of their duty to their God and Creator. (Hear, hear.) Our heavenly Father, in his boundless goodness, has so made his creatures that they should be happy, and in his wisdom has fitted his means to his ends, giving to all of them different qualities and faculties, in using and developing which they fulfil their destiny, and, running their uniform course according to his prescription, they find that happiness which he has intended for them. (Cheers.) Man alone is born into this world with faculties far nobler than the other creatures, reflecting the image of Him who has willed that there should be beings on earth to know and worship Him, but endowed with the power of self-determination, having reason given him for his guide. He can develope his faculties, and obtain that happiness which is offered to him on earth to be completed hereafter in entire union with Him through the mercy of Christ. But he can also leave these faculties unimproved, and miss his mission on earth. He will then sink to the level of the lower animals, forfeit happiness, and live separate from his God, whom he did not know how to find. Gentlemen, I say man has no right to do this. He has no right to throw off the task which is laid upon him for his happiness. It is his duty to fulfil his mission to the utmost of his power; but it is our duty, the duty of those whom Providence has removed from this awful struggle, and placed beyond this fearful danger, manfully, unceasingly, and untiringly, to aid by advice, assistance, and example the great bulk of the people, who, without such aid, must almost inevitably succumb to the difficulty of their task. They will not cast from them any aiding hand, and the Almighty will bless the labours of those who work in his cause." (His Royal Highness sat down amidst loud applause.)

The Rev. J. G. LONSDALE, of the National Society, one of the Joint Secretaries, then read the following report: —

"There has been expended in Great Britain, since the year 1839, through local and voluntary agencies, aided by the State, a sum of more than 2,000,000*l.* on the erection of new school buildings, affording the means of education to more than half a million more children than could before that time have been educated. A sum exceeding one million and a quarter is moreover annually expended in the support of schools for the working classes. Beyond these amounts large sums have been expended in building and maintaining schools by purely private charity, of which no accurate returns have been furnished. This expenditure of money from private and from public sources represents, however, but inadequately the interest taken by the people of England in the education of the working classes; for in almost every locality where schools have been established there are to be found persons who not only contribute money liberally to their support, but devote also to them a large portion of their time and attention. The system of education, based on local sympathies and voluntary agencies, which has thus been provided by the people of England for its working classes, manifests moreover at the present time no signs of exhaustion or decay ; on the contrary, there never was perhaps a time when the opinions prevalent among the upper and middle classes of society were more generally favourable to it, or when those classes were prepared to make greater sacrifices for its extension and development. But these are not the only parties concerned. The concurrence of the working classes, who are to receive it, is equally necessary. It was necessary that schools should in the first instance be erected, that teachers should be specially trained for the instruction of the children who attend them, and that provision should be made for the support of those teachers. These conditions of success being in some measure fulfilled, there remains this further condition, that among those persons whose children are to profit by the schools (numbers of whom have themselves small personal experience of the benefits of education), there should exist a public opinion so far favourable to education as to induce them to make the sacrifices they must make in order that their children may attend the schools. This is the point to which the movement in favour of popular education in England is now brought; but here a difficulty presents itself which it should be the great object of the friends of elementary instruction to remove. The children of the working classes are indeed sent to school from a very early age, but they are said to be taken away at so early an age as in a great measure to defeat the purposes for which the school is established. This is moreover alleged not to be due to the claims of labour, for of the children who are not sent to school only a small portion are at work. It is further asserted, that the evil is not in progress of diminution by the improvements in schools, and the better instruction they now afford. The working classes are indeed said to reason that, as the schools get better, the knowledge necessary for their children (or all that they think necessary) may be got the sooner, and they therefore take them away from school the earlier, so that what is being gained on the one hand by the increased efficiency of schools is being lost on the other by the earlier age at which the education of the children ceases. To inquire to what extent these evils exist, and what expedients, other than legislative, are best calculated to remedy them, is the purpose for which this Conference has been called together. In assembling from all parts of the kingdom persons interested in the work of education, and practically acquainted with its details, the Committee have thought that the extent of this evil might be ascertained, and the success of the expedients which have been tried in various localities for remedying it discussed. It is not, however, thought that in the few days during which this Conference can be kept together the discussion will be exhausted. It belongs, indeed, to such a conference rather to initiate such a discussion than to bring it to a conclusion ; to put forward clearly and distinctly the subject matter of it, together with such evidence thereon as it is able to elicit, and then to leave to the public mind to take up, or not, the argument, and itself to draw the conclusion and work out the result. The committee have acted under the conviction that if the removal of children from school at so early an age as to render the labour of the schoolmaster comparatively fruitless be established, the practical good sense of the people of England will in some way find for this evil a remedy. In order to afford to the Conference an opportunity for receiving all the communications made to it, and discussing, in the short period allotted to its deliberations, all the subjects which claim its attention, the Committee proposes that it should divide into sections. The papers to be read before each section are specified in handbills, copies of which have been distributed in the room. The sections will meet at twelve o'clock to-morrow. The Conference will re-assemble in this room on Wednesday, at eleven o'clock, when resolutions will be proposed, embodying, so far as may be found practicable, any conclusions at which the sections shall have arrived on the several propositions submitted to them. A selection of the papers on which these conclusions may be supposed to have been founded will, moreover, be printed and published."

Lord BROUGHAM, who said he had been forty-six years engaged in promoting the cause of education, gave a short historical account of the progress of the movement during that period, showing that, though falling short of what could be desired, it had been considerable. In 1831 a grant of about 30,000*l.* was made by Government in aid of education; the annual grants now amount to more than half a million. From the experience of mechanics' institutes, he recommended that the management of schools should be placed, to a considerable extent, in the hands of working men.

The Bishop of OXFORD said the difficulty was not to find schools for the children, but children for the schools. It is useless to offer the people education while they (the educators) were divided upon what had to be offered. He hoped the result of this Conference would be to remove or reconcile those differences by a discussion face to face by those who held them. He trusted that the blessing of God would be vouchsafed to their endeavours, being sure that His blessing would not prove fruitless.

The Rev. Canon MOSELEY said, that though great progress had been made in establishing good schools, still the statistics of the census showed, that out of 5,000,000 children who ought to be at school, only 2,000,000 were there; and of the 3,000,000 who were away, only one-third were at work. The great evil was the early age at which children are removed from school, which was on the average $10\frac{1}{2}$ years. He asked how it was possible that an effective education could be given before the age of $10\frac{1}{2}$. The Conference would have to consider whether it should become a permanent body.

H. R. H. the Prince Consort then formally declared the Conference open, and the meeting broke up.

THE SECTIONS.

On the following day the five sections, into which the Conference was divided, met at the Thatched House Tavern, when papers were read, of which the preceding are a selection.

After the reading of the papers valuable and interesting discussions took place, which unfortunately want of space renders it impossible to publish.

The following resolutions were passed in the sections: —

SECTION A.

" 1. That in the opinion of this section of the Conference, the greater number of the children of the working classes in the agricultural, manufacturing, and mining districts are removed from school when from 9 to 10 years old; and that their removal at so early an age, in great measure, destroys the effect of the education provided for them.

" 2. That this section, having inquired into the causes of such early removal, is of opinion that it is not commonly to be traced to the poverty of parents, but in some instances to objections to the rules of the school, in others, to its unpractical character; in others, to an undervaluing of education by parents from the inefficiency of the education which they themselves received; and, as a general rule, to the state of the labour market, which imparts great value to the labour of children, and thus leads—1st. To employers of the parents requiring the labour of the children; 2nd. To dissolute parents living upon the wages of children's labour; 3rd. To a premature and ruinous independence of life and action amongst the very young; all of which causes lead to the withdrawal of the children from school.

" 3. That the section cannot express these conclusions without adding that, in its opinion, whilst some protection of children from too early labour may, in certain cases, become necessary, it is in the improvement of education by moral and religious influences, rather than by legislation, that the greatest remedy for these evils must be found."

SECTION B.

"That it appears that in Germany and Switzerland the regulations in force have produced a very general attendance in primary schools on the part of the children of the labouring classes between the ages of 5 and 14, and that the proportion of children in daily attendance at school is 1 in 6 of the population of Prussia and some other states of Germany, and 1 in 5 in Switzerland.

" In Holland the attendance at school is estimated at 1 in 8 of the population ; and among other regulations for promoting such attendance, the forfeiture of the right of a parent to receive parochial relief, in the event of his having neglected to send his child regularly to school, has been efficacious.

" In France 1 in 8 of the population are in primary elementary schools, exclusive of infant schools, and the age of leaving school is ordinarily regulated by the age at which the children are admitted, if Protestants, to confirmation, and if Roman Catholics, to the administration of the holy communion. That age is most frequently 11 in great towns, and varies from 12 to 15 in other parts of the country.

" Various measures adopted in Central and Northern Europe for the extension and improvement of popular education are deserving of careful consideration, so far as they can be adapted to the circumstances and opinions of this country."

Section C.

" That in the opinion of this section the certificate and prize schemes, adopted in certain localities, are, from their hopeful results, deserving of more extensive trial, as an appeal to parents of elementary scholars, to afford to their children a more regular and longer attendance at school, and to the employers of labour, and to the wealthier classes generally, to encourage the parents of such scholars to make the personal sacrifices requisite for this object.

" That in carrying into execution these schemes, and others brought under the consideration of this section, it is desirable to keep in view the following principles : —

" That such schemes should be regarded only as subsidiary to other agencies for acting upon the irregularity and insufficiency of the time of school attendance.

" That they should aim at enlisting the cooperation of employers of labour, of the Government in its administration of appointments, and of the trustees of apprenticeship funds. That they should be formed with due regard to character and conduct as well as intellectual attainment. That the section regards with peculiar interest the application of prize and certificate schemes to evening schools, which educate young persons from 13 years of age to 20, and which may thus hope to preserve them from degrading and sensual habits."

Section D.

" That in the opinion of this section, the careful examination of the results of instruction in good half-time schools, as compared with the results of instruction for the ordinary full time in the same or the like schools, is fraught with important results affecting the whole scheme for the labouring classes.

" That in large factories or farms the system of relays is advisable each half day ; but that, under circumstances of practical difficulty, the alternate day or week would be preferable.

" That it is expedient to encourage night schools as places of primary or secondary instruction, in which subjects, having relation to the specific labour of the locality, should be taught by certificated or other competent masters. The section believes that the establishment of evening schools of this class will do much towards remedying the deficient state of education amongst both the younger and adult members of the working classes.

" That if the voluntary system is to be worked with success, an appeal must, in the first instance, be addressed to employers, whose preference of instruction will, by stamping a material value upon education, materially tend to secure the co-operation of parents."

Section E.

" That inasmuch as industrial training is calculated — 1st. To impart to the children of the working classes habits of industry ; 2nd. To qualify them by manual exercise for manual employments, which are those by which they are afterwards to live ; 3rd. To enlist the sympathies of the parents by its useful, practical, and remunerative tendency, and thus induce them to keep their children longer at school — it is desirable to encourage to the utmost the introduction of the industrial element in our schools for the working classes."

THE FINAL MEETING.

The final meeting was held on Wednesday, June 24th, at Willis's Rooms, Lord Granville in the chair. There were also present the Marquis of Lansdowne, Earl Nelson, the Right Hon. W. Cowper, M.P., Lord Kinnaird, the Bishop of Oxford, the Bishop of Sodor and Man, the Bishop of St. Asaph, Sir John Pakington, Sir J. K. Shuttleworth, the Hon. and Rev. Grantham H. Yorke, Mr. Akroyd, M.P., Canon Moseley, Canon Girdlestone, the Dean of Salisbury, the Dean of Bristol, Mr. Edward Baines, Mr. Samuel Morley, &c. &c.

The Bishop of OXFORD moved —

" That it is the opinion of this Conference that the greater number of the children of the working classes are removed from school at so early an age as seriously to interfere with their education. That whilst this Conference is precluded from entering on the question of legislative interference, it would call the attention of the friends of education to the positive amount of good which may be effected as to increasing the age to which children continue at school, by the improvement of the schools themselves, and bringing moral and religious influences to bear upon both the parents and children."

The resolution was seconded by Sir J. PAKINGTON, supported by the Marquis of LANSDOWNE, and carried.

The Right Hon. W. COWPER then moved—

" That throughout the north of Europe the children of the working classes remain at school for a longer period and to a riper age than in this country."

Mr. AKROYD, M.P., seconded the motion, and it was carried.

Sir J. K. SHUTTLEWORTH moved—

" That registration, certificate, and prize schemes have been shown to have been applied in certain localities with advantage, and to be worthy of more extensive trial."

Mr. BAINES seconded the resolution, which was supported by Canon GIRDLESTONE, and carried.

The noble Chairman and the Marquis of Lansdowne here left the room, in order to attend a Cabinet Council, and the chair was taken by the Hon. Wm. Cowper.

The Dean of SALISBURY moved —

"That the voluntary half-time schemes have been with success adopted in certain localities, and may be recommended for further trial."

The motion was seconded by Mr. MORLEY, and carried.

The Hon. and Rev. GRANTHAM YORKE moved —

"That this Conference considers the encouragement of industrial education in elementary schools, especially among girls, to be very desirable. and that such instruction is peculiarly important in the reformation of juvenile offenders."

Mr. J. SYMONS seconded the resolution, which was carried.

The Bishop of SODOR and MAN moved the adjournment of the meeting, with a request to the Committee to frame a report to be published, with abstracts of the papers read, and to determine when it should be requisite to again call the Conference together; and congratulated the Conference on its having brought men together of such widely different opinions, all anxious to unite, as far as possible, in the carrying out of the great question of education.

Mr. BRACEBRIDGE seconded the motion, which was carried.

Votes of thanks to the Earl of Granville and the Hon. Mr. Cowper for presiding closed the proceedings, the Conference having lasted upwards of five hours.

N.B.—The Report of the General Committee of the Conference will be published shortly.